D0143732

Key Concepts in
Event Management

Recent volumes include:

Key Concepts in Youth Studies
Mark Cieslik and Donald Simpson

Key Concepts in Hospitality Management
Edited by Roy C. Wood

Key Concepts in Sociology
Peter Braham

Key Concepts in Tourism Research
David Botterill and Vincent Platenkamp

Key Concepts in Sport and Exercise Research Methods
Michael Atkinson

Key Concepts in Media and Communications
Paul Jones and David Holmes

Key Concepts in Sport Psychology
John M. D. Kremer, Aidan Moran, Graham Walker and Cathy Craig

Fifty Key Concepts in Gender Studies
Jane Pilcher and Imelda Whelehan

The SAGE Key Concepts series provides students with accessible and authoritative knowledge of the essential topics in a variety of disciplines. Cross-referenced throughout, the format encourages critical evaluation through understanding. Written by experienced and respected academics, the books are indispensable study aids and guides to comprehension.

Key Concepts in
Event Management

BERNADETTE QUINN

⑤SAGE

Los Angeles | London | New Delhi
Singapore | Washington DC

SEP 16 2013
WITHDRAWN
PROPERTY OF
SENECA COLLEGE
LIBRARIES
KING CAMPUS

Los Angeles | London | New Delhi
Singapore | Washington DC

SAGE Publications Ltd
1 Oliver's Yard
55 City Road
London EC1Y 1SP

SAGE Publications Inc.
2455 Teller Road
Thousand Oaks, California 91320

SAGE Publications India Pvt Ltd
B 1/I 1 Mohan Cooperative Industrial Area
Mathura Road
New Delhi 110 044

SAGE Publications Asia-Pacific Pte Ltd
3 Church Street
#10-04 Samsung Hub
Singapore 049483

Editor: Chris Rojek
Editorial assistant: Martine Jonsrud
Production editor: Katherine Haw
Copyeditor: Jeremy Toynbee
Proofreader: Jacque Woolley
Marketing manager: Alison Borg
Cover design: Wendy Scott
Typeset by: C&M Digitals (P) Ltd, Chennai, India
Printed by: CPI Group (UK) Ltd, Croydon, CR0 4YY

MIX
Paper from
responsible sources
FSC
www.fsc.org   FSC® C013604

© Bernadette Quinn 2013

First published 2013

Apart from any fair dealing for the purposes of research or private study, or criticism or review, as permitted under the Copyright, Designs and Patents Act, 1988, this publication may be reproduced, stored or transmitted in any form, or by any means, only with the prior permission in writing of the publishers, or in the case of reprographic reproduction, in accordance with the terms of licences issued by the Copyright Licensing Agency. Enquiries concerning reproduction outside those terms should be sent to the publishers.

Library of Congress Control Number: 2012946764

British Library Cataloguing in Publication data

A catalogue record for this book is available from the British Library

ISBN 978–1–84920–559–7
ISBN 978–1–84920–560–3 (pbk)

contents

key concepts in
event management

about the author

Bernadette Quinn has a PhD in Human Geography from University College Dublin. She currently lectures and researches in the Department of Tourism at the Dublin Institute of Technology. The nature and meaning of festivals and festivity in contemporary society is one of her key research interests and her work on the topic has been published in a number of international journals including *Urban Studies, Social and Cultural Geography, Tourism Geographies, Event Management* and the *Journal of Policy Research in Tourism, Leisure and Events*. Other research interests include the relationship between culture and tourism, leisure and social inclusion and contemporary forms of tourism mobility. Publications on these topics have appeared in the *Annals of Tourism Research, Gender, Place and Culture* and *Leisure Studies* as well as in various edited book collections. Her teaching interests mirror her research interests and she is involved in undergraduate and postgraduate tourism management and event management programmes teaching modules related to cultural tourism, international festival environments, tourism studies, and tourism and event policy.

acknowledgements

My long-standing interest in festivals and events has been shaped by many people, both practitioners and academics, over the years. These people are too many to mention by name, but I owe all of them a debt of gratitude. While writing this book I was very fortunate to be able to draw on the expertise of colleagues, particularly Lucy Horan and Ruth Craggs, as well as the support and encouragement of my other colleagues at the Dublin Institute of Technology. Finally, a huge thank you to John, Muireann and Aoife for absolutely everything.

key concepts in event management

viii

introduction

In 1991, Getz wrote that festivals and holiday events represented nouveau, alternative tourism (cited in Lee et al., 2008). How times have changed! Such an assertion is simply unimaginable today when, more than 20 years later, finding a city or town without at least one annual **festival** or planned event would be quite a challenge. Does this constitute progress? How do festivals and events contribute to contemporary society? What has the remarkable rise in festivals and events meant for the development of tourism destinations; for the development of economies, be they local, national or international? These and many other questions preoccupy what is now an extremely large, international community of scholars from a range of disciplines who adopt a variety of research approaches to study the complex and profoundly important communal celebrations at the heart of the diverse festivals and events treated in this volume.

While it is difficult to calculate the size of **festival** and event activity, academic, policy and industry commentators everywhere concur that its recent growth across the world in terms of numbers, diversity and popularity has been enormous (Getz, 1991; Finkel, 2009; Thrane, 2002). In the USA it is estimated that there were 10,000 festivals per year, attracting over 31 million visitors by the mid-1990s (Janiskee, 1996; TIA, 2004). In Australia, the government notes that festivals have become ubiquitous, with hundreds being held every year (Australian Government, 2012). In Europe, the growth has been similarly dramatic. According to the International Festival and Event Association (IFEA), the special events industry is estimated to comprise between 4 and 5 million regularly occurring events (Wood, 2012). This significant growth in the practice of festivals and events brought a parallel increase in the emergence and development of the festival and event management profession. It soon also brought a rise in academic interest: closely allied to the development of tourism studies, academics began to take an interest in charting developments in the sector and the literature has burgeoned over the last 20 years. Much of the research is published in tourism studies and specific event-oriented journals, but it also finds expression in a wide range of journals dedicated to management and marketing, urban and place studies, arts and cultural policy, as well as many social sciences-oriented journals. In the majority of cases, festivals and special events are presented as broadly positive phenomena. Throughout the literature, opening paragraphs emphasise the important roles they play in advancing local and regional economies, branding places, attracting visitors, extending the tourism season and fostering community spirit. Yet, festivals and special events, the subject matter at the heart of this book represent a very substantial, complex and dynamic set of activities that can be both deeply rooted and rapidly changing in countries throughout the world. In academia, they are studied from diverse management, social sciences and humanities perspectives. As such, interpretations of their impact and contribution to contemporary economies and societies as well as approaches to valuing, managing and shaping appropriate policies for their advancement are multiple and at times conflicting.

The literature in the field is now enormous and growing all the time. Increasing familiarity with the literature brings an increasing awareness of the unevenness of knowledge, the fractures between academic disciplines and the continuous emergence of new sub-fields. The literature on the **Olympic Games**, for example, is now in and of itself very substantial, yet the extent to which knowledge generated on this particular event translates across into the study of other events that differ by scale and type is very unclear. Getz and Andersson (2010) explained that festival tourism has been studied by many researchers from many perspectives: impact (of varying types), place marketing, travel patterns, displacement effects, motivation, market segmentation, quality and satisfaction, **regional development**, relationship to urban renewal and development, and links to culture and community. However, this sector is nothing if not dynamic and while knowledge gaps are closing in some areas, they continue to open up elsewhere all the time. This book tries to take cognisance of this dynamism in including concepts that would seem very important in terms of future development. The concept of 'risk management', so important from an applied perspective, and that of 'emerging economies', so important from a geographical perspective, are two examples of this.

This volume is tasked with introducing, defining and reviewing the current state of knowledge of the key concepts in the contemporary study of festivals and events. While this involves reviewing literature that is either part of, or closely associated with, tourism studies, in reality, it is a multi-disciplinary task that draws on a wide breadth of discipline areas.

It is well recognised that festivals and special events are important from community, social, cultural, political and economic perspectives. Despite the growth and popularity of festivals and special events, researchers were initially slow in directing research beyond economic impacts and motivations (Gursoy et al., 2004). However, this imbalance is now being corrected. The recent evolution of the academic study of festivals and events cannot be understood in isolation from the simultaneous evolution of the academic study of tourism. As themes of enquiry have emerged and developed within tourism studies, they virtually always evolve into a new theme of enquiry within festival and event studies. This link between the two areas of study is very strong, with tourism studies the primary field of enquiry and festivals and events a large and distinct sub-field within.

The task of advancing knowledge about the meanings, practices and policies associated with festivals and events remains ongoing. As this volume will show, the understanding of core concepts remains uneven, and our knowledge of certain dimensions of festival and event activity far exceeds that of others. Some of the extant gaps are recent, emerging only when contemporary political and societal debates begin to highlight particular concerns. The concept of **innovation** is a case in point: questions as to the role that the festival and event sector plays in promoting, adopting and managing **innovation** are now coming to the fore in the literature. Others, such as the sustainability of the sector's activities have been an issue for longer. Most recently of all, the question as to how **festival** and event activities are affected by global recession has begun to be investigated, in response to the harsh realities negatively affecting the health of the sector in very recent times. The 35 concepts that are discussed in this volume are laid out in alphabetical order.

introduction

1 Authenticity

> *Authenticity has been a central concept in tourism studies since MacCannell (1976) first argued in a highly influential text that the search for the 'authentic' is what drives the modern tourist. It is an equally important concept in festival and event studies because often these are perceived to offer a glimpse into the 'genuine' culture, lifestyle and beliefs of host communities.*

The meaning of authenticity has long been a central question within the social sciences. Early discussions tended to accept the *Concise Oxford Dictionary of Current English* (1964) definition of authenticity as 'reliable, trustworthy, of undisputed origin, genuine'. Over time, however, 'objective authenticity' (Wang, 1999) with its presumption that there is some means of determining what is definitively real or genuine has been strongly challenged by those who argue that reality is socially constructed and continuously negotiated (Bruner, 1994).

Smith et al., writing in a tourism context, define authenticity as 'the value that tourists and hosts place on the development and consumption of what are perceived to be genuine cultural events, products and experiences' (2010: 13). The development of thought about authenticity as a concept in tourism studies has been closely associated with investigations into festival settings. Many festivals, carnivals and other events have 'long traditions and historic continuity that afford them legitimacy' (Sharaby, 2008). Very often festivals and events of a traditional nature are constructed and represented by tourism producers as being the embodiment of authenticity. Traditional events are revived, repackaged, modified and refashioned, while new traditions are invented to attract tourist audiences. Authenticity seeking tourists often actively target festivals and events for the very reasons that MacCannell (1976) suggests. In such settings, traditions and meanings are actively and continuously being re-negotiated, reinvented and reinterpreted. Researchers, such as Müller and Pettersson (2005) and Kim and Jamal (2007), have been keen to explore the nature of the authentic and the construction of meanings of authenticity in festival and event settings. Tourism's role in promoting cultural change and in shaping the nature of the authentic has also been of key interest.

It was MacCannell (1976) who first argued that the search for authentic experience is crucial to the tourist endeavour. In this context, the festival or event is particularly appealing because it is understood to offer 'outsiders' genuine insights into particular 'insider' cultural practices, traditions and heritages. Furthermore, the very nature of festivals entails an overt outward orientation that sees communities of people generate cultural meanings expressly to be read by the outside world (Quinn, 2005). From a tourism supply perspective, festivals offer experiences 'commodified by condensation' in time and place to fit consumption into the busy schedules of visitors, exhibitors and performers (Mykletun, 2009). The problem, however, as expressed early on in the literature, is that in such circumstances, tourists are condemned to experience only a semblance of authenticity. Drawing on Goffman's (1959) models of front and back regions of social space, MacCannell (1976) argued that tourist settings are constructed to comprise six staged settings, all of which tourists strive, and ultimately fail, to 'get behind' in their quest to access the authentic back stages of the host community. MacCannell's theorisation, however, was later criticised because it equates the authentic with some sort of pristine, 'original' state which becomes automatically destroyed upon contact with tourism (Bruner, 1994). Researchers, such as Bruner (1994), Olsen (2002) and Shepherd (2002), have argued instead that authenticity is a socially constructed process and that the critical question is 'How do people themselves think about objects as authentic?' Following this line of thinking, authenticity is no longer seen as a quality of the object but as a cultural value constantly created and reinvented in social processes (Olsen, 2002). Cohen (1988) further elaborates this thinking by arguing the negotiability of authenticity. Being socially constructed, it has many potential forms and so 'a cultural product, or a trait thereof, which is at one point generally judged as contrived or inauthentic may, in the course of time, become generally recognized as authentic, even by experts' (Cohen, 1988: 379).

Thus, within mainstream tourism debates, it is becoming increasingly accepted that there are many reasonable answers to the question of what is authentic (Olsen, 2002); that questions about the meanings of authenticity are always open to negotiation (Timothy and Boyd, 2003); and that it is now necessary to speak of 'competing authenticities, all products of particular social forces engaged in a process of cultural (re)invention and consumption within the context of existing social relations' (Shepherd, 2002: 196). Recent empirical investigations in festival and events settings are moving to reflect this theoretical position although the idea that authenticity pertains to the quality of the object is still being explored. McCartney and Osti (2007: 26), examining the cultural authenticity of the dragon boat races in Macau, discuss the risk of commercialisation diminishing the meaning of an event, transforming it into spectacle or entertainment and 'thereby destroying its cultural authenticity'. Richards (2007), however, following on from the work of researchers, such as Cohen (1988) and Shepherd (2002), explores the value that different event audiences attach to authenticity. The latter explored how residents and visitors view commercialisation processes and authenticity in traditional events and found that while residents and visitors generally agree that the Catalan festival studied, La Mercè, is authentic, their perceptions of authenticity vary. Drawing on Wang (1999), Richards (2007) argues that residents were more likely to emphasise a 'constructive authenticity' based on familiar cultural norms (particularly those related to the role of tradition and language in Catalan society), while visitors tended to appreciate an 'existential authenticity', one reliant on enjoying the festivity and the attendant socialisation. Chang (2006) studied tourist motivations among visitors to an indigenous cultural festival in Wu-tai, the home of the Rukai tribe in Taiwan. She found that contrary to the belief that aboriginal peoples' cultures are a quaint novelty attractive to all tourists (Mark, 2002), not all tourists have the same degree of interest in the cultural experience that a festival provides. In her study, some appeared more interested in experiencing the change of pace associated with the festival and appreciating the rural scenery as well as the novelty value that lay in the use of traditional dress.

Elsewhere, Müller and Pettersson's (2005) analysis of a Swedish festival celebrating Sami heritage shows how different sets of meanings can be produced simultaneously and apparently satisfactorily for both producers and consumers. They describe how the experiences available to tourists, local residents and indigenous peoples range from being variously 'staged' to being 'non-staged'. Furthermore, they conclude that it is probably the co-existence of more or less staged, authorised and unauthorised, representations of Sami heritage that makes the festival attractive to a range of audiences, all of whom can relate to, and engage in, the festival in different ways. Thus, an important theoretical argument becoming established in the literature is that local residents, as producers and as established audiences, can engage meaningfully in festivals in ways that address both their own needs and those of visitors at the same time. More recently Kim and Jamal (2007) debated authenticity in the context of repeat festival attendees. They argued that the notion of existential authenticity is central to understanding the experience of committed, repeat festival attendees. Wang argued that in the context of liminal settings, such as tourism, festival and event arenas, 'people feel that they are themselves much more authentic and more freely self-expressed than they are in everyday life, not because the toured objects are authentic but rather because they are engaging in non-everyday activities, free from the constraints of daily life' (2000: 49–50). Kim and Jamal's findings (2007) supported this theoretical stance, showing how these serious tourists were engaged in 'bonding, friendship, identity-seeking and self-transformation'. They make the point that even though the subjects studied were attending the Texas Renaissance Festival, an example of 'a constructed site of carnivalesque play' (2000: 184) and a commercial tourism event often denigrated as being inauthentic, it actually represented an opportunity for attendees to seek 'self' authenticity.

From an applied perspective, the concept of authenticity and its treatment in the academic literature can appear very complex. Yet, the central idea that festivals and events are prized by attendees (both locals and visitors) because they offer glimpses into the lived cultural and social practices of groups of people, be they artists, athletes, local residents or community groups, continues to be very valid. Recent reporting by the BBC on the difficulties facing the music festival sector in the UK questioned whether 2011 would perhaps mark the end of the proliferation of festivals. It pondered whether, in order to survive, festivals in the future would have to identify and cultivate their uniqueness, those distinguishing elements that identify them as valid and meaningful practices (BBC, 2011).

FURTHER READING

MacCannell, D. (1976) *The Tourist. A New Theory of the Leisure Class.* New York: Schocken Books.

Müller, D.K. and Pettersson, R. (2005) 'What and where is the indigenous at an indigenous festival? Observations from the winter festival in Jokkmokk, Sweden', in C. Ryan and M. Aicken (eds), *Indigenous Tourism: The Commodification and Management of Culture.* Amsterdam: Elsevier. pp. 201–16.

Shepherd, R. (2002) 'Commodification, culture and tourism', *Tourist Studies*, 2 (2): 183–201.

Wang, N. (2000) *Tourism and Modernity: A Sociological Analysis.* Oxford: Pergamon.

2 Bidding

> *The market for large-scale special events is very competitive. Hallmark events, particularly in the sporting domain are in tremendous demand, and cities must compete for the privilege of hosting them. The competition between the aspiring host cities is known as the bidding process.*

Places and communities the world over decide to invest in organising planned events all the time. Frequently, the events that ensue are driven primarily by self-determined needs and achieved through local efforts. For mega/hallmark events, however, the situation is quite different. Hallmark events in sporting (for example, the Commonwealth Games) and cultural (for example, European City of Culture) arenas are internationally mobile and highly prized planned events that countries and regions rigorously compete to host. Many cities and states have established organisations (variously called event agencies or convention bureaux) with a specific remit to attract events into their area. Molotch conceived of cities as growth machines where the desire for growth creates the conditions for consensus to emerge between 'politically mobilised local elites, however split they might be on other issues' (1976: 310). The prospect of re-inventing a city's image, elevating its profile on the global stage, attracting internationally mobile capital and people, over-hauling infrastructures, and igniting widespread popular interest and excitement galvanises local coalitions. As Hall suggested, 'sports mega-events have become integral to the entrepreneurial strategies of cities seeking to gain competitive advantage in the global economy' (2006: 67). To achieve designation, such coalitions must bid to host the event in question and the process of event bidding has now become almost as high profile as the process of hosting events. London, host to the 2012 summer Olympic Games, spent an estimated £15 million on bidding for the event (Benneworth and Dauncey, 2010). As Westerbeek et al. (2002) remarked of the sports arena, only a limited number of hallmark events exist, and this has led to fierce competition among cities wishing to play host. Competition is fierce because cities expect that designation will lead to numerous positive outcomes for the city. These are widely identified in the literature and cross economic, cultural, social, environmental and political domains. Less written about are the cases where successful bids have led cities to accumulate sizeable debts. As Jones (2001) has suggested, the likelihood of securing economic benefits can sometimes be overstated. The Canadian city of Montreal learnt this to its cost after its hosting of the summer Olympics in 1976 resulted in a debt of CAN$2 billion in capital and interest costs (Whitson and Horne, 2006). Other costs can emerge in the guise of price inflation for goods and services, and tax increases to cover the cost of hosting the event (Solberg and Preuss, 2007).

The competition to secure important hallmark events has spiralled into a significant amount of bidding activity and there is now a small but growing literature on this topic alone. In Emery's (2002) discussion on sports event processes, the bidding element forms part of the pre-event phase, following on from the earlier 'ideas and feasibility' element. Within a local authority context, he argued that generally speaking, a bidding process will last for at least 1 year and involves (1) earning the local authority's approval, (2) a competitive bid to the national sports governing body and (3) a competitive bid to the international sports governing body. He makes the point that as each stage advances, the process 'requires further resource commitment, more bureaucracy and greater levels of uncertainty as more stakeholders become involved with the partnership' (2002: 320). Not surprisingly, an important question for researchers is what factors characterise a successful bid? An early contribution came from Westerbeek et al. (2002). They used a sample of 135 events from different countries to identify the factors most critical in the bidding process. Their findings suggest that from the perspective of the event manager, eight factors emerge as particularly important. Above all, it is the ability to organise the event, political support, infrastructure and existing facilities that matter most. Communication and exposure, accountability, bid team composition and relationship marketing are also important but perhaps less vital in the bidding process. Emery's (2002) empirical research found that successful bids were underpinned by five key factors: having relevant professional credibility; fully understanding the brief and the formal/informal decision-making process; not assuming that decision makers are experts; or that they use rational criteria for selection; knowing your strengths and weaknesses relative to your competition.

Competing to host such events as the FIFA World Cup and the Olympic Games means engaging in highly structured and rigorous processes, and some researchers have focused on investigating these. Griffiths (2006) described these processes in the context of a non-sports event, the European City of Culture designation, and analysed the bids prepared by three of the cities in contention for the UK title in 2008. His focus was on the role of culture in urban public policy. For Foley et al. (2012a: 123) successful bids must simultaneously develop a strategy that meets internal stakeholders' needs, meets the priorities of the organising authority (for example, FIFA, International Olympic Committee) and out-manoeuvres other bidders. They draw on researchers, such as Shaw (2008) and Black (2007), who have tried to interpret the kinds of core messages that event bids generally try to communicate. Shaw's (2008) work on the Olympics suggested that internal stakeholders' needs can be addressed with bids that advocate three main 'propositions': (1) a promise of economic gain; (2) an appeal to patriotism; and (3) a homage to idealism and the achievement of dreams. Out-manoeuvring other contenders, according to Foley et al. (2012a), usually takes two main forms: bidders may seek to make their case on the strength on their track record. Glasgow's bid to host the 2014 Commonwealth Games, for example, was strengthened because it had previously hosted a series of diverse sporting and cultural events dating from the **European City of Culture** in 1990 to the UEFA Cup Final in 2007. The second approach to out-manoeuvring other contenders relies on making an emotional appeal to the heartstrings, as in South Africa's bid to host the 2010 World Cup which was presented as a way of strengthening democracy in the country. Bids to host hallmark events like the Commonwealth Games and Olympic Games are years in the making. Foley et al. (2012a) track Glasgow's bid for the 2014 Games back to its selection as Scotland's preferred city by the Commonwealth Games Council for Scotland in 2004.

Within the applied event management literature, where educating future event managers is a key occupation, the bidding process is widely treated. Textbooks, such as that by Allen et al. (2011), discuss this concept, contextualise it in terms of event tourism, describe the various steps and organisations involved in the bidding process, and analyse the reasons for bid failure. Some pay detailed attention to particular hallmark events. Mallen and Adams (2008), for example, discussed the highly formalised process involved in bidding for the Olympic Games. Cities must prepare four key documents for consideration by the

International Olympic Committee (IOC): (1) a feasibility study detailing the capacity of the group and location to host the event; (2) a candidature document outlining the processes being undertaken and the timelines being followed; (3) a bid questionnaire, which responds to a broad series of questions laid down by the IOC concerning everything from legal aspects to the environment and the Olympic village. Finally the bidders must submit (4) a bid dossier, which contains the overall plan and strategy and effectively seeks to make the bid stand apart from its competitors. Closer inspection of all the bidding details is facilitated by a 'bid tour' for those 'would-be' host cities that make it to the short list of cities being considered as potential Olympic Games host cities.

Event bidding is a very risky activity. Only one location can win any given designation and yet so many resources can be invested in the process. Emery (2002) suggests that as more and more local governments engage in bidding for sports events then the bidding process is likely to become even more extravagant, expensive and risky. In order to reduce the levels of risk and the amount of financial debt involved, bidding partnerships are likely to increase in number and complexity. In this context it seems relevant to ask whether a failed bid therefore constitutes a waste of resources? Benneworth and Dauncey (2010) posed this question and suggested that even when bids are not won, engaging in the actual process of bidding can yield positive outcomes. They suggested that the process of bidding for large-scale events can boost a city's self-organisation capacity and support the idea 'that international urban festivals could provide a means for network capacity building in terms of persuading partners to work together on something unambiguously of mutual benefit' (Benneworth and Dauncey, 2010: 1096). Their analysis of Lyon's failed 1968 Olympic bid led them to conclude that, indirectly, it became a catalyst for subsequent change. In reality, fear of failure does not seem to act as a deterrent to cities' continued preoccupation with strategically using events to regenerate, reposition and develop their profiles. Instead, the competitive nature of the event business serves to encourage cities to invest increasing resources into developing their attractiveness as event locations. Dubai, for instance, is a good example of a place that has prioritised major sporting events as a mechanism for advancing tourism and economic development (Smith, 2010). Meanwhile, Liverpool has recently heavily prioritised events as a means of revitalising its economy, profile and reputation through its high profile hosting of the **European City of Culture** in 2008. Showing a commitment to **innovation**, the Liverpool Convention Bureau has recently spearheaded the development of an online bidding tool designed to streamline the process of attracting domestic and international events to the city and to replace the traditional process to making hard copy bids (Liverpool Convention Bureau, 2012).

FURTHER READING

Benneworth, P. and Dauncey, H. (2010) 'International urban festivals as a catalyst for governance capacity building', *Environment and Planning C: Government and Policy*, 28 (6): 1083–100.

Emery, P.R. (2002) 'Bidding to host a major sports event: the local organising committee perspective', *International Journal of Public Sector Management*, 1: 316–35.

Walters, G. (2011) 'Bidding for international sport events: how government supports and undermines national governing bodies of sport', *Sport in Society: Cultures, Commerce, Media, Politics*, 14 (2): 208–22.

Westerbeek, H.M., Turner, P. and Ingerson, L. (2002) 'Key success factors in bidding for hallmark sporting events', *International Marketing Review*, 19 (3): 303–22.

3 Community Festivals

Community festivals are those that emerge from within a place-based community to celebrate some aspect of its identity. There is a substantial literature on 'community festivals', a category of events that has increased in size in recent years

Festivals and planned events can be established as large-scale public ventures with governments of varying levels deciding to use them as vehicles to achieve a variety of policy objectives. However, they are also very likely to emerge as small-scale, localised endeavours, founded by place-based communities of people interested in celebrating something. Such community festivals have proliferated in recent decades (Arcodia and McKinnon, 2004) and key objectives can be to celebrate both group and place identify (de Bres and Davis, 2001). Very often, community festivals exist to commemorate and celebrate moments of importance on the local calendar. These might include the births or deaths of people, momentous happenings, rituals associated with religious practices or the agrarian lifecycle, or social practices of particular significance. Equally, they may emerge in response to a particular local need, perhaps a lack of access to certain forms of art, like jazz music or literature. Festivals can attract artists to places that might be 'off the beaten track' and lacking in a well-developed permanent cultural infrastructure. As such, they can open up access to artists that community audiences might otherwise not have a chance to experience. Clifden Community Arts Week has been pivotal in developing and promoting participation in the arts in a small town in the West of Ireland for the last 36 years. Driven by the desire to widen access and participation in the arts among local people it has contributed by: nurturing artistic participation in a series of ways; developing the town's cultural infrastructure; and through its arts society, programming arts concerts and events year-round. Community festivals may also be stimulated by local authorities seeking to use them as vehicles to achieve a number of aims, usually socio-cultural in nature. As part of its London Olympics 2012 programme, Camden Council in London, for example, established a fund for community festivals and street parties in the Camden district of the city. The fund was aimed at initiatives that engage local communities with cultural activities, support new partnerships and offer opportunities for volunteering or mentoring (Camden Council, 2012).

Gursoy et al. (2004) suggested that generating economic benefits is one of the most important reasons for establishing a festival. However, they also point to the work of sociologists, such as Durkheim (1912) and Turner (1982), who suggested that the main purpose of collective celebrations (such as festivals and events) is to build social cohesion by reinforcing ties within the community. As Derrett (2003) reminds us, a community's sense of both itself and its place is very much constitutive of what makes a festival. Derrett (2003: 51) describes a sense of community as an almost invisible yet critical part of a healthy community. Distinctly intangible in nature, it relates to a community's image, spirit, character and pride, as well as to the relationships and networks that knit it together (Bush, 2000). Researchers are agreed that festivals and events create the conditions and contexts within which groups of people can develop a sense of community: Dunstan (1994), for example, stated that they provide a forum for a shared purpose to become manifest; Wheatley and Kellner-Rogers (1998: 14) suggested that festivals can become the heart of a community as their celebratory nature provides residents with conditions of freedom and connectedness rather than a fixation on the forms and structures of the community. For Derrett they offer opportunities to 'nurture and sustain what is important to their constituency' and demonstrate a sense of community by offering connections, belonging, support, empowerment, participation and safety (2003: 51). These ideas are central to the literature on **social capital** with Chwe (1998), for example, suggesting that public events, such as festivals and special events, play an important role in creating a general common knowledge by providing a communication mechanism for residents to communicate social information and also to build trust. He also suggests that festivals and events provide social incentives for the local community to get actively involved in community activities, so they come to play a role in building social cohesion and trust by reinforcing ties within a community. Ulrich (1998: 157) wrote that community festivals help create communities of values by forging strong and distinct identities. Residents can be the gatekeepers of community values, encouraging some people in, while keeping others out. This last point is linked to the literature reviewed in the section dealing with **power and politics.** This literature is very alert to the politically contested nature of the identity formation processes at issue. As Waterman wrote, events are never 'impromptu or improvised ... and arts festivals in particular, are never spontaneous' (1998: 59). The manner in which multiple divisions may open up within communities that are far from heterogeneous has long been of interest in social sciences research.

From a tourism perspective, as McKercher et al. (2006) argued, small community festivals satisfy sustainability criterion. Organised by, and for the benefit of the local community, community festivals embody the kind of authentic cultural experience so sought after by tourists. They tend to require minimal capital development and take advantage of existing infrastructure. They are generally volunteer intensive and locally controlled. Yet they have the potential to generate substantial returns on small financial investments (Getz, 1993). The 'substantial returns' at issue are those that result from the **tourism** activity that community festivals often come to generate. These can enhance the **identity**-building and civic pride enhancement functions that more localised festivals play. As Getz (1993) pointed out, festivals and special events provide important activities and spending outlets for locals and visitors and enhance the image of local communities. More generally, Jago and Shaw (1998) synopsised the literature and identified a series of reasons explaining communities' interest in hosting planned events. These reasons align with a series of anticipated outcomes including increased visitation to the region, economic injection, improvement of the destination's image and enhanced community pride. Féile an Phobail in West Belfast is a case in point. It was founded in 1988 as a direct response to the conflict in Northern Ireland. Its purpose was 'to celebrate the positive side of the community' and to displace political confrontations with 'a positive display of the community and its creativity' (Féile an Phobail, 2012). From being a 1 week event, the Féile is now the largest community arts festival on the island of Ireland.

In tourism contexts, researchers have been conscious of the role that local community support plays in sustaining festivals. In the tourism literature, research on communities or more particularly on residents has drawn heavily on social exchange theory to investigate differentiation within host populations in respect of engagement in, and attitudes towards, tourism-oriented activities like special events. Getz (2005) discussed the essential importance of **festival** organisers working with local people in order to gain their support; Molloy (2002) argued that in the absence of local volunteers assuming a variety of key organising roles, workers would have to be employed and the costs would become prohibitive. Several researchers have argued that a strong relationship between festival organisers and local residents is vital to long-term viability (Arcodia and Whitford, 2006; Small, 2007). Alienation of the local community has been linked to festival failure (Jago et al., 2003; Molloy, 2002). Meanwhile, alienation and loss of local support has been explained in terms of over-commercialisation (Quinn, 2005; Small et al,. 2005), lack of consultation and disruption (Fredline and Faulkner, 2000). The question of how to promote community participation in festivals has recently been addressed by Rogers and Anastasiadou (2011) in a study undertaken in Edinburgh. They devised a series of community involvement methods that included involving schools, volunteering opportunities, participation in decision making, accessibility of programme and business cooperation.

Measuring residents' perceptions of the social impacts of community festivals and events has been a significant line of research enquiry in the literature. Since 2000, a number of researchers have been actively developing and testing empirical scales to measure and interpret residents' perceptions (Delamere, 2001; Delamere et al., 2001; Fredline et al., 2003; Small 2007). The most recent of these, Small (2007), used the social impact perception (SIP) scale and identified six underlying social impact dimensions including inconvenience, community identity and cohesion, personal frustration, entertainment and socialisation opportunities, community growth and development, and behavioural consequences.

From a management perspective, community festivals experience a number of operational difficulties because of their small scale and limited resources. Arcodia and McKinnon (2004), for example, detailed the challenges faced by rural festivals in Australia because of unexpected rises in public liability insurance. The concept of communities also arises in discussions about event **stakeholders** and the various relationship networks that underpin the production of events. MacKellar's (2006) analysis of the relationship networks between festival, convention and tourism activity drew out the community dimension. She argued that the links created through even just a one-off event created opportunity for people to interact and engage in dialogue about shared commonalities. As discussed elsewhere in this volume, Crespi-Vallbona and Richards (2007) have called for more nuanced understandings of the relationships between different **stakeholders** and specifically raise the question of stakeholders in the context of community groups. One of their key observations is that 'the notion of "community" is usually treated in an abstract fashion, which obscures rather than clarifies the role of different stakeholders' (Crespi-Vallbona and Richards, 2007: 107).

FURTHER READING

Arcodia, C.V. and McKinnon, S.E. (2004) 'Public liability insurance: it's impact on Australian rural festivals', *Journal of Convention and Event Tourism*, 6 (3): 101–10.

De Bres, K. and Davis, J. (2001) 'Celebrating group and place identity: a case study of a new regional festival', *Tourism Geographies*, 3 (3): 326–37.

Derrett, R. (2003) 'Making sense of how festivals demonstrate a community's sense of place', *Event Management*, 8: 49–58.

McKercher, B., Mei, W.S. and Tse, T.S.M. (2006) 'Are short duration cultural festivals tourist attractions?', *Journal of Sustainable Tourism*, 14 (1): 55–66.

4 Definitions

The task of precisely defining the term 'festival' and more especially the term 'planned event' has preoccupied many. Much agreement exists as to what constitutes a festival: it is a communal affair where celebration is always core. Defining 'event' is more complicated because of the enormous variety of criteria, for example, purpose, rationale, size and scale, among others, at issue. At core, planned events are short-lived and transitory. They are special in that they have a particular focus or theme and they are unusual in that they differ from the routine.

As is quite common with young areas of study, such as this one, a certain haziness characterises the definition of festival and event terminology and contributors to the literature have struggled with the task of agreeing definitions. This is partly because researchers have approached the task from different perspectives and partly because of the innate complications involved in establishing what constitutes a planned event. Agreement is unambiguous on one matter: planned events are transitory. They may recur, but while in situ, they last only for a relatively short, defined period of time. If they do recur, it may be in a different location next time, thus for any given place, the significance of playing host is paramount. The title of this volume, *Concepts in Event Management*, means to encompass both festivals and events, as if that is somehow inherently logical. However, it may be noted that while festivals can always be understood as a type of planned event, the reverse does not apply: not all events are festivals. At times, the literature seems confused in its conceptualisation and treatment of these two concepts. Often, for example, the terms are used interchangeably. At other times, an enquiry purporting to be investigating festivals, for example, develops its ideas by reference to the literature on events and vice versa. Sometimes this is appropriate, other times it is less useful.

As Hede (2007) explained, special event research emerged as an area of tourism management research in the mid-1970s, but it was during the 1980s that the study of events began to grow dramatically in academia

(Getz, 2008). It was during these decades that terminology was introduced and meanings debated. The origin of the terms in question emerged
in particular contexts. The marked rise of academic interest in events in
the 1980s, for instance, was closely linked to their role in **place marketing**,
a type of civic boosterism that views culture instrumentally (Loftman and
Nevil, 1996). Undoubtedly, this was an important context shaping
research enquiry into festivals and events from then onwards. While the
use of events as a civic boosterism instrument has been critiqued (Boyle,
1997), it was widely viewed as a positive development among tourism
researchers. Events are seen as an important motivator in tourism (Getz,
2008), and as an effective enhancer of destination image (Hall, 1992;
Ritchie, 1984). Three defining descriptors predominate in the adjectives
commonly used to denote short-term, staged or planned events: *special*,
mega and *hallmark*. According to Shone and Parry (2004: 3), special
events arise from those non-routine occasions which have leisure, cultural,
personal or organisational objectives set apart from the normal activity of
daily life, whose purpose is to enlighten, celebrate, entertain or challenge
the experience of a group of people. A briefer and widely cited definition
of a special event is: 'a onetime or infrequently occurring event outside
the normal programme or activities of the sponsoring or organising body'
(Getz, 1991: 44). The use of 'hallmark' and 'mega' as descriptors implies
large-scale events. In the past, 'hallmark' was a commonly used descriptor
and an early, and much cited, definition of hallmark events came from
Ritchie (1984: 2) who defined them as: 'major one-time or recurring
events of limited duration, developed primarily to enhance the awareness,
appeal and profitability of a tourism destination in the short and/or long
term'. Usually held in city locations, hallmark events were labelled 'our
new image-builders' (Burns and Mules, 1986). Hall defined hallmark
events as 'major fairs, festivals, expositions and cultural and sporting
events which are held on either a regular or a one-off basis' (1992: 1).
Mega-events, meanwhile, have been described by Getz as those which 'by
way of their size and significance … yield extraordinary high levels of
tourism, media coverage, prestige or economic impact for the host community or destination' (1997: 6). Clearly, special events become 'hallmark' or 'mega' in nature once they reach a particular size and scale, but
categorising events by size or scale poses obvious definitional complications. Despite, or perhaps because of this, few contributors have suggested
temporal or scale specifications, although in 1987, the AIEST (Congress
of the Association Internationale d'Experts Scientifique du Tourisme)
suggested that the definition of mega-events should be based on volume

(1 million visits), capital costs (DM750 million [approximately €750 million, current value]) and psychology (it should have a reputation as being a must-see event) (Marris, 1987). Others have introduced dimensions of scale in terms of:

1   impact – according to Roche, 'mega-events are short-term events with long-term consequences for the cities that stage them' (1994: 1);
2   investment – Hall notes that 'the majority of hallmark events have substantial government involvement, whether it be at national, state or local level' (1992: 3);
3   spatial reach – hallmark events are those 'which have an ability to focus national and international attention on the destination' (Ritchie, 1984: 2).

Similarly, Westerbeek et al. (2002) note four defining characteristics: conspicuous governmental involvement; support of domestic/international broadcasting media; superior nature of technological competencies required; and broad support from direct and indirect stakeholders. To further complicate matters, several researchers have introduced the notion of relativity, arguing that smaller-scale events can be understood as being hallmark in terms of their local and regional significance (Getz, 1989; Hall, 1992). In summary, then, it seems clear that the term special events is loosely used as a catch-all term to refer to the broad array of staged or planned events that have proliferated in recent decades. On closer examination, special events are distinguishable by differences of scale, although the specifics of what these differences might be are rarely itemised. However, it seems clear that both the terms 'mega' and 'hallmark' are applied when the profile, investment, and impact involved are very substantial.

Turning then to the festival concept: the explosion in the literature on festivals in the event management and event studies literatures clearly attests to the importance of festivals in this field. The word 'festival' derives from the Latin 'festum', meaning feast (Isar, 1976). As Getz et al. (2010) point out, festivals are socio-cultural constructs and their meanings vary according to where they are produced and by whom. Nevertheless, irrespective of nuances in meaning, the notion of collective, participatory celebration is central. In terms of the subject topic of this book, festivals represent a type of special event that has been known to exist for a very long time. According to Falassi (1987: 1–2), festivals are social phenomena, found in virtually all human cultures, comprising five elements:

1 a sacred or profane time of celebration, marked by special observances;
2 the annual celebration of a notable person or event, or the harvest of an important product;
3 a cultural event consisting of a series of performances of works in the fine arts, often devoted to a single artist of genre;
4 a fair;
5 generic gaiety, conviviality, cheerfulness.

Within the tourism and events literature, festivals are conceptualised as tourism products and tourist attractions. From a broader social science perspective, festivals are social practices that communities have engaged in for generations as a means of expressing beliefs and celebrating identities (Ekman, 1999). In creating opportunities for drawing on shared histories, shared cultural practices and shared ideals, as well as creating settings for social interactions, festivals engender local continuity. They constitute arenas in which local knowledge is produced and reproduced; where the history, cultural inheritance and social structures which distinguish one place from another are revised, rejected or recreated. Overall, 'festival' has proven to be a simpler term to define than 'event', although some confusion exists. Jaeger and Mykletun (2009), for example, point to the difficulties of determining what type of events can be classed as festivals. They suggest that in Norway, for example, the use of the term 'festival' is unclear among both festival organisations and among the population at large. Indeed, a reading of the popular reporting of festivals can sometimes lead to the suggestion that places and communities across the developed world have been inclined to simply add the word 'festival' to any variety of happening, in the hope that it might attract tourists and their associated revenues. Within a place marketing ethos, and from a supply perspective, festivals came to be increasingly defined simply as just one more type of event. Their festive, playful, celebrative qualities were recognised and prized because festivals offer tourists glimpses of local uniqueness (Litvin and Fetter, 2006), diverse cultural experiences (Hall, 1992) and opportunities to participate in distinctive, collective experiences (Getz, 1989). However, there was little attempt to draw on established understandings of festivals as socially and culturally important phenomena involved in the construction of place and community identity (as distinct from image identity). While their reproduction as tourist attraction was sometimes problematised (Greenwood, 1972), critical perspectives such as this has not noticeably influence the emerging event literature.

FURTHER READING

Falassi, A. (1987) *Time out of Time: Essays on the Festival.* Albuquerque, NM: University of New Mexico.

Getz, D. (2008) 'Event tourism: definition, evolution and research', *Tourism Management*, 29 (3): 403–28.

Getz, D. (1991) *Festivals, Special Events and Tourism.* New York: Van Nostrand Reinhold.

Hede, A. (2007) 'Managing special events in the new era of the triple bottom line', *Event Management*, 11: 13–22.

Ritchie, J.R.B. (1984) 'Assessing the impacts of hallmark events: conceptual and research issues', *Journal of Travel Research*, 23 (1): 2–11.

5 Economic Impact

> The literature on the economic impact of events is very substantial. It conceives of festivals and events as activities that can have a series of economic consequences for host locations. The focus of this literature has been to identity, describe and measure these consequences or impacts, which may be both positive and negative in nature.

The concept of impact is omnipresent within event research. It is no exaggeration to say that the early development of event research was overwhelmingly preoccupied with the notion of impact and the literature on impact is now vast in size. Numerous researchers have written about the valuable role that festivals and events play in the lives of local, place-based communities. Often, they do not require extensive capital investment or infrastructural development but can prosper on a foundation of local enthusiasm and local voluntary energies (Getz, 1993; Janiskee, 1994; Turko and Kelsey, 1992). Yet, they can deliver a variety of beneficial returns. The impact literature can be seen to fall into a number of categories covering economic, environmental, social and cultural. Tourism impact and political impact have also been examined. However, it is the literature on economic impacts that is most extensive. While the term 'impact' is pervasive within the literature, researchers also write about '**evaluation**', often in a way that fails to make any distinction between the two. Both impact and evaluation are treated separately in this volume. To complicate matters further, the term 'legacy', is also sometimes used, often in the context of event **leveraging**. At times, this is specifically defined and differentiated from impact, but at other times, it is not. The uneven treatment of these terms in the literature creates a degree of confusion.

The emphasis on impact should be understood in context. Not surprisingly, as festivals and events became increasingly incorporated into urban and regional development agendas, the obvious growth in early academic interest was in management and economics, and research agendas were closely attuned to practitioners' needs. Since at least the 1980s, there has been a pronounced orientation towards understanding the impact of events, and from early on, events came overwhelmingly to be conceived as discrete entities with an ability to uni-directionally create a series of impacts, both positive and negative, on contextual environments. A fundamental idea underpinning the concept of event impact is that events operate on an input–output basis where, as Weed noted, 'the provision of the event is seen as an input and the outcomes, impacts or legacies are seen as an output' (2011: 1). Ritchie's (1984) identification of a range of impacts associated with what he called hallmark events was an important and influential publication. Although he identified a wide range of impact types, most subsequent research attention focused on measuring and evaluating the economic impacts of events on host economies, a development at least partially inspired by the realities of city and regional government needs for justifying investment in festival and event development strategies (Burns et al., 1986; Crompton and McKay, 1994; Dwyer et al., 2000). As early as 1989, researchers were highlighting the need for a broader set of research concerns including 'the anticipation and regulation of the impact of the event on the host community, and the promotion of associated development in a manner which maximises short- and long-term economic, environmental and social benefits' (Hall, 1989: 21). Yet, Gursoy et al. (2004) note that researchers have been very slow in directing research beyond economic impacts and motivations. The overtly 'economic impact' orientation of the literature has been well acknowledged in the literature (Getz, 2008; Hede, 2007; Langen and García, 2009; Moscardo, 2007).

Thus, clearly, festivals and events are valued for their economic benefits. According to Jago and Dwyer 'the economic impact of an event on a region is the net sum of the economic consequence of all of the cash inflows and outflows that occur because of an event' (2006: 7). The measurement of economic outputs has employed a variety of mechanisms. Early research tended to think of impact in post-event terms (O'Sullivan et al., 2009) and three dominant methods for forecasting and evaluating economic impacts in the literature are computable general equilibrium models, input–output analysis and cost–benefit analysis (Andersson et al., 2008; Jackson et al., 2005). The research evidence suggests that large-scale events create both positive and negative impacts in both the short and the long term. Many studies have documented positive outcomes (Decco and Baloglu, 2002; Ritchie and Smith, 1991). Clear positives include the enhancement of the international image of the host community, and the generation of short- and long-term visitor flows. The literature on the **European City of Culture** event is often preoccupied with the **tourism** outcomes of this annual cultural event (Bailey et al., 2004; García, 2005). One of the ECOC's most frequently discussed in the literature, Glasgow 1990, is widely attributed with having transformed the city's image from a rarely visited, depressed, post-industrial city into a lively and attractive city that subsequent to the event increased its inbound tourist flows dramatically. The generation of environmental outcomes in the form of infrastructural legacies is another notable theme in the literature. Large events have come to be seen as catalysts for urban regeneration (García, 2004) although mixed outcomes have been reported in respect of the latter with several acknowledging negative outcomes (Hall and Hodges, 1996; Hiller, 1998; Roche, 1994). Examples of such negativities include the accumulation of large debts for host communities and the displacement of local residents to make way for infrastructural improvements. Some studies have pointed to positive, yet somewhat intangible and often surprising outcomes. Lee and Taylor in an economic impact study, concluded in respect of the 2002 FIFA World Cup held in South Korea that 'the success of the South Korean football team provided the country with a sense of national pride and cohesiveness that no economic impact assessment could ever put a dollar value on' (2005: 602). Lee et al. (2005) make the point that mega sports events, such as the Olympic Games, draw a great deal of international attention to sport and in the process contribute to increased interest in sports tourism.

The economic impact literature is constantly being critiqued and developed. There has been much debate concerning both the robustness of the methodologies and approaches used to determine economic out-comes and the accuracy of gains attributed to events. For example, the limitations of the once well-used input–output analysis are now more clearly understood (Dwyer et al., 2000; Madden, 2002). Many studies have been critiqued for tending to overstate positive impacts while ignoring many negatives (Dwyer et al., 2005; Jackson et al., 2005). Litvin and Fetter (2006), for example, found that the highly successful Spoleto festival, held annually in Charleston, South Carolina, USA, did not benefit the local economy as might have been expected and con-cluded that from a destination perspective, events should seek to com-plement the overall tourism product on offer in a place. Lee and Taylor (2005) critically reviewed the problems that beset economic impact studies, citing critical observations from, inter alia, Crompton (1999), Lee and Kim (1998) and Tyrrell and Johnston (2001). They concluded that on the basis of past research only direct expenditure attributable to an event should be considered in estimating the economic impact of an event. However, elsewhere Wood et al. (2006) argued that a focus on direct expenditure benefits will produce an incomplete picture. Felenstein and Fleischer (2009) acknowledged the difficulties at issue in trying to assess the extent of a festival's contribution to local economic growth. They critiqued existing research on a number of factors: that economic analyses tend to end prematurely with an estimation of mul-tiplier effects; that there is a general absence of interest in demonstrating how these translate into local economic growth; or in examining how public investment in festivals results in a change in local income. Their study, based on empirical research into two Israeli festivals illustrated a practical approach for converting local expenditure into local income change (Felenstein and Fleischer, 2009: 391). Their investigations found that although both festivals generated modest growth benefits, they continued to attract generous public assistance. However, they also con-cluded that the local image creation function of the festival increased the local growth effects. Lee and Taylor (2005) focused on estimating the tourist numbers and expenditure directly attributable to sport tour-ism mega-events. They concluded that existing models fail to adequately conceptualise aversion and diversion effects.

In spite of their proliferation, and the diversity of beneficial outcomes that festivals and events can generate, surprisingly little research has been done on comprehensively identifying and measuring the outcomes at issue (Gursoy et al., 2004). The literature measuring festival and event impact has tended to employ quantitative approaches and to measure impact from one particular perspective at any given time. In addition, studies have tended to take snapshot 'moment in time' approaches and several researchers, writing about different kinds of event contexts have called for more longitudinal perspectives to be employed (Boo and Busser, 2006). In addition, impact research, especially economic impact research has tended to focus on large-scale sporting events. This means that much scope remains for further enquiry into different types of events of differing scales. For example, as Langen and García (2009) note, the rate of growth in the number of cultural festivals and major cultural events is such that their impacts have become increasingly of interest to key stakeholders.

FURTHER READING

Felenstein, D. and Fleischer, A. (2009) 'Local festivals and tourism promotion: the role of public assistance and visitor expenditure', *Journal of Travel Research*, 41: 385–92.

Gursoy, D., Kim, K. and Uysal, M. (2004) 'Perceived impacts of festivals and special events by organizers: an extension and validation', *Tourism Management*, 25: 171–81.

Jago, L. and Dwyer, L. (2006) *Economic Evaluation of Special Events: A Practitioner's Guide*. Altona, Victoria: Common Ground Publishing.

Lee, C. and Taylor, T. (2005) Critical reflections on the economic impact assessment of a mega-event: the case of 2002 FIFA world cup', *Tourism Management*, 26 (4): 595–603.

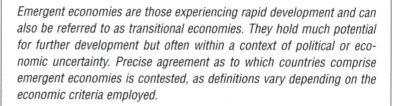

6 Emergent Economies

Emergent economies are those experiencing rapid development and can also be referred to as transitional economies. They hold much potential for further development but often within a context of political or economic uncertainty. Precise agreement as to which countries comprise emergent economies is contested, as definitions vary depending on the economic criteria employed.

The vitality and continued growth of **festival** and event activity world-wide underpins the rationale for writing a book such as this. Yet, the literature reviewed throughout shows an evident Western bias: most of the academic material published on the topic frames its discussions and draws its cases from Western contexts. Even the most cursory search for festival- and event-related articles in any of the international journals will support this assertion. This is a shortcoming that needs redress: festivals and events are growing in number and diversity throughout the world, not just in the West but most noticeably, in emergent economies. As Jago et al. (2010) noted, mega-events have traditionally been the preserve of the developed world, but this is changing. Asian countries have strongly featured in the hosting of mega-events in recent years as has South Africa, while Brazil is about to feature strongly with the Olympic Games and the FIFA World Cup in 2016 and 2014, respectively. As Jones (2012) points out, it is in emergent economies that economic growth is strong, societies are becoming increasingly oriented towards consumption, and youthful populations are driving the demand for leisure pursuits, many of which underpin the festival and event sector.

As UNWTO statistics testify, the greatest dynamism in global tourism flows in recent years has been found in what it terms 'emergent economies'. Asia-Pacific and the Middle East, in particular, have been growing strongly. Average percentage annual growth rates over the period 2000–2010 ranged from 9.6 (Middle East) through 6.4 (Africa), 6.3 (Asia-Pacific) down to 2.1 (Europe) and 1.6 (the Americas) (UNWTO, 2012). The increasing Western demand for long-haul travel into these regions combined with growing intra-regional travel has served to heighten government interest in using tourism as a tool for economic development. As part of this, events have clearly assumed a new strategic significance. In countries such as Abu Dhabi, Dubai and Qatar in the Middle East, for example, event tourism has been actively and strategically developed since the early 2000s. The hosting of the 15th Asian Games in Doha, Qatar in 2006 was the largest ever event held in the Middle East. The Asian Games are the second largest multi-sport event, after the summer Olympic Games. Qatar was the first Arab country to host the Asian Games as well as being the smallest country in the world in modern times to host an event of such scale and complexity. Foley et al. (2012b) investigated the shift in government policies on sport event tourism in the Middle East and Gulf region. South Korea and Japan's joint hosting of 2002 FIFA World Cup and Beijing's hosting of the 2008 **Olympic Games** are examples of very high profile global events held in Asia in recent times. Since the onset of democracy, South Africa has hosted a number of diverse international events ranging from the Rugby World Cup in 1995 and the 2002 World Summit on Sustainable Development to the 2010 FIFA World Cup. All of these events have given South Africa opportunities to rebuild its reputation on the world stage and to benefit from 'massive new investment in infrastructure (for example, stadiums, accommodation, airports, roads, public transport systems) by both the private and the public sector; an upgraded safety and security net and criminal justice system; the introduction of new information and communications technology' (Jago et al., 2010: 221). Not surprisingly the development of festivals and events is supported and promoted by the South African government as part of its economic development strategy (Van Niekerk and Coetzee, 2011). As Cornelissena (2008) put it, hosting a world-class event implies that a country is open to the world for business, and knowledge of this undoubtedly motivated Brazil's successful bid to host the 2016 Olympic Games. Up to this point, Brazil was the only one of the world's 10 biggest economies never to have staged the Olympics. In winning the designation for 2016 it will host the first Olympics ever to be staged in South America. Prior to this, South American cities were notable for their absence from the map of previous host cities, which showed 30 in Europe, 12 in North America and 5 in Asia (Brown, 2009).

For cities throughout the emerging economies, battling in highly competitive conditions to get greater prominence on the world stage, festivals and events are important **place marketing** strategies. Shin (2004), for instance, presented the case of the Gwangju Biennale Festival as being representative of recent cultural festivals in South Korea, where the image of a 'city of art' was one of the standardised images developed by local governments to reshape the images of several South Korean cities. With an interesting combination of research questions, Lamberti et al. (2011) examined the Shanghai World Expo to see what effect it had on fostering community participation in tourism development. They explained how the hosting of the Expo was related to the Chinese government's desire to profile the burgeoning Chinese economy on the world stage, to affirm Shanghai's position as a leading city and to develop tourism. Their findings shed light on the evolutionary nature of community participation and concluded that in this case, the event was instrumental in broadening community involvement in general as well as in decision making. The effect of this was to enlarge the elite group that make decisions and to spread the benefits.

As Jago et al. (2010) pointed out, however, the capacity of developing countries to profit optimally from the opportunities offered by the hosting of events is sometimes constrained. They refer to the employment generated during both the construction and operational phases of mega-events, and suggest that the skill legacy created is often limited because much of the higher skilled labour inputs are sourced from outside the country. Accordingly, they highlight the need for training programmes to ensure that skills are transferred.

Beyond this, an interest in festivals, as distinct from events, has predominated in the literature pertaining to developing countries. Festivals are widespread cultural practices that have been found to exist for centuries in societies throughout the world (Turner, 1982). In contrast, planned events pursuing economic and development-oriented agenda, have been much more associated with advanced capitalist societies until relatively recently times. The sociological and anthropological literatures that have been interested in festivals have often focused on community development and on social capital issues, and a central argument has been that festivals serve to build social cohesion by reinforcing ties within a community. In essence, this research supports sociological arguments about how collective celebrations like festivals, while providing public entertainment, serve profoundly important opportunities for communities to reify their group identity (Durkheim, 1912). One study contributing to this line of argument comes from Shukla (1997) who reached into the imagined communities of the diaspora in exploring the 1991 Cultural Festival of India, organised by Indian immigrants in New Jersey, USA. The 'spectacular exhibition' of Indian culture studied was found to simultaneously reify Indian culture, portray idealised Indian values and celebrate technological innovation, building in the process, both national and transnational diasporic communities.

As noted elsewhere, the interest in the link between festivals, events and **social capital** is growing. As Torche and Valenzuela (2011) remark, it is everywhere regarded as a source of economic development and social integration while in the developing world it is also regarded as a means of overcoming poverty and consolidating democratic rule. According to Rao (2001), any institution that serves to reinforce ties within a community, whether by generating common knowledge or by building trust or by some other means, is building **social capital** by facilitating the formation of networks and increasing social cohesion. In emergent economy contexts where poverty alleviation can be a fundamental concern, there is much scope for ensuring that the economic benefits generated by special events trickle down to local populations and that overall, the development of events forms part of a wider strategy to combat poverty. Okech (2011), writing about a cultural festival in Lamu, Kenya, makes this point. Equally, in such contexts, developing understandings of the processes by which households gain access to social capital, or about how **social capital** is built and sustained within a community is vitally important. Rao (2001) argued that such processes differ from culture to culture and are deeply conditioned by social norms and constraints. Understanding how social capital works requires an understanding of the social mechanisms that underlie it, and knowledge of how these mechanisms interact with economic decisions. Rao (2001) suggested that festivals are examples of such mechanisms. He explained how village festivals provide a space within which households can express their sociability by, for example, making a direct contribution to the temple committee, or for poorer households, by dressing up, making special food, participating in common events and otherwise spending money in a visible manner that enhances the 'festival experience' for the entire village. Festivity is a highly associational activity and so by participating, a family signals its commitment to being an active member of the community; a 'good' citizen, a potential partner in mutually beneficial reciprocal relationships. Thus, Rao (2001) argued, at the village level, festivals enhance social cohesion and build social capital, while at the family level, they provide households with an opportunity to access social networks and generate returns from investments in social capital. This does not happen without a cost: according to Rao (2001), contributions to festival activities accounted for 15% of the annual income of village families in his study. Households gain returns on their investments, however. Those who spend more on festivals, whether as contributions to the village or in private celebrations, receive tangible private returns in the guise of higher social status, access to larger networks through which they get lower prices on food and more invitations to meals. Relatedly, Narayan and Pritchett (1999) found that villages which have higher levels of social capital tend to have more households with higher incomes, and also benefit from better school and faster rates of technology adoption. Others, like Chwe (1998), have argued that public events like ceremonies and festivals solve coordination problems by producing common knowledge and thus play an important role in communicating information.

FURTHER READING

Foley, M., McGillivray, D. and McPherson, G. (2012) 'Policy pragmatism: Qatar and the global events circuit', *International Journal of Event and Festival Management*, 3 (1): 101–15.

Jago, L., Dwyer, L., Lipman, G., van Lill, D. and Vorster, S. (2010) 'Optimising the potential of mega-events: an overview', *International Journal of Event and Festival Management*, 1 (3): 220–37.

Lamberti, L., Noci, G., Guo, J. and Zhu, S. (2011) 'Mega-events as drivers of community participation in developing countries: the case of Shanghai world expo', *Tourism Management*, 32: 1474–83.

Rao, V. (2001) 'Celebrations as social investments: festival expenditures, unit price variation and social status in rural India', *Journal of Development Studies*, 38 (1): 71–97.

Shin, H. (2004) 'Cultural festivals and regional identities in South Korea', *Environment and Planning D: Society and Space*, 22: 619–32.

7 European City of Culture

> The European City of Culture event, which started in 1985, is an initiative of the European Commission. It is a year-long cultural event, awarded annually to a designated city within the European Union, and its stated purpose is to celebrate European cultural diversity.

As discussed elsewhere in this book, national governments have strong vested interests in the events sector. So too do supranational governments such as the European Union (EU). An initiative of the Education and Culture Directorate General, the origins of the European City/Capital of Culture (ECOC) date to 1985. It was initially an inter-governmental scheme designed to raise the profile of culture, art and creativity within the EU. The idea was that individual EU member states would annually host what is in effect a year-round, large-scale cultural event. The intention was not to develop the initiative through the major, capital cities of Europe, but rather to use it to highlight the diverse cultural riches of Europe through its lesser known, smaller cities. The initiative has undergone a number of changes since its inception, and since 1999 the ECOC has had the status of a Community Action. A list of EU member states responsible for nominating ECOCs has been identified for the period 2005–2019 (Palmer/Rae Associates, 2004) and competition for securing designation is so intense that it has been compared with that surrounding the Olympic Games nomination (Richards, 2000).

The ECOC event has occurred annually in at least one European city every year since 1985, yet it has received relatively little attention from event management researchers. It has, however, been of growing interest to researchers within urban, cultural and tourism studies. As such, the questions posed have not tended to be concerned with the workings of the organisations set up to organise the ECOCs in host cities themselves, but rather about the event's broader environmental contexts. Researchers have been keen to investigate how it: fits within the context of urban policymaking; contributes to tourism; shapes destination positioning; advances the workings of the cultural sector; and promotes access to and participation in culture among various societal groups including residents and tourists. The literature tends to be critical in tone, querying the assumptions and values underpinning the event and unravelling the power dynamics at play as the annual events unfold within different European cities.

One of the interesting aspects of the literature on ECOCs is that it introduces a breadth of geographical coverage not often seen in the research on other types of events. While the academic literature on festivals and events are full of cases and examples from English-speaking nations, notably, the USA, UK, Canada and Australia, insights into these activities in continental Europe are less easily obtainable through English-language sources. The literature on the ECOC helps to redress this imbalance.

Recent years have seen a small but growing academic interest in investigating the meanings and outcomes of the ECOC. Not least among the reasons for this growing interest is the fact that the ECOC has become absorbed into the culture-led urban regeneration agenda now widely evident across Europe, as elsewhere. In effect, the majority of ECOCs use the designation to improve their international profile, generate visitor flows, enhance a sense of pride in their city, promote themselves and their countries as cultural centres, and secure their place on the cultural map of Europe (Palmer/Rae Associates, 2004). Following an examination of ECOCs from 1990–2000, these authors concluded that while cities tend to invest multiple objectives in the year, the main strategic focus has been on obtaining economic benefits through tourism, image enhancement, urban revitalisation and the development of the creative industries. O'Callaghan and Linehan (2007) have made a similar argument about the Cork 2005 ECOC.

Much of the emphasis in the literature on ECOCs has concerned the impacts and subsequent legacies that have been left behind. A diverse array of impacts has been noted. Glasgow 1990 is an ECOC that is constantly referred to in the literature. 'Unquestionable achievements' associated with Glasgow as identified by García (2004: 319) include the use of a wide definition of culture that extended beyond the arts to incorporate such areas as design, engineering, architecture, shipbuilding, religion and sport, and the balance that it struck between: using venues across the city as opposed to just the city-centre for reasons inspired by social inclusion and broadening access; planning flagship national companies and international stars, alongside emerging local artists and grassroots organisations; and allocating funding to both temporary events and more permanent cultural infrastructures. Research on other ECOCs includes that by Sjøholt (1999) who concluded that the lasting value of the ECOC in general might lie in the international contacts and networks created in the course of the year. Balsas (2004) suggested that Porto 2001 succeeded in widening the cultural audience in the city. He further cited Santos et al.'s (2003) assertion that the ECOC can lead to the creation of new domestic and international networks for cultural programming and training. Sacco and Blessi (2007) argued that the Lille 2004 designation resulted in increased media attendance and a 39% increase in annual cultural visits. Quinn's (2010) research on Cork 2005 suggested that legacies can include contributions to social capital, capacity building and the enhancement of well-being within a city's cultural sector.

Some ECOC-related research has focused on local residents. Boyko (2008) investigated how events affect local people's sense of their own place. His study of the Brugge 2002 event concluded that many residents of the city felt that their needs were not being met by the year. In contrast, most of them believed that the year was aimed at tourists. This was despite the insistence of organisers that visitors and residents were both targeted. Kuzgun et al. (2010) studied the perceptions of Istanbul residents towards the city's designation as ECOC in 2010. They found that monthly household income and education were significant indicators of levels of awareness and culture involvement in the event. They concluded by suggesting that more efforts should be made to broaden awareness of the event among local people. Very recently, a 5-year research programme 'Impacts 08' undertaken at the University of Liverpool concluded that Liverpool benefited greatly from its designation as ECOC 2008. Visitor arrivals to the city reached 9.7 million, an increase of 34%, and generated £753.8 million for the economy. Visitor arrivals to the city's seven largest attractions rose to 5.5 million in 2008. Media coverage of the city increased substantially, with positive images predominating, creating a picture of a city as a modern, multi-dimensional place with a vibrant and diverse cultural life (Carter, 2010). Following the success of the Liverpool event, the UK government has introduced a 'UK City of Culture' event. Following a competitive process between four cities, Derry/Londonderry is the city that will hold the designation for the first time in 2013. The hope is that the city will 'follow Liverpool and show what impact, what step change, a year in the media spotlight can bring' (Redmond, 2010).

While the work included above shows that the outcomes of the ECOC have been a subject of enquiry, there is a general acknowledgement that the methodologies and even the language developed to investigate cultural impacts remain underdeveloped (García, 2005). A key problem with cultural outcomes in particular is their purported intangibility. It is measurable, tangible outcomes (for example, tourism revenue or job creation) that are most often sought by **stakeholders** like city authorities and funding agencies. Yet other 'softer' outcomes, such as capacity building, community empowerment, image enhancement and relationship building, may be no less important. These sorts of indicators tend not to be immediately apparent, in that they generally cannot be easily calculated and presented to an outside authority, such as a city council, by way of manifestly demonstrating that an event has made an impact. An overt manifestation of impact may only materialise after the cultural event or intervention has taken place. Thus, researchers such as Evans and Shaw (2004) have argued that investigating cultural outcomes requires a longitudinal approach, and this, unfortunately, poses methodological difficulties. The research void that exists pertains not only to the identification and measurement of these outcomes but also to a more coherent understanding of the processes that lead to their materialisation.

For example, once the spectacular has faded and the routine takes over again, how are the outcomes of cities' engagement with the ECOC initiative to be sustained? This is a key problem raised in the literature. Richards (2000) suggested that the event often fails to consider ways of sustaining developments initiated in the course of the year. With specific reference to the Glasgow year, García (2005) argued that the experience was seriously tainted by a lack of provision to sustain cultural legacies into the longer term. The event organisers failed to establish partnerships and workforce structures that could survive the year and be applied, on a smaller scale, outside an event scenario. In line with García (2004, 2005), Quinn (2010) found the Cork 2005 year to be lacking in a strategic approach to developing the cultural sector. She found that the absence of a clearly thought-out and operationalised approach to developing the 'process' or developmental potential of the 2005 event led to what Deffner and Labrianidis (2005) had earlier identified as the ECOC's tendency to lead to 'missed opportunities'. Indeed, assessments of individual ECOC experiences tend to converge on one conclusion: that of unrealistic expectations and missed opportunities in the face of hugely contested cultural domains (Deffner and Labriandis, 2005; García, 2005; Hitters, 2000; Quinn, 2010).

As such, an important context for research enquiries into the ECOC has become the extent to which competing agendas seek to capitalise on the potential of the event. In spite of the apparent rhetoric surrounding this 'cultural' event, it may be that valuing culture for culture's sake may not be of central importance for host cities themselves. Instead, city authorities prize them for the marketing opportunities they offer to improve city image and for the regeneration tool they represent for infrastructures and districts within the city (Cogliandro, 2001). As the ECOC event becomes instrumentally embedded into urban policy strategies across Europe, a key outcome has been a heightening of tensions and conflicts amid an array of competing discourses within the city. While several studies have identified a number of positive outcomes for ECOC host cities, as Griffiths has summarised, 'in many cases the organizational and financial demands of mounting a programme of unprecedented scale and complexity have placed serious strains on the delicate web of relationships between the city's cultural institutions and the multiplicity of independent groups and artists that form the basis of its cultural landscape' (2006: 419).

García, B. (2005) 'De-constructing the city of culture: the long term cultural legacies of Glasgow 1990', *Urban Studies*, 42 (5–6): 1–28.

Palmer/Rae Associates (2004) *Study on European Cities and Capitals of Culture 1995 – 2004*. Brussels: European Commission.

Quinn, B. (2010) 'The European capital of culture initiative and cultural legacy: an analysis of the cultural sector in the aftermath of Cork 2005', *Event Management*, 13: 249–64.

Richards, G. (2000) 'The European cultural capital event: strategic weapon in the cultural arms race?', *International Journal of Cultural Policy*, 6 (2): 159–81.

8 Evaluation

> *Event evaluation is a process of assessing whether an event organisation has been successful in achieving the objectives that it set out to achieve.*

key concepts in event management

32

It is through evaluation that answers to the question as to what constitutes a successful event can be found. According to Goldblatt and Supovitz (1999), success equates to the accomplishment of the festival organisers' predetermined aims, and evaluation is viewed as a way of determining success, by reviewing what has been achieved in the light of predetermined objectives (Williams and Bowdin, 2008). Recently, numerous researchers have commented upon the growing involvement of public agencies, at local, regional and national levels, in organising and supporting festivals and events (Rolfe, 1992; O'Sullivan et al., 2009). The increased investment of public funds that this involvement has generated heightens the need for appropriate mechanisms to comprehensively measure the returns on investment generated. Hence, the last decade has seen growing attention being paid to the question of festival and event evaluation and in this context 'impact' and 'legacy' are key terms. In this volume, **economic impact** and **social impact** have dedicated sections, while legacy is treated in some detail within the section on **leveraging**.

According to Getz (2005), evaluation directs an organisation's marketing and planning functions, enables it to learn about its own operations and to devise in the process, ways of improving its management. Hall (1997), meanwhile, describes it as an extension of the management control function, which assists the development and management of processes for the next hosting of the event in question. Getz (2005) introduced the idea that event evaluation takes three basic forms (in chronological format): formative (pre-event); process (during event); and outcome (post-event). Williams and Bowdin (2008) suggest that it may be driven by either internal management requirements (for example, financial spend, use of resources, audience satisfaction) or by external stakeholders (for example, economic or environmental impacts). To date, most attention from practitioners and academics has been paid to post-event outcomes. Relatively few researchers have taken an organisational perspective in terms of investigating approaches to evaluation (Williams and Bowdin, 2007). In addition, it is helpful to recognise that evaluation in festival and event contexts has tended to adopt a singular focus on either economic, socio-cultural or environmental matters, with the overwhelming focus of attention, particularly in the past, being on the former. It is only very recently that attempts to measure all of these simultaneously have begun to emerge.

Early approaches to event evaluation very definitely focused on capturing the economic value of events. According to Jago and Dwyer 'the economic impact of an event on a region is the net sum of the economic consequence of all of the cash inflows and outflows that occur because of an event' (2006: 7). Researchers tended to think of evaluation in post-event terms and to use adjustable input–output (IO) analysis to generate multipliers (O'Sullivan et al., 2009). However, many have been critiqued for tending to overstate positive impacts while ignoring many negatives (Dwyer et al., 2005). Felenstein and Fleischer are two authors who suggest that evaluation studies in the past have tended to over-exaggerate the benefits, stating that 'invariably, results are favourable and are then used to bolster the demand for public support for the festival' (2009: 285). This notwithstanding, the displacement effect (Allen et al., 1999; Hultkrantz, 1998), understood as the tendency for a mega-event to dissuade potential tourism and locals from visiting during the course of an event (because of fears about overcrowding, congestion, price inflation and so on), has been discussed in connection with several large-scale events. The overall conclusion has been that either regional tourism or other tourism sectors have suffered collateral damage as a result of the hosting of a mega-event. For example, Hultkrantz's (1998) study of Göteborg's hosting of the World Athletics Championship in 1995 found that while visitors to the city itself received a boost, overall arrivals to Sweden fell as visitors avoided the country because of the event.

Early economic evaluation research tended to focus on large scale, usually sporting events like Grand Prix races and the Olympics Games. More recently, the focus has started to widen to incorporate smaller-scale events with researchers, such as Whitford (2004), arguing that it is at the local level that support for festivals and special events is thought to make a fundamental difference. Jackson et al. (2005) deemed the IO model to be most suitable for evaluating the economic impact of transient, small regional festivals. They analysed a DIY economic impact assessment kit developed for use by regional festivals in the Australian state of Victoria. The introduction of the kit represents an acknowledgement of the difficulties presented by the need for public agencies to evaluate the effectiveness of funding a number of small-scale festivals. Seven festivals that were early adopters of the DIY kit were included in the study which found that ease of use, the availability of training and a help desk were key factors in the successful use of the kit.

At the same time, researchers have commented on the plethora of approaches used to measure economic impact and the lack of consistency in the methodologies employed (Dwyer et al., 2000). In addition, Jackson et al. (2005) argued that objective and comparable methods of measurement have been lacking and this has been problematic. In response, Getz argued that 'a more standardised methodology for evaluating events and their impacts, more comprehensive methods and measures of values must be used' (2000: 21). Jackson et al.'s (2005) response was to develop a 'Do-it-Yourself' economic assessment kit, aimed at enabling festival organisers to evaluate the economic impacts of their festivals using readily available and accessible software. Yet the lack of comparability continues to be problematic. Williams and Bowdin, in a study of approaches to evaluation among seven arts festivals, concluded that the effectiveness of methodologies employed was 'difficult to determine due to the range of methods used and the subjectivity of arts appreciation' (2007: 200). Thomas and Wood (2003), meanwhile, argued that local authorities' festival and special event evaluations were likely to be ad hoc, unsystematic and often subjective. More recently

Wood (2005), in a study of local authority events in England, found that while festivals and events are used to further a variety of objectives, the measurement of their achievements is rarely systematic and objective. Others have noted that the type of evaluation employed can be ill-matched to the task of measuring the degree to which the organisation's stated objectives were achieved. O'Sullivan et al. (2009), for example, undertook a study of unitary authorities (UA) in Wales, seeking to investigate the links between the purpose of festivals and events, the reasons underpinning their evaluation and the nature of what was being measured. They found that while UA support was generally premised on furthering socio-cultural aims, the actual evaluation undertaken focused on improving processes.

In terms of post-event outcomes, there has been a growing awareness of the need for evaluation to be increasingly broadly defined. The literature is peppered with calls for researchers to move beyond the economic domain into other equally fruitful terrains where social, cultural and political issues can be addressed (Bowden et al., 2006; Gnoth and Anwar, 2000; Moscardo, 2007; Wood et al., 2006). Recent work on evaluating and assessing the impacts associated with events has reflected this awareness. It has also been influenced by developments in the literature on the social impact of tourism more generally (Lankford and Howard, 1994) and an upsurge of publications on the topic is now evident. Outcomes found to be associated with events are both positive and nature and include for example, enhanced place image and social cohesion on the positive side, with traffic congestion and the promotion of socially deviant behaviour on the negative side. Early research came from Fredline and Faulkner (2000), and from Delamere et al. (2001) who developed a festival social impact attitude scale (FSIAS) to measure resident attitudes towards the social impact of events. Soon after, Fredline et al. (2003) and Fredline (2006) progressed scale development, still focusing on resident attitudes. More recently, there has been a growing awareness that events can also be associated with environmental outcomes, again both positive and negative. However, this is a very new area of research and relatively little empirical research has been conducted. It seems reasonable to suggest while that the identification of potential environmental impacts is beginning to emerge, much progress needs to be made in gathering longitudinal and comparable data in order to comprehensively evaluate and thus manage such impacts (Jones, 2008).

The initial preoccupation with thinking singularly about just one kind of impact or output, namely economic, has now broadened to thinking about how to apply the triple bottom line (TBL) concept. The concept of the TBL, developed by John Elkington in the 1980s, calls for a recognition of the economic, social and environmental impacts of events. As Hede notes, 'research on event evaluation is currently focused on amalgamating the economic, social and environmental forms of evaluation into one framework' (2007: 14). 'The rationale behind TBL reporting is to illuminate the externalities associated with business activities and therefore to promote sustainability through planning and management practices that ameliorate negative outcomes and promote positive ones' (Fredline et al., 2005: 3). This is proving to be a complex challenge and while understandings of the complexities at issue in evaluating the broad range of outcomes associated with events is advancing, progress remains hampered by incomplete understandings of how to factor in differences of scale and underlying policy objectives, and so on.

Accordingly, researchers' attempts to evaluate events, while broadening in focus, do not always seek to simultaneously address all three areas of impact. Pasanen et al.'s (2009) reporting of the FEET (Finnish event evaluation tool), designed to generate comparable data on the economic and socio-cultural effects of events in Finland is a case in point. Its main interest is investigating the tourism expenditure caused by an event and it seeks to determine how much economic activity is generated when visitors are attracted into a region because of an event. In line with existing studies, the spending of local residents, being of no incremental benefit, is not considered. In addition to measuring tourist expenditure, the tool examines entrepreneurs' assessments of the event's impact, and the expenditures of the organisation hosting the event to calculate the economic impact. The tool also tries to measure socio-cultural effects by seeking the opinions of a variety of stakeholder groups including residents, entrepreneurs, organisers and policymakers. The authors draw on existing research to devise a series of one-part, Likert-type scale statements, to elicit information from these different groups.

FURTHER READING

Getz, D. (2005) *Event Management and Event Tourism*, 2nd edn. New York: Cognizant Communication Corporation.

O'Sullivan, D., Pickernell, D. and Senyard, J. (2009) 'Public sector evaluation of festivals and special events', *Journal of Policy Research in Tourism, Leisure and Events*, 1 (1): 19–36.

Pasanen, K., Taskinen, H. and Mikkonen, J. (2009) 'Impacts of cultural events in Eastern Finland – development of a Finnish event evaluation tool', *Scandinavian Journal of Hospitality and Tourism*, 9 (2–3): 112–129.

Williams, M. and Bowdin, G.A.J. (2008) 'Festival evaluation: an evaluation of seven UK arts festivals', in M. Robertson and E. Frew (eds), *Events and Festivals*. Abingdon, Oxon: Routledge. pp. 86–121.

9 Event Management

The events industry has now become so extensive that specific management practices have been adapted to meet its needs. Events management is the professional business of managing these 'extraordinary' phenomena.

The rhythm of human civilisations has always been punctuated by moments of celebration, when collectively, people locally, nationally and internationally mark momentous happenings of spiritual, sporting, artistic, agrarian and other natures. In recent decades, countries throughout the world have seen the planning of such celebrations proliferate and become transformed into an industry of very sizeable proportions. Today, celebrations like the Olympic Games, the FIFA World Cup, the MTV Music Awards, the Academy Awards and St Patrick's Day are commonly referred to as 'special events'. According to Getz a special event is 'a one-time or infrequently occurring event outside the normal program or activities of the sponsoring body' and 'an opportunity for an experience outside the normal range of choices or beyond every day experience' (2007: 16). The term 'event management' refers to the practice of managing events. For Goldblatt it involves 'researching, designing, planning, coordinating and evaluating events' (2002: 7). Defined narrowly, special events management involves designing, planning, marketing and staging events, managing the logistics, legal compliance and risk issues involved, and evaluating and reporting after the event.

More broadly, event management researchers and educators have long been cognisant of the wider economic environment within which events operate, recognising the interplay between the discrete event and the wider economy through the study of **economic impact**. More recently, a growing concern with how events 'fit' holistically into their wider environments has seen greater attention being paid to such matters as **stakeholders**, environmental sustainability, **social capital** and **regional development**. In an academic sense, the term 'event management' refers to the literature that approaches the study of events and festivals from a management perspective. A great deal of event management material is now available in the shape of text-books. This is applied in nature, aiming to take the learner through the entire management process from understanding the context, to planning, operations and evaluation (Allen et al., 2011; Bowden et al., 2006). Those publications aspiring to capture the 'core text book' market are all-encompassing in the type of events that they refer to illustratively, drawing on examples and cases ranging from those organised by small community groups, to local authorities and inter-national sports federations and, from events that celebrate a breadth of activities from folk arts, food, community and sports, to meetings, business and corporate. Increasingly now as well, textbooks take a more focused and in-depth approach, specialising in a particular type of event sector, for example, meetings and conventions (Silvers, 2008); a particular dimension of event activity, for example, enter-tainment (Sonder, 2004) or; on strategic or operational issues to a greater or lesser degree. Also, in applied terms, event management is now a distinctive part of the tourism and hospitality industries as evidenced in the formation of industry associations, specific training courses and accreditation schemes (Allen et al., 1999).

The event management research literature published in journals such as the *International Journal of Event and Festival Management* and *Journal of Convention and Event Tourism* is now enormous. At this stage, several literature reviews assessing the state of knowledge in the field have been published (Formica, 1998; Getz, 2000; Harris et al., 2001) and they all largely concur on the priorities that have domi-nated research enquiry. Most attention has been paid to the evaluat-ing the effects, especially the economic impacts of events. Marketing and sponsorship are other well developed themes. Management itself and management areas like risk, human resources and operations are much less frequently treated, despite the fact that these areas are priorities for user groups including practitioners and policymakers (Harris et al., 2001). Is this because the needs of the event sector are met within the general management literature? A number of authors would not agree, asserting that managing events differs from other management areas. According to Mules (2004: 95), its uniqueness is twofold: '(1) events have a unique and all-consuming climax, untypical of other management areas and, (2) most events are a form of entertainment and require staging'. Very recently, Getz et al. (2010) suggested that managing festivals was even more different for a number of reasons. Prime among these is the fact that festivals are often produced within the non-for-profit sector and typically seek to serve a breadth of diverse and sometimes conflicting policy goals stretching from culture to tourism and place branding. In addition, they suggested that the need for a distinctive management framework and approach stems from a number of factors, not least of which is their 'celebratory core' (Getz et al., 2010: 31). Despite this apparent need for a distinctive management approach, there does seem to be a real gap in the literature here. The question of strategic management is a case in point. According to Viljoen and Dann (2000) the articulation of a vision and mission is a core element of strategic management. For Mules, strategy management is 'the process by which an organisation's mission is articulated, reviewed and specified. [It] forces the individuals engaged to turn their attention away from their specialist area and to focus on where the organization as a whole is going' (2004: 970). He notes that it does not seem to be covered in event management texts. Carlsen and Andersson concur, arguing that 'the field of festival and event studies is largely devoid of any literature with reference to management strategies or detailed analysis of the management challenges that festivals face' (2011: 83–4). Their findings suggested that a strategic SWOT analysis provides a useful means of identifying the challenges that festivals face and the management strategies that could be usefully adopted to meet these challenges. In somewhat related fashion, a number of researchers, notably Chacko and Schaffer (1993), Getz (1989), Goldblatt (1997), Grimes (1994), Hall (1992), Mayfield and Crompton (1995), have considered the factors underpinning event success. Lade and Jackson (2004) suggested that these might be said to fall into the three very broad categories of community

involvement and support; management and planning functions; and marketing strategies. Mayfield and Crompton (1995) focused on the nature of market orientation evident, arguing that the early adoption of a strong market orientation, as opposed to product orientation, can be strongly associated with success. This literature can inform the development of management strategies.

A number of researchers note that while the literature tends to conceive of festivals as a somewhat homogeneous group there is 'obvious variation in management processes, resources and capacity' (Carlsen and Andersson, 2011: 84). This point had earlier been made by Andersson and Getz (2009), who drew attention to the fact that internationally, the festival and event sector tends to be a mixed industry. Activity tends to be dominated by not-for-profit organisations, who frequently argue that they merit public subsidies because they deliver services that governments should be providing. However, in its entirety, the creators and suppliers of festivals and special events include private firms, public agencies and not-for-profit organisations. In a mixed industry environment, a pertinent research question is whether the nature or the type of organisation in question is influential in shaping such matters as the quality, efficiency and profitability of the service being offered. Andersson and Getz (2009) systematically compared four samples of three different types of festivals (193 in total) in different countries. They found that while all three types of festivals offered similar types of experiences, there were a number of differences including cost to consumers, emphasis on high output quality and efficiency.

Other elements of the event management process are dealt with to varying degrees in the literature. Processes like **risk management**, human resources, procurement, **marketing**, logistics and several others tend to be well covered in textbook material. Some of these have been the subject of detailed research and increasingly feature in academic journals. The topic of food safety is a case in point. Lee et al. (2010) have noted how concerns about food safety have been the subject of considerable research attention (Cote et al., 1995). In general, these studies are concerned to raise the standards of food safety and to contribute to applied knowledge as to how improvements might be effected. Boo et al. (2000) found that consumers perceived the food served at fairs and festivals to be significantly less safe than that served in cafeterias and restaurants, while Worsfold (2003) suggested that food vendors need greater hygiene awareness. Lee et al. (2010) gathered data at one of Indiana's largest festivals, the Feast of the Hunter's Moon, in 2006 and 2008. They found some food vendors' knowledge of food safety to be inadequate and recommended a series of training initiatives. **Risk management** is another topic that is of growing interest to researchers and a sizeable literature (treated elsewhere in this volume) is beginning to emerge.

Other topics have not been so well served. Time management is one example. According to Goldblatt, time is a mismanaged resource, something that has largely been taken for granted, when really it needs to be managed in the 'most minute segments' (2005: 59). The importance of managing time effectively is heightened in event contexts where the transience of the event is paramount in its planning. Emery (2003), talks about the particularly high levels of uncertainty and complexity that characterise sports events. He points to the many dimensions that make them highly uncontrollable: spectator fervour, intense live media coverage, unscripted performance outcomes, and a diverse array of stakeholder interests. Information technology (IT) and its application in the sector is another topic that is both underdeveloped in practice and under-researched in the literature. Knox (2004) argued that very little IT has formally been incorporated into the working practices of event managers. This is, however, changing, and Knox outlines a number of ways in which information technology can be used to make the processes of event planning, promotion and evaluation more efficient. Beaven and Laws (2004) is one of the few studies to investigate the impact of the adaptation of new technologies. They focus on virtual ticket distribution of live music events.

FURTHER READING

Carlsen, J. and Andersson, T. (2011) 'Strategic SWOT analysis of public, private and not-for-profit festival organisations', *International Journal of Event and Festival Management*, 2 (1): 83–97.

Formica, S. (1998) 'The development of festivals and special events studies', *Festival Management and Event Tourism*, 5 (3): 131–37.

Goldblatt, J. (2002) *Special Events: Twenty-First Century Global Event Management*, 3rd edn. The Wiley Management Series. New York: Wiley.

Mules, T. (2004) 'Evolution in event management: the God coast's Wintersun festival', *Event Management*, 9: 95–101.

10 Experience

> The concept of experience is important in the study of festivals and events because they give people the opportunity of experiencing something that is different to the routine and the ordinary. The intangibility of the event 'service' adds to the complexities at issue in delivering unique, positive, memorable experiences.

As discussed elsewhere in this volume, festival and event attendees have long been the centre of research attention in the literature on **motivation**. This literature acknowledges that a key driver underpinning the motivation to attend events is the desire to engage in an experience that is somehow novel or exciting (Scott, 1996; Tomlijenovic et al., 2001; Uysal et al., 1993). In recent years, there has been a growing interest in understanding how people experience, engage in, and perform their roles as festival and event attendees, audiences and spectators. Getz (2007) has argued that the experience, and its associated meanings, is central to the planned event. The very proliferation of the event phenomenon in recent decades has been linked to the rise of the experience economy (Pine and Gilmore, 1999) and this in turn has stimulated much of the growth in the mainstream **event management** literature.

The question as to how people experience festivals and events is being approached in different ways in the literature. Within event management there is a real interest in understanding attendees' experiences because they relate to satisfaction: as Winkle and Backman (2009) remind us, it is quality experiences that will encourage attendees to return and to speak well of the event to their friends and family. Something that complicates enquiries is the fact that intangibility is a key characteristic of the service on offer. Festivals and events are said to offer 'unique, different or new experiences' (Axelsen and Swan, 2010: 437), and this is why they are so sought after. Morgan (2009) examined festival experience using a combination of both external (managerial) and internal (experiential) perspectives. He drew on Kapferer's brand identity prism to conceptualise the event experience using the elements of 'design and programming', 'physical organization', 'social interaction', 'personal benefits', 'symbolic meanings' and 'cultural communication'.

key concepts in event management

42

Very usefully, Morgan (2008) points to the different approaches adopted by researchers as they study how consumers evaluate events, noting a distinction between those that assume that satisfaction derives from a cognitive evaluation and those who acknowledge that service experience is 'inherently interpretative, subjective and affective (Arnould and Price, 1993, cited in Morgan, 2009: 84). Pegg and Patterson's (2010) study of a country music festival audience in Tamworth, Australia, is an example of the latter. They found that while the love of country music was the main reason for attending the festival, it was the variety of activities and festival atmosphere that was considered as being the most important aspect of their participation. They found that atmosphere was continuously mentioned by audience members and they linked this to Pine and Gilmore's (1999) argument that positive visitor experiences result from engaging in memorable offerings that have an enduring affective element to them. The concept of atmosphere, defined by Makins as a 'general pervasive feeling or mood' (1992: 77), is undoubtedly very important in the context of understanding experience. It has been found to be integral to the success of any festival (Taylor and Shanka, 2002). Yet as Frew and Ali-Knight (2009) note, atmosphere is little researched in the literature, in most cases, receiving only a passing mention. Morgan (2008) supports Pegg and Patterson's (2010) line of thinking, arguing that the key to a successful festival is to find ways to create space for social interaction and to facilitate visitors' ability to have personal experiences. The extent to which festival-goers shared the cultural values of the performance, a sense of 'communitas' with other festival-goers and developed personal satisfaction during the course of the festival were formative factors in shaping memorable experiences. Prentice and Andersen (2003) pointed out that socialising with family and others, gregariousness and the enjoyment of company more generally, have been found frequently as a dimension of festival consumption. They suggest that the recurring importance of gregariousness may imply that the festival itself becomes a destination, rather than simply an attraction of place-based destinations. The experience of gregariousness may ultimately be independent of any specific place, and what makes festivals special has been found to centre on uniqueness and quality, as well as atmosphere (Getz and Cheyne, 1997).

While this affective dimension of event attendance seems to be attracting growing attention, the literature on 'consumption experiences' is actually already well-established in the services marketing literature. Lee and Kyle (2012) drew on Richins' (1997) consumption emotion scale containing six dimensions of emotion (love, joy, surprise, anger, sadness and fear) to investigate emotions across time and settings and visitors' recall of their emotional experiences at festivals over time. They found that love and joy were the most commonly experienced emotions with neutral and negative emotions being felt infrequently. In terms of recall, they found that the memories reported inaccurately reflected the actual emotions experienced, with visitors tending to underrate their positive emotions. Their findings were only partially consistent with previous research leading to an affirmation of Richins' (1997) conclusion that understandings of emotions are context specific.

Researchers drawing on other theoretical reference points are also contributing to our understanding of festival and event experiences. Very commonly, researchers use the concept of experience to try to understand how attendees draw meaning from engaging in events. Packer and Ballantyne (2010: 2), for example, have recently identified a need to investigate the nature and outcomes of music festival experiences. They suggest that the health and well-being benefits associated with engagement in music more generally (Bailey and Davidson, 2005) might also apply in music festival contexts. Their analysis, which focused on adolescents, found the music festival experience to comprise four distinct aspects: the music experience, the festival experience, the social experience and the separation experience. All of these led to a series of positive outcomes related to interpersonal relationships, identity and to a lesser extent, agency. They outlined a conceptual model that could potentially guide future research and called for further enquiry into the relationship between music festival attendance and psychological and social well-being.

Gration et al. (2011) approach the question of experience from the perspective of consumer behaviour and examine the idea of festival attendance and self-concept. Self-concept theory refers to the total ideal of how one sees oneself, and can be understood as a basic motivation to achieve the ideal self in either private or public contexts (Chaudhuri, 2006). Its relevance to festival settings lies in the suggestion that in attending festivals, people are seeking a better 'other' and to affirm the nature of their self (Douglas et al., 2001). Gration et al.'s empirical study of festival-goers at a folk festival in Queensland, Australia, supports extant knowledge in finding that these consumers actively disassociate themselves from what they perceive to be the negative 'tourist' label. Rather, they saw themselves as distinct individuals who' enjoyed the social, cultural and environmental.

It would seem that the concept of experience deserves a great deal more attention from researchers. The concept of experience is not usually dealt with in the applied event management textbooks and this needs to be redressed. That having been said, experience features in discussion on event design. This is an important part of the event production process (Berridge, 2006). Event designers work to develop aspects of the event like the setting, theme, programme, consumables and service delivery to create particular kinds of effects. As Pettersson and Getz point out 'experiences cannot be fully designed as they are both personal (that is, psychological) constructs that vary with the individual, as well as being social and cultural constructs related to the individual and the (often) social nature of events' (2009: 310). Nevertheless, event designers seek to shape the kind of experiences delivered with the express intent of making them positive, lasting and memorable. Beyond the applied literature, while research on the topic is growing, and the theoretical frameworks being employed to shape enquiry are developing, many avenues remain unexplored. To date, the attention has focused overwhelmingly on participants as audiences but as Getz (2007) points out, while event audiences/consumers are most prominent in this respect, several different cohorts of people, including volunteers, artists/performers, organisers, media and affected residents experience events. All of these groups are typically overlooked. Furthermore, as yet, there has been relatively little interest in understanding how the changing dynamics of contemporary festivals might be influencing participant experiences. Research presented by Bengry Howell at the British Psychological Society's annual conference in 2010 drew a link between recent developments in experiential marketing and event audience experiences. Bengry Howell (2010) pointed out that most of the major UK music festivals are now owned by an international live entertainment company and argued that 'these events have become commercially branded experiences, run, promoted or sponsored by particular drinks or telephone companies, as they see festivals as opportunities for experiential and emotional marketing and stimulating brand commitments among captive audiences'. Accordingly, these events are characterised by substantial levels of commercial involvement and an environment in which consumption is often managed and regulated. If a particular drinks company is the lead or title sponsor of an event, then usually only the products owned by that company can be sold on-site. Bengry Howell (2010) argued that this regulated environment conflicted with how the young people surveyed in the research understood the festival: they 'saw festivals as an opportunity to escape from the obligations and responsibilities of daily life, and as a chance to be free – an opportunity to wander, to disappear into the crowd, a place where time isn't managed and can't be wasted, where they can let go'. As companies, such as the international drinks groups Diageo and Red Bull, increasingly move away from sponsoring event organisations and invest in organising events themselves, as part of their experiential marketing strategies, it may be interesting to investigate what this means for event experience.

FURTHER READING

Arnould, E.J. and Price, L.L. (1993) 'River magic: extraordinary experience and the extended service encounter', *Journal of Consumer Research*, 20: 24–35.

Gelder, G. and Robinson, P. (2009) 'Critical comparative study of visitor motivations for attending music festivals: a case study of Glastonbury and V Festival', *Event Management*, 13: 181–96.

Morgan, M. (2008) 'What makes a good festival? Understanding the event experience', *Event Management*, 12 (2): 81–93.

Pegg, S. and Patterson, I. (2010) 'Rethinking music festivals as a staged event: gaining insights from understanding visitor motivations and the experiences they seek', *Journal of Convention & Event Tourism*, 11: 85–99.

Pine, B.J. and Gilmore, J.H. (1999) *The Experience Economy. Work Is Theatre & Every Business a Stage*. Boston, MA: Harvard Business School Press.

.... 11 Festival ....

'What is a festival? ... First of all it's a celebration. It's something exceptional, something out of the ordinary ... something which must create a special atmosphere that stems not only from the quality of the art and its production, but from the countryside, the ambience of a city and the traditions ... of a region.' (de Rougement, in Isar, 1976: 131, author's translation)[1]

---

[1] 'C'est quoi, une festival? C'est d'abord une fête. C'est quelque chose d'exceptionnel, qui sort de la routine ... et qui doit créer une atmosphère spéciale, à laquelle contribuent non seulement la qualité des oeuvres et de leur exécution, mais le paysage, l'ambiance d'une cité et la tradition ... d'une région.'

As the above quotation makes clear, festivals embody communal celebration. The phenomena being celebrated can be very diverse, with festivals being used to celebrate everything from the arts to food, religious happenings and kinship. The word 'festival' derives from the Latin *festum*, meaning feast (Isar, 1976), and the notion of collective, participatory, celebration is a central meaning of festival. In terms of the subject topic of this book, festivals represent a type of special event that has been known to exist for a very long time. Turner (1982), for example, suggests that people have recognised the need to set aside certain times and spaces for celebratory use for centuries. Falassi (1987), meanwhile, explains that festivals have been found to exist in virtually all human cultures. A festival is a social practice through which communities express beliefs and celebrate identities (Ekman, 1999). In creating opportunities for drawing on shared histories, shared cultural practices and shared ideals, as well as creating settings for social interactions, festivals engender local continuity. They constitute arenas where local knowledge is produced and reproduced; where the history, cultural inheritance and social structures, which distinguish one place from another, are revised, rejected or recreated.

The act of producing a festival is clearly a social phenomenon, and underlying much of the fascination that geographers, sociologists, anthropologists, folklorists and others have found in festivals is their collective dimension. Numerous scholars in these disciplines have sought to explore the 'social drama' enacted in festival sites to gain insights into how groups of people view their place in society and interact together to variously contest and reproduce the social structures and value systems that bind them together. Indeed, as Duvignaud (1976) has discussed, there has been a long-standing conceptualisation of festivals as the ultimate, most intense manifestation of the collective being. Social scientists have tried to interpret the social meanings in the public ritual and display evident in festivals. Many have viewed public festivities as representing a polar opposite to conventional social life, as a 'time out of time', or as a temporary release from those environments highly regulated and structured by ordinary time. Indeed, Duvignaud (1976) asserts that all observers agree that the festival involves a powerful denial of the established order. Such interpretations are perhaps most clearly drawn out in Bahktin's (1968) work on the related concept of carnival. Anthropologists, such as Geertz (1993), have conceptualised festivals as complex cultural practices that can be considered as cultural texts, one of the many ensembles of texts, themselves ensembles, which comprise a people's culture. He understands culture to be 'webs of significance' that people have themselves spun and within which they are suspended (Geertz, 1993: 5). His view that unravelling and understanding these webs is best advanced by adopting an interpretative search for meaning, as opposed to an explanatory search for laws, has predominated among the social science literature on festivals.

Historically, festivals were often allied to the rhythms of agrarian society (Rolfe, 1992). Very often there were religious underpinnings, as in many of the festivals that Fox Gotham (2005) reminds us existed in the Middle Ages. Researchers consistently point to the fact that throughout earlier periods, festivals 'encapsulate identity in terms of the nation-state, a sense of place, and the personal and heterogeneous identities of a people' (Matheson, 2005: 4). Festivals have long been implicitly involved in the creation of place identity to further tourism interests. Gold and Gold (2005: 268) for example, describe how the recognition of Greenwich as the fulcrum of the earth's time zones in 1884 inspired the hosting of a year long festival intended to boost international tourism to London. Adams (1986) discusses how, as long ago as 1859, the Handel Centenary Festival held in London's Crystal Palace was marketed as a tourist attraction with the organisers distributing 50,000 prospectuses in the European offices of the railway companies serving Crystal Palace.

While festivals have long been the subject of academic enquiry, there has been a growth of interest in the topic since the late 1990s. This has mirrored their flourishing in contemporary society (Quinn, 2005), following a decline from the mid-20th century onwards (Boissevain, 1992). Their proliferation is strongly allied to their tourism potential and is underpinned by a series of demand- and production-driven factors. In terms of the former, socialisation needs, the growth of serious leisure (Prentice and Andersen, 2003) and the move towards the consumption of experiences (Getz, 2008) have been important. On the production side, key drivers have been their potential to deliver a series of development outcomes in terms of economic restructuring and revitalisation, destination repositioning, inward investment and tourism revenue generation. Thus, festivals (as events) have become part of a wider range of 'cultural strategies' (Fox Gotham, 2005; Shin, 2004) used to regenerate and orient post-production economies towards consumption (Zukin, 1995) where leisure, entertainment and tourism underpin an 'experience economy' (Pine and Gilmore, 1999). While festivals have always displayed an outward orientation designed to communicate cultural meanings to the outside world, now festivals are increasingly of interest to both practitioners and academics because of their association with tourism. Undoubtedly, there is a very strong link between festivals and tourism. Festivals create 'product', enliven a destination, animate static attractions and promise a glimpse into the authentic culture of a place. Meanwhile, for festivals, tourist audiences create new forms of demand, box office income and means of widening their repute. There is abundant evidence showing that countless festivals are marketed as tourist attractions and generate sizeable flows of tourist numbers and associated revenue (Getz, 1991; O'Sullivan and Jackson, 2002). Indeed, recent years have seen the term 'festival tourism' enter the tourism lexicon (Arnold, 2000; O'Sullivan and Jackson, 2002). Fundamental conceptualisations here have tended to reflect Uysal and Gitelson's (1994) definition of festivals as traditional events staged to increase touristic appeal to potential visitors. Prevalent research topics have been marketing, audience motivation, visitor management and **economic impact**. Much of the research has been applied in nature, with a key priority being advancing the strategic development and management of festivals as tourist attractions.

Simultaneously, however, social scientists and humanities researchers have remained cognisant that festivals have a deep social and cultural complexity and have adopted a more critical approach to conceptualising the relationship between festivals and tourism. Perhaps most obviously, festivals have featured prominently in debates about the role that tourism plays in affecting cultural change, often providing empirical contexts. Greenwood's (1972) analysis of a Basque festival was highly influential, initiating still ongoing discussions about **authenticity, tourism** and commoditisation. Originally, a core question asked was whether the commoditisation of festivals through tourism renders these cultural practices, and the social relations inherent therein, inauthentic (Matheson 2005). More recently, however, Shepherd (2002: 195) has argued that commodification within the sphere of culture is a social fact, and suggests that discussion should now focus less on what has been commodified and more on how authenticity becomes constructed and decided. This argument has tended to influence subsequent research enquiries (Müller and Pettersson, 2005; Richards, 2007).

Festivals have also been investigated because they offer insights into the close relationship between identity and place in different spatial spheres. Hall (1992), for example, has written about the role of events in developing and maintaining community or regional **identity**. De Bres and Davis (2001) and Derrett (2003) discuss how festivals can promote a sense of pride, kinship and community among local residents. Moscardo (2007), meanwhile, has considered the role that festivals play in **regional development**. The inevitable tensions that arise as neo-liberal agendas instrumentally employ festivals to further place positioning strategies are a key problematic in the investigation of place identity (McCarthy, 2005; Waitt, 2008). The interplay of global homogeneity and local heterogeneity that characterise modern capitalism (Fox Gotham, 2005) are plain to see in festival settings. Isar's assertion that genuine festivals must be 'rooted in society, in real life' (1976: 126) can be overlooked in the bid to achieve **place marketing** and related goals. Thus some authors have critiqued the advent of 'homogenisation' (Richards and Wilson, 2006) as 'destinations jostle to reproduce successful themed festivals of their own' (McCartney and Osti, 2007: 26). Yet others argue that festivals are in reality reproduced through a complex interplay of externally and locally sourced influences (Fox Gotham, 2005; Quinn, 2003).

A further important theme in the festival literature is the power dynamics that shape their reproduction. Waterman reminds us that events are never impromptu or improvised and that 'arts festivals in particular, are never spontaneous' (1998: 59). Power divisions have many, often multiple, bases including social class, race, gender and sexuality. Research by De Bres and Davies (2001), Shin (2004), Jamieson (2004), Quinn (2005b) and Waitt (2005) argues that the construction of festivals involves the elevation of selective cultural details/social positions and community voices to symbolic status and the simultaneous downgrading or silencing of others. This process unfolds not simply in the interest of constructing a desirable image of place to be represented in the international tourism marketplace, but also more profoundly for the sake of promoting vested interests, maintaining social order and the cultural status quo. More recently, in a move away from emphasising the tensions and dichotomies that can often characterise festival setting, Crespi-Vallbona and Richards (2007) have argued for greater attention to be paid to the ways in which particular constituencies of actors active in the reproduction of festivals may actually share meanings and consensus.

In conclusion, festivals constitute an important subject of academic enquiry across a number of disciplines. Clearly they have an important tourism function and their ability to further regeneration and place marketing strategies warrants serious critical attention. However, festivals

remain, at their core, extremely important occasions of communal creativity, expression and celebration that have characterised human populations for centuries. As such, investigations into festival practices and
settings yields invaluable insights into how people live in places, generate
cultural meanings and reproduce social relations.

FURTHER READING

De Bres, K. and Davis, J. (2001) 'Celebrating group and place identity: a case study of
    a new regional festival', *Tourism Geographies*, 3 (3): 326–37.
Falassi, A. (1987) *Time out of Time: Essays on the Festival*. Albuquerque, NM:
    University of New Mexico.
O'Sullivan, D. and Jackson, M. (2002) 'Festival tourism: a contributor to sustainable
    local economic development?', *Journal of Sustainable Tourism*, 10 (4): 325–42.
Quinn, B. (2005a) 'Arts festivals and the city', *Urban Studies*, 42 (5–6): 927–43.

12 Identity

> *Identity is hugely significant for a wide range of academic disciplines
> but it is not an easy concept to define. It relates to a sense of self,
> both individually, and also collectively, in respect of a wider social
> group.*

Festivals and events have long been of interest to researchers because
they constitute a vehicle for forging identities: collective identities
with particular groups of people; and identity with place. Premised on
collective assembly and on celebrating unity, societies and peoples
everywhere have long defined themselves through spectacle and festivals. Etzioni (2000) drew on the work of Durkheim to argue that
secular, routine, daily life leads to a weakening of shared commitments to beliefs and to social bonds and to an enhancement of centrifugal individualism (Etzioni, 2000). The importance of rituals lies
in the fact that they provide an important mechanism through which

society can be recreated, as members of society collectively share experiences, thus deepening social bonds. Since the beginning of recorded history, community festivals have served to create and express collective identity (Bergmann, 1999: 2). Festivals in particular have been a focus for empirically investigating how people connect with their place and with other people through their festival practices (Aldskogius, 1993; Ekman, 1999; Lavenda, 1997; Lewis and Pile, 1996). Turning to the literature on place identity first, the kind of identity in question can be linked to different spatial spheres, ranging from the local to the international. Ultimately, however, festivals occur in specific localities and offer representations of certain elements of those localities, resulting in the creation of a powerful sense of place (Jeong and Almeida Santos, 2004). As discussed elsewhere in this volume, there is a sizeable literature on **place marketing** that is most often interested in mega-events and in country or major city destinations, but equally, a breadth of spatial spheres have been studied and from a variety of perspectives.

The relationship between place-based communities and festivals cannot be captured simply through a unilinear investigation of how festivals impact upon communities. Rather, as Derrett (2003) reminds us, a community's sense of both itself and its place is very much constitutive of what makes a festival. Derrett (2003: 51) describes a sense of community as an almost invisible yet critical part of a healthy community. Although hard to define, it includes a community's image, spirit, character, pride, relationships and networking (Bush, 2000). Festivals and events provide a forum for a shared purpose to be manifest (Dunstan 1994) and offer connections, belonging, support, empowerment, participation and safety (Derrett, 2003: 52). According to Wheatley and Kellner-Rogers (1998: 14) they can provide the heart of a community, as their celebratory nature provides residents with conditions of freedom and connectedness rather than a fixation on the forms and structures of the community. Festivals offer opportunities to 'nurture and sustain what is important to their constituency' (Derrett, 2003: 51); an opportunity for community cultural development (Getz, 1997). This sort of informal participation provides residents with a sound overall view of their community and perhaps creates an environment where they can be more willing to contribute to the solution of community problems. This in effect, is **social capital**. Residents can be the gatekeepers of community values, encouraging some people in; keeping others out.

Festivals occur in specific localities and researchers are at one in attesting to the important role they play in continuously re-making and re-inventing their host places. For Gotham (2005), festivals can be a mechanism for creating and maintaining place character, articulating local identities and generating place-specific forms of collective action. Jeong and Almeida Santos (2004) offered insights into how festivals selectively offer representations of certain elements of host localities, resulting in the creation of a powerful sense of place. De Bres and Davis (2001) discussed how a Kansas River Festival helped to promote a sense of pride, kinship and community among the river communities involved. While Moscardo (2007) examined 36 case studies of regional festivals and events, seeking to broaden understanding of how events contribute to regional development.

There is also a long-standing literature on the role played by festivals and events in the process of nation-building and national identity formation. Sometimes, this role is overtly intentional, as for example, in the case of the Festival of American Folklore, known as the Smithsonian Folklore Festival since 1998. This was founded in 1967 as 'an annual exhibition of living cultural heritage from across the United States and around the world' (Kurin, 2001: 6). A key impetus was 'to stimulate a sense of ownership and identification with the national patrimony' (Kurin, 2001: 8), through 'a somewhat counter-cultural experiment' that challenges the curatorial voice, 'foregrounding instead the authentic voices of its participants' (Kurin, 2006: 10). Matheson (2005) wrote about how the monarchy served as a vehicle to embody and symbolise the nation-state during the UK monarch's Golden Jubilee celebrations in 2002. At other times, the role played by festivals and events is only part of a much more complex cultural process. This is the case in Azara and Crouch's (2006) research on La Cavalcata Sarda, an annual folkloric festival held each May in the northern Sardinian town of Sassari. They described how historical images of Sardinia, built up through the writings of colonisers and travellers in general, were defined by 'otherness': 'different, savage, primitive, untouched by civilisation, inferior but also as a living fossil; intriguing, exotic' (2006: 35). In this context, they went on to describe how the festival has functioned to diffuse and institutionalise these competing narratives of the 'otherness' of Sardinia since the late 19th century. In terms of nation-building, Snowball and Webb (2008) investigated the connection between arts festivals and a county's cultural capital. They interpreted the value of cultural goods to lie in its common good, drawing on Klamer (2004) who defined common goods as those that are shared by a group of people without a clear definition of ownership as distinct from public goods, when it is possible to exclude non-members. The empirical context for their work was South Africa, a nation in the throes of re-building itself in the aftermath of apartheid. Their research measured the cultural value of the South African National Arts Festival on the basis of four indicators: (1) the extent to which the festival played a role in maintaining the stock of diverse South African cultural capital, where diversity is defined as the cultural variety of performers, artists, artistic performances and artefacts; (2) the role of the festival in building new cultural capital, where cultural capital is understood to be a form of South Africa's wealth, but is primarily related to the education and inclusion of young South African artists; (3) the extent to which the festival acted as an outlet for the expression of political and social resistance and (4) the festival's role in the 'valorisation' of cultural expression by artists, agents and audiences (Klamer, 2004). They concluded that the national arts festival had clearly become increasingly important in maintaining the stock of all South African arts and cultures and thus in strengthening the nation-rebuilding process.

There is a further category of events whose role in maintaining and perpetuating cultural identity within geographically dispersed groups is very important. Brewster et al. (2009) examined the Scottish Highland Games, an event staged not just in Scotland but across the world where Scottish diaspora are to be found. The Games, which date back to around 1820, have assumed importance for the global diaspora of Scottish migrants who seek to retain such aspects of their Scottish heritage as music, dance and other distinctly Scottish cultural traditions. While events such as these build and maintain community ties across the boundaries of place, they also represent a means through which sometimes marginalised immigrant groups can demonstrate and consolidate community power in the context of uneven social relations in their new place of residence (Marston, 1989, 2002).

The festival as a site of group identity formation, contestation and negotiation has been of keen interest in the literature. Sometimes enquiries have sought to investigate and characterise audiences for particular genre of arts festivals, as Burland and Pitts (2010) have recently done in the case of jazz festival audiences. In such instances, the festival represents an opportunity for artists to reach audiences and for audiences to explore the meanings that the art form plays in their lives and identities. The primary research interest often lies with the particular type of art in question, as opposed to with any particular festival dynamics as such. Often, however, the enquiry focuses on cultural meanings more broadly. Cohen (1986) argued that public events are boundary-making mechanisms through which people can declare their differences. Smith echoed this argument, commenting that 'boundaries are constructed to celebrate difference, in doing so they often signal inequality' (1995: 161). Waterman (1998) noted that arts festivals are used by elites to establish social distance between themselves and others, and Blau (1996) recognised that in general, the arts have been part of the process through which social elites define themselves as the dominant class and establish social distance between themselves and the rest of the population, drawing on the distinction between popular and high culture to bolster class differences. Identity struggles, for example, on ethnic grounds, can be played out through festival sites, as discussed by Matthews-Salazar (2006), in her analysis of an indigenous Indian festival in Argentina.

The identity-building potential of festivals has perhaps been most apparent when marginal cultures have been at issue (Kates and Belk, 2001). Festivals and events like carnivals and parades have long been conceptualised as social spaces, and sites of consumption characterised by politically motivated contestation, resistance and negotiation. A growing literature on gay and lesbian events investigates how the ritual aspects of festivity facilitate the expression of a variety of meanings through how, when and where people partake and consume festival practices. Kates and Belk (2001) investigated consumption meanings and ritual aspects of the Lesbian and Gay Pride Day through an ethnographic study of gay men involved in the Toronto celebrations between 1993 and 1997. Their analysis suggested how festive moments like these represent opportunities to challenge, subvert and invert hegemonic, socially accepted cultural tradition, norms and discourses. Jeong and Almeida Santos' (2004) investigations into the Kangnung Dano festival showed how it is a means through which a dominant group defines regional identity by actively excluding marginalised members of the community. They further noted that as cultural festivals reconstruct regional identity and heritage, the process involved entails selecting particular traditions and cultures above others. Those that are selected reflect and perpetuate the ideologies

12 identity

of the dominant group. Rarely can the outcomes of encounters in festival sites be interpreted in simple, dichotomous terms. As several researchers have pointed out, the reproduction of meanings in festival settings is heavily characterised by ambiguities and ambivalences in ways that both constrain and facilitate the identity-building potential of festivals (Nagle, 2005). One area of literature where the need for nuanced interpretations has been underlined is that dealing with gay and lesbian identities (Kates and Belk, 2001; Markwell and Waitt, 2009). Markwell and Waitt (2009) examined the spatiality of four Australian Gay Pride parades and highlighted the multiplicity of narratives about the meanings of sexuality that emerge through the reproduction of the parades.

Finally, globalisation provides a very dynamic and powerful context within which researchers have sought to understand the nature of identity formation. Gotham (2005) challenged the assertion that when festivals encounter tourism, the latter serves overwhelmingly to standardise and homogenise. Instead, his empirical analysis of the New Orleans Mardi Gras demonstrates a multitude of ways in which people 'reinforce place differences, maintain local character and construct new forms of local uniqueness' through the carnival (2005: 322). Jeong and Almeida Santos (2004: 653) argued that the new and growing challenges of tourism development, globalisation and commercialisation act as potent forces which encourage places to negotiate new identities less rigorously bound by local traditions. They argued that these shifts can 'empower marginalised groups, such as women and youth, who value innovation and the broadening of the festival's identity over the preservation of dominant traditions that function to exclude them' (Jeong and Almeida Santos 2004: 653).

FURTHER READING

Derrett, R. (2003) 'Making sense of how festivals demonstrate a community's sense of place', *Event Management*, 8: 49–58.

Gotham, F.K. (2005) 'Tourism from above and below: globalization, localization and New Orlean's Mardi Gras', *International Journal of Urban and Regional Research*, 29 (2): 309–26.

Jeong, S. and Almeida Santos, C. (2004) 'Cultural politics and contested place identity', *Annals of Tourism Research*, 31 (3): 640–56.

Markwell, K. and Waitt, G. (2009) 'Festivals, space and sexuality: gay pride in Australia', *Tourism Geographies*, 11 (2): 143–68.

13 Innovation

> Innovation is a concept that is defined in several different ways but in essence it concerns the search for newness, change and improvement not simply to products and services, but also to the processes underpinning the entire business of organising, sourcing, producing, marketing and delivery.

In straightened economic times, innovation assumes greater priority for economic policymakers. In Europe, six cities have come together to develop a festival as one part of a strategy to develop new and better innovation policies for regions and countries across Europe. Organised in Barcelona, Kortrijk, Milan, Lisbon, Vilnius and Tallinn, the Innovation Festival is a tool to raise consciousness of the need for innovation and a celebration of European innovativeness. While an innovation festival may appear a novel concept, the idea of using a special event to promote innovativeness can be said to echo the origins of world fairs and international expositions where the circulation, dissemination and showcasing of new ideas was always a strong underlying principle.

Within the event sector, when competition tightens and resources become scarcer, the need to be innovative becomes ever more pressing and a focus on continuously seeking to renew programme content and improve organisational processes becomes increasingly pertinent. Continuous innovation is stressed by Porter as being important as a competitive strategy. Festivals and events are obviously linked to innovation in the sense that in recent decades, they have represented a significant 'new idea' that thousands of places the world over have strategically invested in to advance place marketing, economic restructuring and international repositioning agendas. For governments throughout the world, innovation has become of crucial strategic importance. As Nordfors (2009) notes, expanding economies no longer produce more of the same products, but rather ever more new products with additional value. Festivals and events are examples of 'new' services with additional value that have flourished in recent times. Getz defines creativity as 'the mental process of generating new ideas or concepts' (2007: 210). To date, however, innovation is not a topic that has been widely investigated in festival and event settings. According to Carlsen et al. (2010), the closest body of relevant work is that dealing with innovation and small tourism businesses. Perhaps this has to do with Mules' (2004) observation about festivals and events being interested in nostalgia (often events celebrate tradition of one kind or another), whereas innovation is all about newness and change. Extant literature tends to fall into one of two categories: one looking at innovation in the context of a festival seeking to reinvent some aspect of its own operations and; the other looking at how festivals can act as innovative entities and serve to reinvent their host economy/region.

Carlsen et al. (2010) considered that in festival settings, the drive to innovate relates not only to product and service innovation, but also to organisational innovation, market innovation and festival participant innovation. Research on innovation to date has highlighted the need for festivals to renew themselves constantly. Mules' (2004) study of the Wintersun festival on Australia's Goldcoast found that survival and success was related to regular updating and diversification of the festival offerings in order to provide new reasons for audiences to attend. Getz's (2002) study of why festivals fail found that stagnation in the festival programme and an inability to improve festival quality were key explanatory factors. Getz (1998) found that going to other events was the most common way for event managers to get new ideas. Larson (2011) discussed how festival organisations, which stage their operations on a recurrent basis, face a problem that is inherent in the 'innovation paradox'. This refers to the fact that, while recurring projects seem to have the potential to develop and reinvent their ways of working, this tends not to happen. Instead the work becomes institutionalised and the workers largely do as they have always done. Thus innovation may be limited. This innovation paradox can apply to events held on a recurring basis. Larson (2011) investigated three Swedish festivals to identify precisely how this problem can be avoided and how festival processes can be renewed. She identified different processes of renewal: institutionalised, where repetitive tasks, planned and intentional (for example, engaging performers) reproduce the event but with little overall change and; emergent, where innovation occurs, either proactively or reactively, in response to changed circumstances.

Recent research on innovation in the festival and event sector has tended to emphasise the highly cooperative nature of the activity

(Larson, 2009a). As discussed elsewhere in this volume, festivals and events require the collaboration of multiple **stakeholders** that may include government, businesses, not-for-profit organisations as well as employees, volunteers, residents and tourists (Getz, 2008; Getz et al., 2007; Telfer, 2000). Thus, rather than viewing **festivals** and events in isolation, it makes more sense to conceive of them as forming part of an inter-organisational network (Larson, 2009a). According to Carlsen et al. (2010), however, there is little evidence to suggest that festival organisations are availing of opportunities to partner and network with available and appropriate organisations like destination management organisations or with creative communities to add value to various parts of a festival's endeavours. Yet there are some instances where networking activities are being undertaken with implications for innovation capacity. Mackellar (2006), for example, used a case study of a regional festival, the Northern Rivers Herb Festival in Lismore, Australia, to investigate innovation and network interaction. This event was founded in 2001 to promote a culture of natural living, incorporating herbs and related products, cuisine and environmental sustainability. Mackellar found that through its networking activities with a variety of actors, the festival organisation proved to be an incubator for different types of innovation especially product, marketing, process and social. Service and organisational innovations were also identified. Adapting Trott's (2002) typology of innovation to the study of events, and expanding it to include social innovation, she identified innovative activity that had been made possible only by the inter-relations of actors within the festival network studied. The main beneficiaries were found to be small- and medium-sized businesses in their first years of operation, where the festival offered a new marketplace to showcase products and engage with new and existing customers.

The kind of linkages and relationships that evolve between festivals and other agencies is a key concern of the literature investigating the role played by events in stimulating innovation in the wider economy. Hjalager's (2009) study of the Roskilde rock music festival in Denmark explicitly investigated the extent to which the festival could be analysed as an innovation system. The idea that festivals, in this case, music festivals, are part of a wider music economy and need to be conceptualised as such was fundamental to the enquiry. Hjalager drew on the work of Frey (1994) who explained how the recording industry uses festivals to give artists exposure and how festivals constitute stages where recording companies scout for new and emerging talent. His work draws on the idea of innovation as an interactive, cumulative process to analyse the way in which the festival is at the centre of a web of relationships with other agents and institutions. The system has produced, and continues to produce a series of diverse spin-offs and innovations, which she identifies in terms of professionalisation; tourism; leisure, sports and culture; education; management; and business. Key characteristics underpinning the successful functioning of the festival innovation system as well as key policy issues in need of addressing in the future are discussed. More recently, Jóhannesson (2010) allied actor network theory with an empirical analysis of a local village festival in Iceland to investigate the kind of interactivity and networking that happens between festivals and other entities in particular places in order for innovation to emerge. Freire-Gibb and Lorentzen (2011) posed similar questions in a study of the Lighting Festival in Frederikshavn, Denmark. They concluded that the festival strengthened local socio-economic networks, extended business networks, promoted local products and services, and improved technical education. They noted, however, that the relationships involved in the networks were not conflict free and changed continuously. Somewhat relatedly, Carlsen et al. (2010) pointed out the folly of dichotomously thinking that innovative festivals are inevitably successful. Rather, they pointed to the simultaneity and co-dependency of innovation and failure, arguing that a greater awareness of this is needed in research approaches to festival management.

In applied terms, hallmark events like the Olympic Games and the FIFA Football World Cup create enormous investment opportunities in large-scale infrastructural projects. These offer tremendous scope for applying innovative techniques in engineering, design, construction and related fields. The design of the Olympic Park for the London 2012 Olympic and Paralympics Games, for example, incorporated footfall energy harvesting whereby the feet of spectators walking from West Ham station to the Park supply the energy used to power 12 LED spotlights illuminating the walkway both day and night (Zervos, 2012). Among practitioners in the industry, the need for festivals and event to be innovative in everything that they do has become increasingly recognised. Edinburgh Festivals, the recently established umbrella organisation covering 12 major festivals in Edinburgh has established an

Innovation Lab. Its aims are: embedding innovation as a festival mindset; testing models and processes for innovation; creating a dynamic portfolio of projects, which explore new digital opportunities, and changing the conversation about how the cultural sector engages with technology (Festivalslab, 2012). Initiatives like this may well be the way of the future.

FURTHER READING

Hjalager, A.M. (2009) 'Cultural tourism innovation systems – the Roskilde festival', *Scandinavian Journal of Hospitality and Tourism*, 9 (2–3): 266–87.

Larson, M. (2009) 'Festival innovation: complex and dynamic network interaction', *Scandinavian Journal of Hospitality and Tourism*, 9 (2–3): 288–307.

Larson, M. (2011) 'Innovation and creativity in festival organisations', *Journal of Hospitality Marketing & Management*, 20 (3/4): 287–310.

MacKellar, J. (2006) 'An integrated view of innovation emerging from a regional festival', *International Journal of Event Management Research*, 2 (1): 37–48.

14 Leveraging

The concept of event leverage relates to the long-term aftermath of events and specifically to the idea of strategically using an event to optimise a series of desired outcomes over the long term. It differs from 'legacy' or 'impact' in the manner in which it involves a strategic, pro-active approach that envisages interventions and initiatives before, during and possibly after the event. Leveraging is concerned with ensuring that positive effects generated by the event continue to be felt into the long term.

As part of the very substantial literature on event impacts, some attention has been paid to the concept of leveraging, but it can be argued that the leveraging concept is neither very well defined nor used to great effect within the literature. While some researchers, such as

Chalip (2004) and Smith (2010), clearly explain it, situate its relevance and treat it singularly, the vast bulk of literature simply incorporates the concept within its treatment of impact more generally. Researchers often implicitly treat the concept of leverage without actually mentioning it, while others specifically seek to draw out the leveraging dimensions of the event outcome scenario. Does one infer from this that leveraging is not so very important? Or is it rather a case that its significance has been overlooked?

According to Chalip, leveraging is 'those activities that need to be undertaken around the event itself, which seek to maximise the long-term benefits from events' (2004: 228). Leveraging is concerned with planning beyond the event so that positive impacts (for example, increased business activity, enhanced destination reputation, strong voluntary commitment) can be sustained into the future. Thus, at issue here are the processes and outcomes that relate not simply to the actual event itself but to the wider activities sparked off by the hosting of the event. It may be that these are initiatives developed in parallel with the event, and which have used their association with the event to generate publicity, good will, funding and so on. Event leveraging, according to O'Brien and Chalip (2007) is a strategic approach, one that focuses on processes and interventions prior to, and during, the event. It is in effect, an approach that instead of waiting for outcomes to occur, seeks to proactively achieve a set of pre-identified, intended benefits. The importance of effective leveraging lies in the undoubted potential that events offer as vehicles for developing their host places. In general, the literature has identified a wide range of positive benefits that can be leveraged: several researchers explain cities' interest in hosting large-scale events in terms of their ability to accelerate infrastructure projects, enhance destination profile, generate sizeable visitor flows and attract international media attention. Local and regional economies can be stimulated through employment creation and the generation of additional spending. Chalip (2004) identified four ways of maximising trade and revenue from an event: enticing visitor spending; lengthening visitor stays; retaining event expenditure; and using the event to enhance regional and business relationships. Equally, hosting large-scale events can generate significant costs, creating large-scale debt, as experienced by Montreal in 1976 (Whitson and Horne, 2006). When this happens, cities are forced to raise taxes and/or make cut backs in areas of the public sector like education and health (Toohey, 2008).

Sometimes there is no attempt to leverage benefits from events because of a basic lack of knowledge: Connell and Page (2005), for example, found that when the World Medical and Health Games were being held in Stirling, Scotland, 26.4 per cent of businesses were unaware of the event. In terms of strategically seeking to benefit from the hosting of events, it can be argued that events are best employed when they are used to advance existing urban development plans. However, this may not be the reality. Quinn's (2010) study of the Cork 2005 European Capital of Culture event found that while the event was actively used to speed up the local government's existing urban regeneration priorities the event organisers made no attempt to further the city's existing cultural plan through the event. Thus, implementing a planning process is critical if the full potential of hosting an event is to be realised. Chalip (2004) noted that if benefits are to be effectively leveraged they must be incorporated into the event strategic planning process. The concept of leverage assumes, first, a knowledge as to the potential that events offer in terms of generating a series of beneficial outcomes and, second, an intent to actively seek to profit from them. As Smith notes, the many outcomes that can emerge from events may not happen automatically, 'initiatives need to be implemented to capitalise on the goodwill, civic engagement and publicity that major events can generate' (2010: 163).

For Karadakis et al. (2010) an important starting point is to undertake a SWOT (strengths, weaknesses, opportunities, challenges) analysis of the host location. They suggested that key strengths are having certain infrastructures, proper security, an ability to attract volunteers, a background in hosting large-scale events, a strong economy and a stable political and economic environment. Weaknesses, conversely, may include a deficit in necessary infrastructures, the size of the country, economic and political instability, a lack of historical involvement in sport, a lack of local support and a bid lacking in detail. Undertaking and learning from a SWOT analysis lays a strong basis for planning and can 'assist all stakeholders involved in the bidding, preparation, delivery and post-games management to target and prepare much more efficiently with the long-term needs of the host city' (Karadakis et al., 2010: 182). Jago et al. (2010) argued that if benefits are to be experienced in the long term, then the preparation for, and construction of, the event and associated facilities must be viewed as part of a long-term destination development strategy. Legacy is receiving increasing attention as the role of the event as catalyst becomes more and more appreciated. O'Brien (2006: 241) made a very important point in acknowledging that the mere decision to host a major event such as the **Olympic Games** introduces widespread environmental change in the host economy and that local economic actors need to learn to effectively adapt. He undertook a study of 'Business Club Australia', a programme, targeted specifically at facilitating longer-term business opportunities arising from the hosting of the Sydney Olympics in 2000. This was the first time that the federal government of a host city ever funded such an initiative. O'Brien (2006) examined the implementation of this programme and investigated how, under its auspices, business network linkages were formed and these linkages leading to supplementary webs of contacts were initiated. Legacy committees have become the norm within the organising structures of large-scale events such as the Olympic Games, FIFA World Cup and other very large sports events. The local organising committee of the 2010 FIFA World Cup held in South Africa, for example set up the African Legacy Programme in November 2006 with the aim of improving Africa's global image. Jago et al. (2010) reported the efforts made in South Africa to spread the opportunities offered by the event. One government initiative was an active support programme for assisting emerging entrepreneurs. As part of this, 10,000 of the 55,000 rooms contracted by the 2010 FIFA World Cup were allocated to rooms in small non-hotel tourism businesses.

A key question in the literature on leveraging has been how best to generate both immediate tourism impacts and also future tourism value in terms of flow-on tourism and repeat visitation (Chalip, 2004). A key factor in this regard has been identified as the effective **marketing** of events (Taks et al., 2009), especially given that Weed (2003) found that traditionally, sport organisations and tourism organisations tend not to work together very well. While some of the above show a preoccupation with leveraging to effect economic benefits, other contributors stress an approach that is more integrative and holistic in nature. Foley et al. (2012a) briefly reviewed some of the studies that have critiqued events on the basis of failing to facilitate meaningful engagement for local populations and in so doing suggested the need for a more strategic approach to leveraging the social benefits of events. Chalip (2004) argued that effective leveraging is best served by providing networking opportunities among key event stakeholders. Ziakas (2010) pointed to the need to manage event portfolios existing within any given destination and argued that analysing events in terms of their interrelationships is vital if beneficial synergies are to be produced. His analysis of the event portfolio in a rural community in Texas, USA, led him to conclude that the absence of a strategic approach leads to unexploited potential to leverage benefits, especially in terms of creating synergies between beneficial economic and social outcomes. He called for a more holistic approach that advocates integration in three ways: conceptual connectivity to communicate core messages and meanings to event audiences; functional integration that emphasises collaboration possibilities between event organisations; a policy framework that acknowledges and facilitates the multiple objectives and orientations of the event organisations in question. Smith (2010) discussed leverage from the perspective of spatially diffusing event benefits. He used the case of the 2002 Commonwealth Games held in Manchester, UK, to illustrate how locations peripheral to the central location (north western England) also benefited through a planned approach to leveraging benefits.

In much of the literature discussed above the leverage in question was in effect, 'economic leverage'. Chalip (2006) has stressed the need to also develop the concept of social leverage. He draws on anthropological work to argue that the liminality and heightened sense of community (or communitas) engendered by festivals and events promotes social interaction and sociability, helps breaks down social barriers (perhaps temporarily) and generates a sense of good will among event attendees and participants. If harnessed effectively, these social aspects of festival and event settings can be strategically cultivated to help strengthen the social fabric of particular communities and social groups and to build up stores of **social capital**.

FURTHER READING

Chalip, L. (2004) 'Beyond impact: a general model for sport event leverage', in B.W. Ritchie and D. Adair (eds), *Sport Tourism: Interrelationships, Impacts and Issues*. Clevedon: Channel View Publications. pp. 226–52.

Foley, M., McGillivray, D. and McPherson, G. (2012a) *Event Policy. From Theory to Strategy*. Oxon: Routledge.

O'Brien, D. (2006) 'Event business leveraging: the Sydney 2000 Olympic Games', *Annals of Tourism Research*, 33 (1): 240–61.

Smith, A. (2010) 'Leveraging benefits from major events: maximising opportunities for peripheral urban areas', *Managing Leisure*, 15 (3): 161–80.

14 leveraging

> *The process of marketing festivals and events concerns how the organisation engages with all its stakeholders. Organisations need to understand the needs and motivations not only of their consumers, but also of the staff and volunteers who work within the organisation and with all of the other organisations with whom they relate. Crucially, they need to be able to communicate effectively with all of these **stakeholders** and ultimately, to satisfy the diverse needs and sustain the diverse relationships at issue.*

While the marketing process may relate to how an organisation engages with all its **stakeholders**, the key relationship dealt with in the literature on event marketing is that between the event organisation and the consumer. Wale and Ridal wrote that the marketer's task is to 'create, promote and stage event experiences that satisfy customer needs and that customers choose over other competitors in the marketplace' (2010: 137). Organisations carry out market research in order to analyse their markets and to learn about their specific needs, motivations, likes and dislikes, and choice-making processes. They target, segment and improve their offerings accordingly, seeking to produce event experiences that will match as close as possible with what consumers are seeking. Simultaneously, they use various marketing communications tools in the marketplace to attract the attention of would-be consumers and ultimately to stimulate the desire to purchase their services. Increasingly, event marketing is understood as experiential marketing. As Schmitt (1999) wrote, experiential marketing focuses on consumer experiences and treats emotionally and rationally driven consumption as a holistic experience.

Marketing is a core topic covered in the applied literature. Core text books treat marketing in-depth, explaining the need for marketing and taking learners through the process of strategic marketing. The notion that events need to be developed and marketed as experiences is a key idea. As Allen et al. (2011) explained, the production, delivery and consumption of an event are inseparable, usually happening simultaneously. The

key concepts in event management

immediacy of the service consumption that this entails creates a whole series of challenges for the organisation. The intangibility of the experience, and the active and complex role that consumers themselves play in shaping that experience, are further factors of which event marketers must be cognisant. Ultimately, the task of the marketer is to maintain existing customers and win new ones. To communicate messages about their products and services they use a variety of tools, including advertising, direct advertising, sales promotion, personal selling and public relations. The relative importance and precise nature of these tools has evolved over time, heavily influenced by changing technologies. As Bowden et al. (2006) explained, a reliance on 'promotion' has been overtaken by the use of 'integrated marketing communication'. In the latter, all sources of contact that a consumer has with an event are considered 'as potential delivery channels for messages' (Shimp, 2003: 8). Thus every opportunity possible is used to communicate the event brand. Brand is defined by Duncan as 'an integrated bundle of information and experiences' that distinguish it not only from other events but from the vast array of competing leisure experience possibilities (2002: 13). Duncan explained that there are four types of brand messages: (1) planned messages such as media releases, advertising, e-newsletters, websites and all the other promotional activities undertaken by the event organisation; (2) unplanned messages, which are the unanticipated messages that emerge as a result of, for example, complaints, media coverage, dissatisfied customers' comments; (3) product messages are those that relate to information about the event, for example, programme content and venue information; (4) service messages are those that relate to information about event services, for example, details about transport and catering services available. In the midst of all of these possibly conflicting messages, the event's marketing team must try to manage the event brand. The precise combination of marketing communication tools used will be strongly informed by the organisation's knowledge about its target market as well as about its consumers and potential consumers.

Understanding changing consumer behaviour and how consumers reach decisions to purchase services like events is a fundamental task for marketers. In this context, the rapid and continuing rise of virtual social connectivity and social interaction has been a forceful stimulus promoting the rise of social media in contemporary marketing practice. The use of social media, that is those Internet-based applications that permit the creation and exchange of user generated information (Kaplan and Haenlein, 2009) is one of the most striking features of marketing activity and event marketing is no exception (Wortham, 2009). It can take many forms including blogs, podcasts, internet forums, wikis and videos. Some of the most popular applications, for example, Twitter, flickr, YouTube and Facebook, are now household names and used by millions of users worldwide. Event organisations are increasingly using social media to market their events. Festival Edinburgh, for example, communicate messages from 12 Edinburgh arts and cultural festivals through its own online television station, edinburghfestival.tv, with some material partially broadcast via the Internet on sites like YouTube and MySpace (Carrell, 2009). Developments like this attest to a growing understanding of the role that social media play in everyday lifestyles, which sees people continuously report and update their engagement in, and experience of, all kinds of events and happenings via Twitter or Facebook. O'Leary Analytics (2011) examined how Oxegen 2011, a music festival held at Punchestown Racecourse in Ireland and one of the biggest music festivals in Europe, featured in social media commentary during an 11-day period covering the run-up to the event, the weekend event itself and a few days afterwards. There were 34,000 mentions of the festival across all media during the period with more than 25,000 of these appearing as tweets and the greatest number appearing 2 days before the festival began. Analysing data like this clearly helps an event organisation to develop a better understanding of its customer base. It can also be of value in helping event organisations become better prepared to seek sponsorship deals.

To date, however, relatively little is known about how social media is being used or managed in the sector. Rothschild (2011) investigated the use of social media among US venues (for example, convention/exhibition centres, stadia, amphitheatres). He found that a significant number of venue managers were beginning to make effective use of social media in their marketing efforts. Commonly used methods included using email newsletters and using various mechanisms, such as YouTube, Facebook and Twitter, to communicate with consumers. While it was found that those venues with a defined social media strategy were noticing revenue increases relative to those without such a strategy, managing social media was not without its challenges: not having enough staff to manage the process, for example, was found to be problematic. Davidson's (2011) findings were not dissimilar. His online survey of 10 large purpose-built conference centres in the UK found that the rate of adoption of web 2.0 applications varied, with the more committed venues using five or six tools (Twitter, Facebook, podcasts, Flickr) in their marketing communications strategies.

While the literature reviewed above relates to the business of marketing events and festivals, there is also a need to realise that events and festivals are themselves used to market products and experiences that are both related and unrelated to their focus of celebration. It is now widely recognised that consumers have become less responsive to traditional advertising methods and so marketers must find new ways of communicating with target audiences. Through event **sponsorship**, companies seek to influence brand attitude and buying intention among event audiences. Under sponsorship arrangements, companies reach agreements as to how an event organisation will convey its messages to a defined target group. A more recent development has seen companies themselves get involved in the organisation of events for the purpose of advertising their products. An example of this is the worldwide series of Red Bull Flugtag events, which began in Austria in 1991 and saw the 100th event being staged in Dublin in 2011 (Red Bull, 2011). As Drengner et al. explained, the popularity of companies staging their own events is that, unlike with event sponsorship, the company can communicate detailed product information because of the 'active participation of the target group and their intense social interaction with the company' (2008: 139). In all of these cases, a notable research interest has been in trying to identify the manner in which companies' engagement with events impacts upon brand image and brand awareness (Drengner et al., 2008; Martensen et al. 2007) either through sponsorship or through involvement in event organisation. A feature of this form of marketing is that through sponsoring/organising events, companies seek to engage their target groups in experiential activities. Some research on this has been done in respect of wine and food festivals. Food and wine events, according to Hall and Sharples are 'fairs, festivals, expositions, cultural, consumer and industry events which are held on either a regular or one-off basis' (2008: 4). Their importance as effective tourist attractions has been increasingly realised in recent years as part of the drive to develop cultural tourism offerings, particularly in rural regions (Hall and Mitchell, 2001; Hjalager and Richards, 2002). Festivals and events have been noticeably to the fore in plans to develop and market what is variously described as gourmet, gastronomic or culinary tourism. Yuan and Jang (2008) investigated the role played by festivals in promoting wineries and their products. They examined the relationships between festival quality, satisfaction with the festival, subsequent awareness of local wines and future purchasing intentions. Axelsen and Swan (2010) extended this work by investigating which festival attributes are key in altering consumers' perceptions of the quality of wine products. Their study of a Moonlight Wine Tour, an annual food and wine festival held in Brisbane, Australia, found the new experiences encountered by festival visitors and the hype and glamour associated with a festival to be the most significant in this respect.

Another dimension of the literature on marketing and events relates to the role that the hype and glamour play in promoting destinations. As the discussions on **tourism** and on **place marketing** in this volume suggest, events are increasingly being used to signal destination distinctiveness, quality and brand values (Getz, 2008). Very frequently, festivals and events are strategically used to help tourism destinations stand out in the crowded tourism marketplace. As Ferrari and Resciniti noted, 'events can influence the image of the locality where they are made and, therefore, can be considered as fundamental elements of differentiation, especially if based on distinctive and unique local resources' (2007: 387). Simeon and Buonincontri (2011) discussed the case of the Ravello festival, and how it functions as the main marketing tool for the Amalfi coast of Italy. It dates to 1953 and is predominantly a music festival that attracted almost 80,000 visitors in 2008. It has an important role to play in defining an image for the area, positioning it in the international marketplace and contributing to the local economy. Edinburgh is another example. In 2009, Edinburgh City Council, the Scottish Government, EventScotland and Scottish Enterprise came together to develop the 'Festival Edinburgh' marketing campaign and logo in a strategic attempt to promote Edinburgh as a year-round festival city. Since 2009, all 12 of Edinburgh's arts and culture festivals have come together under the 'Festivals Edinburgh' umbrella. The festivals developed a joint festivals website and a 'single-entry' ticketing site for all the festivals box offices in the attempt to increase ticket sales. As discussed in the entry on **place marketing**, events are used by national governments to enhance, boost or variously reposition their countries' image in the international marketplace. Marketing researchers have been interested in investigating the mechanics of how this actually works from a marketing perspective. Florek and Insch (2011), for example, used a product–country image fit matrix to investigate destination and event image congruence. They presented several cases of destination and event pairings, discussing the extent to which the match was positive or not. Favourable examples include the hosting of the Nobel Prize Award ceremonies in Stockholm and Oslo. Unfavourable ones are 2008 Beijing Olympic Games and the 2002 Miss World contest held in Nigeria. Germany's hosting of the 2006 FIFA World Cup was analysed and interpreted as having had the very positive effect of re-balancing Germany's international image as a country.

FURTHER READING

Allen, J., O'Toole, W., Harris, R. and McDonnell, I. (2011) *Festivals & Special Event Management*, 5th edn. Milton, Queensland: John Wiley & Sons Australia.

Bowden, G., Allen, J., O'Toole, W., Harris, R. and McDonnell, I. (2006) *Events Management*, 2nd edn. Oxford: Butterworth-Heinemann.

Martensen, A., Grønholdt, Bendtsen, L. and Jensen, M.J. (2007) 'Application of a model for the effectiveness of event marketing', *Journal of Advertising Research*, 47 (3): 283–301.

Rothschild, P.C. (2011) 'Social media use in sports and entertainment venues', *International Journal of Event and Festival Management*, 2 (2): 139–50.

16 MICE/MEEC

> *The meetings, incentives, conventions and exhibitions (MICE) industry (otherwise known as the meetings, expositions, events and conventions [MEEC] industry) represents a very important part of international tourism activity. Sometimes MICE are referred to as 'business events'.*

The meetings, incentives, conventions and exhibitions that comprise the MICE sector all aim to bring together people 'whose purpose is to share updated information and ideas, to sell or buy new products, or to launch new products to reach a consensus on various challenges' (Kim et al., 2011: 86). At its core is the need to facilitate communication, and MICE activity is now key to the wider world of international business and trade, as it is to international tourism. The cluster of events encapsulated in the term MICE is in itself quite diverse. All of them are meetings, and there has been a proposal that this activity should be referred to simply as the meetings industry. Brief definitions of individual MICE activities follow.

- Conferences: are meetings used by any group/association/organisation to 'meet and exchange views, convey a message, open a debate or give publicity to some area of opinion on a specific issue' (Convention Industry Committee, 2003, cited in Bowden et al., 2006: 21). They vary tremendously in size from relatively localised, small events to global conferences attracting tens of thousands of delegates, some national in scale (political party conferences), others international (international medical conferences).
- Incentive travel: a motivational tool used by management to acknowledge and reward performance in pursuit of organisational goals. The Society of Incentive Travel Executives (SITE), dedicated to connecting motivational experiences with business results, now has a global network of 35 chapters and 2100 members in 87 countries (Society of incentive Travel Executives [SITE], 2012).
- Corporate events: include a variety of activities associated with corporate activity including incentive travel, meetings, client and staff entertainment and conferences (Rogers, 2003).
- Exhibitions: defined in Bowden et al. as 'a presentation of products or services to an invited audience with the object of inducing a sale or informing the visitor' (2006: 21). According to the European Major Exhibition Centres Association (EMECA, 2012) more than 36 million visitors and more than 330,000 exhibitors take part in approximately 1000 exhibitions affiliated to EMECA.

As Rogers (2003) notes, the development of the modern conference and convention industry dates from the middle to later part of the 20th century. The growth of this activity was stimulated by the rise in the formation of trade associations and since the 1960s, the practice of hosting meetings, conferences, conventions has expanded not only in Europe and North America, but outwards to virtually all parts of the world. Roger (2003) notes the scale of investment and commitment that governments in countries such as the UK, Australia, South Africa, Thailand and Dubai have made in developing infrastructures to accommodate this activity. Its expansion into developing world countries has accompanied broader economic development and, frequently, has grown in line with an increasing emphasis on tourism development. The industry's expansion into the Asia-Pacific region has been particularly dramatic, driven by economic development in the region, the development of state-of-the-art infrastructure and the marketing activities of such agencies as the Asian Association of Convention and Visitor Bureaux. The development of MICE activity in the Middle East has also been noteworthy with countries like Dubai strategically developing an event-led development strategy not just for MICE activity but for other special event activity especially in the sports domain. Investing in infrastructures, development initiatives and marketing activities has been a top policy priority.

Notwithstanding the negative effects of the 2001 economic downturn and the 9/11 terrorist attacks, activity within this sector has grown significantly in recent years. According to the international congress and convention association, meetings activity is increasing. Its country and city rankings data show that 9120 events were held in 2010, an increase of 826 events on the previous year, which had been, at the time, an all-time record. In 2010, the USA, Germany and Spain were the countries with the highest number of meetings, while in terms of cities, it was Vienna, Barcelona and Paris that topped the rankings. Among the cities showing the biggest increase in activity were Madrid, Istanbul, Sydney and Taipei (ICCA, 2012).

The activities of the MICE industry clearly constitute examples of planned events, hence their inclusion in this book. However, they differ from other special events in a number of ways. Unlike other areas, research on MICE has tended to emanate from within hospitality as opposed to tourism studies. This reflects the role played by hotels in the earlier days of this industry's evolution. More importantly, the size and scale of this activity internationally, and the degree to which it is organised at destination level, is now such that it can be regarded as constituting a separate sphere of activity, quite distinct from other special events. MICE activity is particularly lucrative. As Kim et al. (2011) explained, visitor flows generated by MICE activity tend to give a much higher economic return than general tourist flows: convention travellers tend to stay longer and to spend more per capita. US figures for 2004 suggest that it accounted for US$122.3 billion in direct spend (Convention Industry Council, n.d.). Dimmock and Tiyce (2001) suggested that conferences can lead to: increased personal and business income, investment and sponsorship, tax revenue, employment and training, increased business opportunities, improved destination image and increased visitor numbers. The benefits that destinations stand to gain from MICE mean that it is a very competitive industry, and multiple destinations compete to be selected as locations for MICE activity. The lucrative nature of this industry has led many countries to identify its development as being of strategic importance. Increasingly, destinations develop appropriate infrastructures and establish Convention and Visitor Bureaus to enhance their prospects of attracting MICE business.

The highly competitive nature of the sector is a key theme in the literature. In recent times, Western countries' traditional dominance of the global market has come under challenge from strong growth elsewhere, particularly in Asia. Kim et al. (2011) related that Asian countries had a 14.6 per cent share of the market in 2005. Governments in countries such as China, South Korea and Japan are actively pursuing strategies to develop their convention industries and promote their countries as leading MICE destinations. Strategies include constructing state-of-the-art convention centres, promoting the development of associated service activity in retail, accommodation and entertainment, and establishing convention development laws. Kim et al. (2010) identifies Korea as a good example of this. The convention industry in Korean has grown to become one of the most important segments of the tourism industry, the country having hosted a number of mega-events since the 1980s. Hotels are a key component of the venue infrastructure with 47.3 per cent of international conferences held in the country in 2007 using hotels as venues.

Not surprisingly, the relative competitiveness of MICE destinations and the reasons determining why particular destinations get selected above others have long stimulated research enquiry. From the event planners' perspective, the choice of location is one of the biggest decisions that they have to make. It will often determine the number of attendees that decide to attend the event and this in turn will strongly influence how successful the outcome of the meeting will be (Lee and Black, 2005). It is no surprise then that the destination selection process has been a key focus of academic enquiry. Understanding event planners and the criteria they consider in deciding where to locate meetings is critical for both meeting buyers and suppliers (Vogt et al., 1994). An early study was Oppermann's (1996) analysis of the images of 30 convention destinations in North America as perceived by association meeting planners. Key selection factors identified here were meeting rooms/facilities, hotel service quality, hotel room availability, clean/attractive location, safety/security, air transportation access, food and lodging costs, overall affordability, city image, transportation costs, restaurant facilities, exhibition facilities, scenery/sightseeing opportunities, climate and nightlife. More recently, extant research synopsised by DiPietro et al. (2008) identified that key selection criteria include: accessibility, availability of facilities, quality of service, affordability, destination image, attractions/entertainment, and safety and security. Lee's (2010) recent Korean study supported this assertion finding that purpose-built conference facilities, excellent service and competitively priced room rates were very important attributes that organisers look for when considering which hotels to select as conference venues. While a lot of the literature has focused on explaining the selection of particular destinations, or on comparing destinations within a particular country, as Baloglu and Love (2005) did with five convention cities in the USA, a more recent development has been to compare across international boundaries. Kim et al. (2011) compared competitiveness among five cities in East Asia, Seoul, Hong Kong, Beijing, Shanghai and Tokyo.

As Lee (2010) explained, the MICE sector is very complex with a multiplicity of stakeholders involved as suppliers and buyers, but also in a variety of marketing, training, funding and regulatory capacities. As Lee (2009) found, conference organisers can differ in their requirements from those, like hotels, who supply venues. The complexity of convention activity was acknowledged early on by Oppermann and Chon (1997) in their Conference Participation Decision-Making Model. Some studies have tried to investigate the question of venue and destination selection from the perspective of both suppliers and buyers. Kang et al. (2005), is a case in point. They analysed the competitiveness of Asian international meeting destinations, including Bangkok, Hong Kong, Singapore, Seoul and Tokyo, basing their study on the perceptions of both meeting planners and buying centres.

Somewhat surprisingly, little research has been conducted on a key stakeholder group, the meeting planners themselves. As Beaulieu and Love (2005) point out, this is a relatively new profession, with industry certification and continuing education only developing over recent decades. There were, however, some 32,000 people identified as Meeting and Convention Planners by the US Department of Labor in 2000 (Beaulieu and Love, 2005).

FURTHER READING

Bowden, G., Allen, J., O'Toole, W., Harris, R. and McDonnell, I. (2006) *Events Management*, 2nd edn. Oxford: Butterworth-Heinemann.

DiPietro, R.B., Breiter, D., Rompf, P. and Godlewska, M. (2008) 'An exploratory study of differences among meeting and exhibition planners in their destination selection criteria', *Journal of Convention & Event Tourism*, 9 (4): 258–76.

Lee, T.J. (2010) 'The successful conference venue: perceptions of conference organisers and hotel managers', *Event Management*, 13: 223–32.

Rogers, T. (2003) *Conferences and Conventions: A Global Industry*. Oxford: Butterworth-Heinemann.

17 Motivation

Research on motivation in festival and event contexts is very well established and seeks to understand and explain what drives people to attend festivals and events, and what benefits they are seeking to derive through their attendance.

Just as the question: 'Why do people travel?', has been a long standing query in tourism studies, so too has the question: 'Why do people attend festivals and events?', long preoccupied festival and event researchers. From a tourism perspective, events clearly require audiences. As Faulkner et al. (2001) argued, the destination development engendered by an event is largely driven by the attendance it is expected to generate. Thus, the promotion and marketing of events is a key area of interest, and the question as to what motivates people to attend events has been an important social psychological question dating back to the early 1990s. There is now a substantial literature on the topic, including a recent comprehensive literature review by Li and Petrick (2006). This is not surprising. An in-depth knowledge of visitors' motives for attending festivals and events is a prerequisite for planning and marketing events effectively (Crompton and McKay, 1997). Yet, this is an immensely complicated topic and even after extensive research there continue to be criticisms that existing knowledge of audience behaviours is descriptive, relies on ad hoc, illustrative case studies (Li and Petrick, 2006) and requires a more systematic and comprehensive approach (Nicholson and Pearce, 2001). Gyimóthy (2009), drawing on Li and Petrick (2006), called for researchers to draw on conceptual and methodological insights from other disciplines to advance understanding.

To date, the complexity of motives at issue has been debated in general (Crompton and McKay, 1997) as well as in specific areas like sports events (Gibson, 1998, 2006) and business and convention events (Rittichainuwat et al., 2001). The importance of understanding constraints has been discussed as has the importance of market segmentation, with Formica and Uysal (1998) demonstrating that successful promotion depends on effective segmentation. Indeed, the literature on segmentation alone has now grown to be quite sizeable and is considered elsewhere in this volume. It is notable that virtually all of the motivation literature conceives of the event solely in tourism terms and focuses on the motivations of visitors attending as audience members, as opposed to residents. This emphasis on understanding visitors' motivations has in turn meant a preoccupation with large-scale events, to the neglect of smaller-scale, often rural-based events (Li et al., 2009).

Much of the early motivation research was driven by researchers based in the USA. Ralston and Crompton's (1988) research into the motivation of visitors attending a festival in Texas was one such early study. They generated a set of motivation statements that laid the basis for later research into the topic. Accordingly, the early 1990s saw a number of researchers employ quantitative techniques in North American contexts to investigate and delineate dimensions of motivation. Overall, a number of dimensions including: socialisation/sociability; family togetherness; novelty; excitement; escape; have been identified in a number of these studies (Mohr et al., 1993; Uysal et al., 1993). A scale developed by Uysal et al. (1993) has been widely used. Prentice and Andersen (2003) point out that the enjoyment of company as gregariousness is a recurrent motive for attending festivals, while socialisation has been found frequently as a dimension of festival consumption. They suggest that the recurring importance of gregariousness may imply that the festival itself becomes a destination, rather than simply an attraction of place-based destinations. The experience of gregariousness may ultimately be independent of any specific place, and what makes festivals special has been found to centre around uniqueness and quality, as well as atmosphere (Getz and Cheyne, 1997). While researchers agree on the prevalence of socialisation as a motive, Nicholson and Pearce (2001) concluded that the kind of socialisation at issue can vary.

Schneider and Backman (1996) undertook a motivation study in Jordan, interested to see whether the motivation scales developed in the North American context could be applied to different national contexts. They found them to be applicable to the Arabic festival that they studied in Jordan (Lee et al., 2004), while Jeong and Park (1997) equally found application of the novelty scale in their South Korean study. By 2004, Lee et al. (2004) in a review of the literature on festival motivation summarised earlier work and concluded that a core set of motives for event participation existed irrespective of event theme or location and inclusive of a range of different nationalities. They further deduced from their review of motivation studies that 'participation related variables were more likely to elicit differences in motivations than were traditional demographics'. Their study of Korean and international visitors to the 2000 Kyongju World Culture Expo investigated the differences between these two groups through profiling them by segment clusters. The existence of differences between the two groups, they argued, is evidence that event managers need to pay close attention to the needs and wants of non-local participants. Lee (2000) investigated the factors that motivated people to attend an international event, namely the Kyongju World Cultural Expo, and explored whether motivations differed between Caucasian and Asian visitors. One of their key findings was that the motivation items and scales measured in North America and Europe could be also applied to Asian countries.

Reflecting developments in the wider tourism studies literature, event motivations can be interpreted in terms of 'push and pull' factors. The key dimensions of socialisation, novelty, excitement, escape and so on mentioned above all relate to Iso-Ahola's (1980, 1983) theoretical ideas about leisure as escapism. Getz (2008) suggested that events exert a 'pull' on visitors particularly when special interests are involved, as when serous athletes seek out events in which to compete.

Given the longstanding nature of event motivational research, the literature has developed several sub-themes. Researchers have investigated motivations in the context of different types of events, for example. Extant research on cultural tourists' motivations has tended to indicate a propensity for tourists to come from higher socio-economic backgrounds with relatively high cultural capital. Kim et al. (2007) supported this finding in their analysis of Canadian data, which found that participation at 'festivals and musical attractions' (not local festivals and fairs) was positively influenced by both education and income variables. Research into the motives of sports events attendees is another identifiable area with investigating the motivations associated with active and passive sports tourists. A further dimension of event motivation studies has been an enquiry into the characteristics of first-time and repeat visitors. Festivals have been found to attract particularly high levels of repeat visitors (Van der Wagen, 2005). The value of attracting repeat visitors as a desirable stable revenue source and a significant reference group for prospective visitors is well acknowledged in the literature (Anwar and Sohail, 2004; Fallon and Schofield, 2004; Getz, 1991). Festivals have been associated with levels of repeat visitation that exceed those associated with tourism activities more generally. Yet it is not well understood what explains customer loyalty/repeat visitation. The question as to what factors explain repeat festival visitation has been raised by Grappi and Montanari (2011) in respect of a cultural festival. They investigated six different environmental dimensions including programme content, staff behaviours, places and atmosphere, information and facilities, hotel and restaurant offers, and souvenir availability. They found that programme content was what festival attendees paid most attention to. They further found that social identification played a role in determining repeat visitation, arguing that the more an attendee identifies with the usual group of attendees, the more likely they are inclined to make a return visit to the festival (Grappi and Montanari, 2011). Findings like this support the dominant emphasis on socialisation found in extant motivational literature. They also link into the literature on **service quality**, where 'repeat visitation' is construed as 'consumer loyalty'.

Given that most research has focused on visitors, there is a knowledge deficit as to what motivates local residents to attend festivals and events hosted in their home areas, whether locally oriented or international in scale. Formica and Uysal's (1998) study of motivations for people attending the Umbria Jazz festival in Italy is an exception. They found that motivations differed between residents and non-residents. So too, did McDowall (2010), whose Thai study found that while residents and non-residents were similarly motivated by local culture and family, they differed in other respects. Van Zyl and Botha (2004) is one of the few exceptions to look solely at the factors that motivate local residents' attendance. They point to the importance to the host community in sustaining a festival as justification for studying residents' engagement.

FURTHER READING

Gibson, H. (2006) *Sport Tourism: Concepts and Theories*. London: Routledge.

Lee, C., Lee, Y. and Wicks, B.E. (2004) 'Segmentation of festival motivation by nationality and satisfaction', *Tourism Management*, 25: 61–70.

Li, R. and Petrick, J. (2006) 'A review of festival and event motivation studies', *Event Management*, 9 (4): 239–45.

McDowall, S. (2010) 'A comparison between Thai residents and non-residents in their motivations, performance evaluations and overall satisfaction with a domestic festival', *Journal of Vacation Marketing*, 16 (3): 217–33.

18 Olympic Games

With a history dating back millennia, the Olympic Games is the world's largest sporting event. Hosted every 4 years in major cities located thoughout the world, the summer Olympics features competitive sports and constitutes a mega-event of unparalleled size and scale. The winter Olympics, featuring winter sports, is also held every 4 years. The Games are organised by the International Olympic Committee.

While there is a degree of fuzziness about the precise meaning of terms and definitions employed in the festival and event literature, there is no doubt that the summer Olympic Games constitutes a mega-event. According to Liao and Pitts (2006), each summer Games might draw 15,000 athletes and officials, a further 15,000 media representatives and anywhere between 400,000 and 1 million visitors. These sorts of numbers are unrivalled by any other event, with the FIFA World Cup being the only event remotely comparable. The scale of the Olympic Games, and that of their potential impacts, is massive in event terms. This is the case for all aspects of the actual hosting of the event, and also for the extensive planning required. The Games are global in their reach and involve an immensely competitive, costly and politically charged bidding process. The time period involved in **bidding** and

key concepts in event management

then in planning the Games themselves is very lengthy. This gives research-ers scope to undertake various types of longitudinal, comparative investiga-tions, in a way that is not possible with smaller-scale events.

While the literature on this mega-event has been criticised for being both limited and insufficiently systematic from an **event management** perspective (Faulkner et al., 2001), it is important to note that a very substantial literature on the Olympics has been produced by researchers working in many fields. The Olympics are urban phenomena and con-stitute significant urban development projects. Accordingly, there has been a great deal written about the Olympics within urban studies. Equally, there is a substantial body of literature on the Olympics, both past and present, in the sports studies literature.

Within event management studies, the academic field concerned with organised events, the Olympic Games stand out because of their longevity and their continuity over time. Liao and Pitts' (2006) his-torical review traces the evolution of the modern Games back to 1896. During this period, 25 summer Games were staged in 21 cities spread across 17 countries. As an event, the Games also stand out because of the pivotal role that they play in reproducing and reshaping their host locations. Liao and Pitts (2006) use the term 'Olympic urbanisation' to describe the relationship between the Games and the evolution of urbanisation. This has evolved through a series of identifiable phases. The first of these they identify as the relatively low-key, modest 'Modern Olympia' of 1896–1904. The period 1908–1928 marked the beginnings of greater international attention and the period when cities began seriously planning and developing sports infrastructure. In the next phase, 1932–1956, the idea that physical developments would centre on an Olympic 'quarter' emerged. In the most recent period, 1960–2012, the Games came to be synonymous with extensive urban transformation.

Research on the Games has had a few notable emphases, with impacts being most dominant. Always, the hosting of the Olympic Games gener-ates a wealth of debate and discussion about the potential legacies of these mega-events, not just for the host city but for the country and possibly even the wider international region. Extant research shows that legacies can be broad-ranging, but also diverse and highly variable in terms of value. The Games' potential to generate legacy has been an enormous preoccu-pation for event researchers. As elsewhere, the question of economics has dominated and continues to persists: Weed and Dowse, recently argued that 'notwithstanding the range of actors commenting on the 2012 Games

(London), the dominant public discourse has been about the potential to develop economic legacies' (2009: 170). Nevertheless, there has been a broadening of enquiry into domains beyond the economic in the literature over time.

The emphasis on the economic is understandable: cities host the Olympic Games because they anticipate a host of positive economic outcomes. Faulkner et al. (2001) reviewed the literature on the tourism impacts of the Sydney 2000 Games and identified three broad themes: visitor numbers associated with the Games; longer-term effects; and organisational responses. However, research has shown that pre-Games expectations of economic outcomes are not always borne out. Conclusions as to the longer-term impacts of the Games have been tempered by research that has found promotional benefits to be significant but transitory (Ritchie and Smith, 1991) and that acknowledges that most Games take place in cities that are already well known (Hiller 1998). Faulkner et al.'s (2001) review of existing research concluded that the effect of the Games on visitor numbers can be more modest than expected when diversion and time-switching effects are considered. Still on the subject of the Sydney Games, Madden's (2002) computable general equilibrium analysis found that over a 12-year period (1994/5–2005/6) the estimated impact of the Games on Australian GDP was quite small: only 0.12 per cent higher than if Sydney had not hosted the Games. Furthermore, as already noted, one of the shortcomings of the event literature is that inferences in respect of matters such as economic impact have sometimes been transferred and applied very loosely across very different event contexts. Yet, relating findings from hallmark-event contexts to more minor arenas should proceed with caution. Madden (2002) argues that the type of macro-economic shock generated by the Olympics is only likely to accompany similar, unanticipated hallmark events, as opposed to smaller events that occur perhaps on an annual basis.

In terms of longer-term effects, the Olympics offer the potential for cities not only to reposition themselves as tourist destinations but to re-invent and represent themselves on the global stage as economic power houses, and as stable and open societies. Hosting the Olympics gives a country tremendous international exposure. The size of the television audiences drawn by events like the summer Olympic Games is vast and growing. Nielsen (2008) reports that television coverage of the 2008 Beijing Games attracted 4.7 billion viewers (70 per cent of the world's population), an increase on the

3.9 billion who watched the 2004 Athens Games and the 3.6 billion who watched the 2000 Sydney Games. Not surprisingly then, researchers have been interested in investigating the relationship between the hosting of events and country image (Mossberg and Hallberg, 1999; Hede, 2005; Gripsund et al., 2010); and between the hosting of events and future consumer intent with respect to product and holiday purchasing. Nebenzahl and Jaffe (1991), for example, found that electronic products heavily promoted through the Seoul Olympics developed a better image among Israeli consumers in consequence. Gripsund et al. (2010) saliently pointed out that the hosting of major sports events, the 2006 Turin Winter Olympics in their empirical case, can have a negative image effect and that managing and controlling branding in the event context is both an opportunity and a challenge.

Courtesy of their tremendously high media profile, the political implications of the Games are immense. Robinson et al. (2010) used the case of the 2008 Beijing Olympics to suggest that the logistical success of the Beijing event was very important in overcoming some of the very mixed perceptions of China portrayed in the international media in the lead-in to the Games. Concerns about diverse matters ranging from air pollution to human rights violations, religious persecution and state surveillance and control on media and media access had been widely reported. In the aftermath of the Games, they suggest that domestic support for the Chinese government increased and that tourism development was a key benefit. Waitt (2003: 197–8) suggested that for Sydney, the 2000 Games offered the city's entrepreneurs and politicians an event to both reposition the city as a global city and to restructure the local economy in 'creative' industries. The Games were located on a largely government owned brownsite, providing an opportunity to materially and symbolically transform a marginal redundant space associated with noxious industries, an abattoir and an armament depot into a 'central, clean, green economic base sustained by consumptive practices of culture economies, primarily sport' (Waitt, 2003: 189). More recently, Dansero and Puttilli (2010) applied a territorialisation approach (Raffestin, 1980) to a study of the Torino 2006 Winter Olympic Games. Their findings suggest that the legacy of a sports mega-event like the Olympic Games can be seen to produce an increase in what they term local 'territorial capital'. The focus of their approach advocates planning and managing the mega-event's legacy as part of the general planning of the territory and resources, as distinct from viewing the legacy of the event in isolation.

Relatively little is known about the social impact of the Olympic Games (Waitt, 2003). Fredline and Faulkner (2000) argue that far greater concern has been given to evaluating the political, cultural, economic and environmental consequences. Historically, social impact assessments often relied on secondary data sources or investigated resident attitudes towards an event. In the latter respect, a 'snapshot' as opposed to a longitudinal approach was usually employed. Waitt's (2003) study of the 2000 Sydney Olympics tried to address some of these deficiencies in the literature. He examined the temporal dynamics of the social impacts of Sydney 2000 using two telephone surveys, one 24 months before and the other during the Games. Theoretically, he used social exchange theory, which has been widely used to explain resident assessments of tourism impacts. As Ap (1992) explained, residents who perceive rewards of either maintenance and/or improvement of their social and economic well-being are overall likely to evaluate the event positively. Sadd (2010) argued that research into the social legacy impacts of events is becoming increasingly important and makes reference to the work of several authors including Fredline et al. (2003). García (2001) has written about the cultural programmes associated with Olympic Games. She argued that the role of arts activities in enhancing the marketing potential of sports events like the Olympics has yet to be fully appreciated.

In terms of environmental impact, the literature on the Olympic Games shows mixed findings. Positive impacts identified include the use of sustainable practices during the operation of the Games themselves and preservation of the physical environment and local heritage post event (Deccio and Baloglu, 2002). Negative impacts reported include inconvenience, traffic congestion and associated pollution during the preparation stages, longer-term damage in terms of destruction of forest areas and disturbance to wildlife and open spaces (Girginov and Parry, 2005). The 1992 Winter Games in Albertville constituted something of an environmental disaster and was instrumental in bringing about the introduction of an Olympic Games environmental policy. Since 1996 the IOC's Sport and Environment Commission has made environmental initiatives a standard requirement, although according to Konstantaki and Wickens (2010) this requirement is not always met. The organising committee of the 2012 London summer Olympics emphasised its commitment to sustainability and to legacy producing *The London 2012 Sustainability Plan* in 2007 and actively seeking to comply with the British Standard for Sustainable Events, introduced in 2007. However, the planning period preceding an Olympic Games is very lengthy and the influence of changing economic and political contexts can be very forceful. Since 2007, the global economy has taken a serious downturn with market uncertainties continuing to prevail into 2012. Simultaneously, there was a change in government in the UK in 2010 with a corresponding shift in political priorities. When the sustainability plan for London 2012 was updated in December 2010, the five priority themes identified in the 2007 document (climate change, waste, biodiversity, inclusion and healthy living) had become four key areas of focus (harnessing the UK's passion for sport, exploiting economic opportunities, promoting community engagement and regenerating East London). While legacy continued to be emphasised, the articulation of objectives in respect of sustainability was much less apparent.

FURTHER READING

Liao, H. and Pitts, A. (2006) 'A brief historical review of Olympic urbanization', *The International Journal of the History of Sport*, 23 (7): 1232–52.

Madden, J.R. (2002) 'The economic consequences of the Sydney Olympics: the CREA/Arthur Andersen study', *Current Issues in Tourism*, 5 (1): 7–21.

Waitt, G. (2003) 'Social impacts of the Sydney Olympics', *Annals of Tourism Research*, 30 (1): 194–215.

Weed, M. and Dowse, S. (2009) 'A missed opportunity waiting to happen? The social legacy potential of the London 2010 Paralympic Games', *Journal of Policy Research in Tourism, Leisure and Events*, 1 (2): 170–4.

19 Place Marketing

Place marketing is the business of setting a particular place apart from others; of creating an image for a place such that it appears more attractive to a wide array of inward flows of capital, revenue, skills, human capital, tourists and so on. Destination marketing has a similar meaning, except that it is more specifically oriented towards attracting tourists and developing tourism activity.

There is no doubt but that the advent of globalisation has meant that places need to become adept at marketing themselves to attract visitors, residents and workers, businesses, industry alike. Festivals and events have proliferated accordingly, as part of place marketing strategies intended to cultivate strong images and distinguish locations from international competition. Westerbeek et al. explain how city marketing is a way of branding a city so that 'consumers can give meaning to the attributes, values, benefits or activities which that city offers' (2002: 305). This brand sets the city apart from others. The intense desire to host large-scale events, such as the Olympics and the FIFA World Cup, is closely related to the anticipated international exposure that accrues to the nations hosting such events. The extent to which this international exposure influences destination image, awareness of destinations and future intention to visit has been investigated by several researchers (Hede, 2005; Mossberg and Hallberg, 1999).

Festivals and events are particularly associated with cities. According to Ilczuk and Kulikowska (2007: 7) the geographic distribution of international arts festivals in Europe disproportionately favours urban areas. They are now well acknowledged as providing useful vehicles for creating a city brand, and the focus of event celebration, be it sport, arts or some other form of culture, create attractive and eye-catching images that align well with cities' aspirations to appear as 'creative cities'. As Jamieson (2004) suggested, festivals and events serve as discourses of 'city branding' and the 'creative industries' in a competitive global context where 'culture' provides the discursive linchpin linking creative practices, formerly regarded as 'the arts', with economic-led, post-industrial, globalised urban repertoires.

A key driver for the growth and reinvention of festivals and events internationally has been their potential to deliver a series of development outcomes in terms of economic restructuring and revitalisation, destination repositioning, inward investment and tourism revenue generation. For example, Schuster (2001) has argued that festivals and events staged as urban ephemera or urban spectacle yield economic benefits by raising the profile of places, their products and institutions and attracting flows of tourists, capital and inward investment. For many western cities, a key motivation in developing festival and event strategies has been to recover from long-term economic decline. Festivals and events have been part of a wider range of new 'cultural strategies' (Gotham, 2005) used to regenerate and orient post-production economies towards consumption where leisure, entertainment and tourism underpin an 'experience economy' (Pine and Gilmore, 1999). Hallmark events, in particular, have stimulated tourist flows and encouraged public investment in infrastructure (Magdalinski and Nauright, 2004).

As Waitt (2008) points out, urban festivals are not new and have long been used to advance particular urban agenda and promote the ideologies of elite social groups. Muñoz (2006) cites the great exhibitions and Olympic urbanism as two examples of how architecture and urban planning are used to communicate a specific urban image. Benedict (1983) discussed the World Fairs as politically intentioned displays and Roche (2000) makes this point about the Olympics. Today, Edinburgh defines itself visually either by images of the castle or of the city during its festival season (Jamieson, 2004: 65). Prentice and Andersen (2003: 3) wrote about how Edinburgh has worked to position itself as 'the Festival City' rather than solely as Scotland's capital, thereby offering creativity, as well as heritage, as unique selling points. In 2011, the official Edinburgh Festivals website described Edinburgh as 'Scotland's beautiful capital, known throughout the world as the Festival City. Visitors come to Edinburgh every year to experience the eight summer festivals' which present a diverse variety of artists and events: 'There is something for everyone so come to Edinburgh and be inspired' (Edinburgh Festivals, 2011). The role that the festival has played in setting the city apart is lengthy. The original 'Edinburgh International Festival of Music and Drama', held in 1945 served both to re-establish the civilising high cultural values of pre-war Europe and to stand firm in the face of the threat of the Americanised culture industry. Over time as Jamieson (2004) pointed out, the high cultural ideals of the early festival came to be contested by newer, alternative perspectives which emerged in the form of the Edinburgh Festival Fringe.

It is now understood that festivals and events are very important from the specific perspective of destination marketing. Felenstein and Fleischer (2009) are just two of many authors who note the recent proliferation of the use of festivals as tools to generate tourism activity. While sometimes it can be a question of existing festive practice being recreated or repackaged as tourist attractions, it can equally involve the establishment of new festivals with the specific intention of furthering tourism goals. Creating interest and attracting attention as they invigorate and enliven places, the tourism functions that festivals play are now well rehearsed: they attract tourists, generate tourist expenditure, help to revitalise destination image and assist with combating seasonality problems. To date, the literature on place marketing has tended to focus on larger-scale events located in urban areas. However, with the growth of niche festivals there has been growing interest in using festivals to market regions. As Axelsen and Swan's (2010: 436) brief literature review noted, wine and food festivals provide opportunities for creating awareness of regional wine brands, promoting the attractiveness of wine-growing regions and encouraging repeat tourist visitation to a region.

The literature on festivals, events and place-making has often been critical in tone. Some researchers have stressed how the widespread ascendancy of festivals as urban regeneration tools fits with the neo-liberal logic of governing through a 'conjunction of business, play and fantasy' (Waitt, 2008: 513). As such, festivals as place marketing tools must be understood in the context of the contemporary politics of entrepreneurialism. Neoliberal economics advocates minimising state intervention and valuing public–private partnerships, private enterprise and the operation of free market forces (Waitt, 2008: 517). Frequently, the creative industries are a pillar of this so-called 'new urban politics' (Cox, 1993) which places great store on city re-invention through cultural districts, cultural icons, creative clusters and cultural festivals of all description. In similar vein, Eisinger (2000: 316–17) explained how city regimes now 'devote enormous energies and resources not simply to the basic and traditional municipal functions but also to the task of making cities, in the words of Judd and Fainstein (1999), "places to play"'. In contrast to cities' investment in service provision (clean water, free schools, public libraries and parks and public health facilities) in the late 19th century, contemporary investment is aimed at the middle classes, and often at the visiting middle classes, who can afford to 'eat in the new outdoor cafés, attend trade and professional conventions, shop in the festival malls, and patronise the high- and middle-brow arts' (Eisinger, 2000: 317). Eisinger (2000) problematises this approach, arguing that the hierarchy of interests being served here places the needs of commuters, day-trippers, tourists and business travellers above those of residents.

The reductionist tendencies of place marketing approaches have also been highlighted. McClinchey's (2008) investigation of ethnic festivals in Toronto pointed to the changing nature of host communities and host places and to the particularities both of cultural meanings, community needs and place identities at issue. In the context of such multi-layered complexities she raised questions about the monotone ways in which festivals are used to marketplace. Elsewhere, Gauthier's (2009: 656) interpretation of the representation of the Canadian province of Alberta in the Smithsonian Institution's annual Folklife Festival in 2006 was that 'the objectives of cultural conservation were overshadowed by business and technology'. In addition, writing in the context of destination branding and sports events, Gripsund et al. (2010) pointed out that the image effect of hosting a major event may be negative, and that the host nation cannot guarantee that it will be otherwise.

Notwithstanding the critical tone of some of the academic literature on place marketing and events, in practice, place marketing is a term that clearly resonates with event marketing professionals. Nationally, many countries have increasingly incorporated events into their product development and destination branding campaigns. Fáilte Ireland, the Irish tourism development authority, for example, has used events to partially spearhead its development of sport and cultural tourism since the start of the 2000s. Using the capacity to attract international visitors as a criterion, it offers a range of funding initiatives, business development assistance, marketing supports and advisory services to the sector. Getz (2007) suggested that Australian practice represents the 'state of the art' in the business of developing events. He highlighted EventsCorp Western Australia and Queensland Events Corp as examples of organisations with strategies, policies and programmes for 'attracting, bidding, developing and assisting events' primarily for tourism purposes.

FURTHER READING

Gripsund, G., Nes, E.B. and Olsson, U.H. (2010) 'Effects of hosting a mega-sport event on country image', *Event Management*, 14: 193–204.

Mossberg, L. and Hallberg, A. (1999) 'The presence of a mega-event: effects of destination image and product country images', *Pacific Tourism Review*, 3: 213–25.

Waitt, G. (2008) 'Urban festivals: geographies of hype, helplessness and hope', *Geography Compass*, 2 (2) 513–37.

Westerbeek, H.M., Turner, P. and Ingerson, L. (2002) 'Key success factors in bidding for hallmark sporting events', *International Marketing Review*, 19 (3): 303–22.

19 place marketing

> *Event planning concerns the anticipation and regulation of the event environment. It is future-oriented and intended to ensure that the event unfolds as intended, achieves its stated goals and creates the desired impacts.*

The literature on event planning is not as sizeable as one might have thought. The topic is dealt with within the management literature where the focus is on the event organisation and the planning requirements faced as the event moves from the inception of an idea right through to the complete execution and evaluation of the event. It is also investigated in a variety of other literatures including tourism studies, planning, geography and urban studies. Here, events are investigated within their wider contexts and questions are asked about how they fit into the cultural or regional development plans in the host location. The governance of the host location and the perspective of stakeholder groups within the host location are often central to research enquiries here.

The **event management** literature on event planning is strongly influenced by the mainstream management literature on strategy and planning. Johnson et al.'s (2008) writings on strategy, for example, have been related to the event sector. They distinguished between different levels of strategy: corporate, business and operational. Corporate strategy pertains to the overall context; business strategy relates to how individual business units within the organisation can best compete within the appropriate marketplace and; operational strategy relates to how corporate strategy can be translated into the organisation's delivery of goods and services. The event literature itself typically models the event planning process, breaks it down into phases, and identifies and describes the tasks associated with each phase. Usually, two distinct types of planning are identified: strategic and operational (Bowden et al., 2006). Strategic planning pertains to the setting of an overall strategy for the event and involves devising a mission statement and objectives, determining policies, identifying funding and devising an overall strategy to ensure that the mission is achievable. A close analysis of the broader environment in which the event is to take place is a key part of strategic planning. Event organisers use various tools to ascertain their relative position in the marketplace and to scan their current and future environments. SWOT (strengths, weaknesses, opportunities, threats) or PEST (political, economic, social, techno-logical) analyses are commonly used to examine external as well as internal environments with a view to minimising any potential risks facing the event and to maximise the chances of successfully achiev-ing its objectives. As Getz (2007) points out, adaptability is a key element of strategic planning. Events and the environments in which they operate are in a constant state of change and it is important that event organisations be flexible in their objectives and policies. Discussions on planning often incorporate treatment of leadership as an important concept. Leadership is a key consideration in strate-gic planning, given that leadership involves providing direction. For Goldblatt (2004), leaders in the event sector should have integrity, confidence, persistence, vision as well as the ability to collaborate, problem solve and communicate.

In contrast to strategic planning, operational planning relates to more routine, specific, individual procedures or dimensions of the event. According to Getz (2007) these generally are customer-oriented (traffic, queuing, ticketing, information and so on); supplier-oriented (utilities, infrastructure, equipment, scheduling, accreditation and so on) and communications. Shone and Parry (2004) acknowledged a number of operational stages: objectives and getting started; plan-ning; organising and preparing the event; implementing and running the event and divestment/legacies/evaluation. Getz's (2005) model of events operations planning outlines a variety of factors that can influence an event. These include programming, theming, experien-tial goals, management, site and venue and any other constraints. Based on an awareness and analysis of these comes the detailing of specific goals and plans 'for the venue or setting, food and beverages, technical support, and service quality' (Getz, 2007: 275). Some researchers, like Tum et al. (2006) further compartmentalise the phases involved in operational planning. They conceptualise opera-tions in terms of: the analysis phase (environmental scanning and situational analysis), the operations planning phase (strategic and delivery), implementation and delivery, and performance evaluation.

Closely allied to the requirements of operational planning are such processes as logistics, procurement and supply-chain management, task scheduling and people movement. In recent decades, advances in information and communication technologies have revolutionised the management of event operations, especially in large-scale events where capacity and resources exist to avail of such advances (Papagiannopoulos et al., 2009).

While the literature on event planning draws heavily on business planning more generally, the specific characteristics of the festival and event business lead to a whole series of particular planning requirements. The particular temporal characteristics of events, which can range from a once off, never-to-be-repeated event, to an annual event of a few day's duration, to one of up to 1 year's duration (for example, the **European City of Culture**), demand a particular emphasis on time planning. The critical need for risk assessment and **risk management** is another key feature of event planning. Allen et al. (2002) defined risk in event management as the likelihood of the special event or festival not fulfilling its objectives. More generally, definitions of risk are associated with the possibility of adverse outcomes, although as Laybourn (2004) pointed out, risk is actually most often associated with the assessment and management of potential hazards. These hazards may come under the following categories as identified by Shone and Parry (2004): staff and others; health and safety; catering; crowd management; security; and transport. The likelihood of adverse outcomes occurring increases in line with the complexity of the event. Indeed, as Laybourn remarks, 'one reason an event is special is because of risk – it has not been done before!' (2004: 302). The reliance on factors beyond an event organisation's control such as weather and currency fluctuations create a wide variety of uncertainties. For this reason, contingency planning is critically important in event contexts.

In the foregoing discussion, the workings of the event organisation itself are the focus. However, as recent decades have seen cities and regions increasingly build marketing and development strategies around events, interest has grown in investigating how events fit within planning scenarios more broadly. This shift has been encouraged by the growing understanding that events generate impacts and that these impacts can be negative as well as positive, unanticipated as well as expected. Thus, beyond the specific domain of event management, an extensive literature now investigates Hall's argument that event planning should be 'concerned with the anticipation and regulation of the impact of the event on the host community, and the promotion of associated development in a manner which maximises short- and long-term economic, environmental and social benefits' (1989: 21). This line of thinking moves into the event's external environment, and holds that event planning should have a collaborative, participative orientation towards key actors (local government, community interests, residents, the private sector) within the host and wider environment. An underpinning argument for involving residents in event planning relates to the fact that if residents' quality of life is adversely affected by the staging of events, then visiting tourist populations may be adversely affected in consequence because of the ensuing animosity or ill-feeling. Public participation in the planning process is thus often advocated as a mechanism for implementing social justice through reconciling host residents and tourism development objectives (Lankford and Howard, 1994). According to Waitt (2003: 196), residents are more likely to have positive perceptions if they have a sense of participation in planning policies and trust in the event organisers. Gursoy and Kendall (2006) argue that hallmark decision making/political planning is gradually being abandoned as key decision makers realise the value of local involvement and support. There is also growing awareness that strategically conceiving of the links between events and their external environments can lead to opportunities for **leveraging** as many benefits as possible for the host economy/community (Pugh and Wood, 2004). The literature on collaborative planning overlaps with the growing body of work on **stakeholders,** where the politics involved in achieving consensus are a key theme and where the concept of sustainability is central.

FURTHER READING

Getz, D. (2007) *Event Studies. Theory, Research and Policy for Planned Events.* Oxford: Butterworth-Heinemann.

Hall, C.M. (1989) 'The definition and analysis of hallmark tourist events', *Geojournal,* 19 (3): 263–8.

Pugh, C. and Wood, E. (2004) 'The strategic use of events within local government: a study of London borough councils', *Event Management,* 9 (1): 61–71.

Shone, A. and Parry, B. (2004) *Successful Event Management: a Practical Handbook.* London: Thomson.

20 planning

> The meaning of policy in festival and event contexts is no different to elsewhere: policy is about setting a vision that encapsulates the direction in which festival and event organisations seek to follow; it is about setting goals and objectives which they strive to achieve. Beyond the organisational context, festivals and events influence, and are influenced by public policy in a variety of ways. Public policy is the domain of government and relates to how governments and agencies of the state make decisions, or fail to make decisions, about the festival and event sector and related environments.

It is routine for individual festival and event organisations to develop specific policies relating to particular areas of their operations. Often policy development is a requirement, as in areas such as health and safety where organisations are required by the state to conform to particular legislation. At other times policy development is not a requirement but rather relates to the development of good practice, in cognisance of the wider competitive and other environmental influences and pressures faced by these organisations. The development of environmental policies such as those produced by the Edinburgh Festivals is a case in point. The majority of the policy literature in the festival and event domain, however, relates to public policy in some shape or form, and conceives of the festival or event organisation from an external viewpoint.

The literature on policy in the festival and event domain is to date quite limited. Indeed, relative to its importance, alongside the other concepts in this volume, it is the idea of policy that is perhaps most under-researched both in applied, real-world festival and event settings, and in academic debates and empirical investigations. Festival policy is simply defined by Ilczuk and Kulikowska as 'coherent, intentional action undertaken by any level of public authorities concerning festivals' (2007: 7). In a study of international arts festival policies of public authorities in Europe, Ilczuk and Kulikowska (2007) found that half of the 20 national experts surveyed reported that a coherent public policy towards festivals did not exist in their country. Instead, they concluded that festivals tended to come under the broader cultural policy pertaining to their particular genre/niche. For example, theatre festivals came under the remit of theatre policy. Alternatively, festivals tended to be classed within a motley grouping of 'other' events, quite diverse in nature. The void in knowledge about policymaking and festivals and events has become ever more apparent since the sharp increase in government involvement and support for the sector witnessed in recent decades. While a range of justifications for public intervention have been forthcoming, including arguments related to public good, social equity, return on investment and market failure, growing public involvement has not translated into corresponding policy development and policy frameworks. This has been noted as being problematic in the academic literature for some time now. Hall and Rusher (2004) asserted that little attention had been paid to the policy settings and structures within which events take place. Whitford wrote: 'alarmingly, event policies are often inconsistent and vague due to, among other things, the ad hoc approach to the development of event policy adopted by numerous governments' (2009: 674). Her analysis of 219 event policies produced by 19 local authorities in Australia over the period 1974–2004 concluded that they represented 'an ad hoc disparate approach to the development of policy which arguably, has been utilised as a platform for rhetoric' (Whitford, 2009: 676).

It seems obvious to ask why does this void exist? Historically, many festivals and events grew within the broader policy arena shaping their particular focus of activity (Quinn, 2010). Thus, arts festivals, for example, typically emerged within the domain of their respective arts discipline (music, opera or theatre) and responded to the needs identified therein. Their origins may have been prompted by the need to escape the confines of the institutionalised and conformist national sites of cultural production as described by Frey (1994) or to start, in bottom-up fashion, the process of developing cultural infrastructure. Cultural policymakers envisaged differing roles for cultural festivals at different periods, reflecting and informing changing societal dynamics and priorities. Thus, over time, the artistic role of festivals broadened out to assume social dimensions in terms of cultural democracy and access; and economic dimensions as agents of economic revitalisation and wealth generation. Writing about France in the 1990s, for example, Autissier (2009) explained that the cultural policy remit attached to festivals was

21 policy

threefold: asserting territorial distinction or identity; attracting tourists; and promoting access to culture. While cultural policies shaping the evolution of cultural festivals in particular jurisdictions have not escaped criticism, no less than sports or other policies, the sorts of critiques aired in the contemporary literature do not apply.

Recent critiques include those referred to above from Whitford (2009) and Getz who wrote that 'public policy pertaining to festivals and other planned events is generally fractionalised ... not comprehensive ... and fails to integrate events effectively with all the relevant policy domains' (2009: 62). These critiques refer to the changed world of festivals and events where in recent decades events have speedily risen up political agendas. Irrespective of their focus, be it sporting, cultural or artistic, their potential to deliver a variety of beneficial outcomes has seen them increasingly embraced by governments in national, city and regional domains. The haste to incorporate them instrumentally into other policy domains, be it culture, urban regeneration, sport or place marketing, has rarely been accompanied by a determined effort to think though a cohesive policy pathway. Meanwhile, the multiplicity of **stakeholder** perspectives involved in any given particular policy domain (such as the sporting arena) becomes increasingly complex once allied to, for example, an urban policy domain intent on furthering broader agenda, such as physical regeneration or cultural inclusion. Policy aims tend not to be cherished equally: usually, according to Getz (2009), public policymakers' interest in the sector is most likely to be driven by tourism, place marketing and economic development ambitions, with cultural considerations coming later. Writing about local authority support for arts-related festivals and events, Ilczuk and Kulikowska claimed that public authorities are often 'far less interested in the artistic dimensions of the festivals than in other benefits such as economic value' (2007: 10). In the literature on the **European City of Culture** initiative there are many echoes of this claim. This multiplicity and diversity of stakeholders, with its attendant diversity of philosophical approaches and policy visions, necessarily mitigates against the emergence of a singular, clear policy focus and indeed problematises the very wisdom of seeking to attain a singular focus. Accordingly and not surprisingly, a key theme in recent literature is the contested nature of the festival and event public policy arena with commentators conceiving of individual policy realms in opposing camps, with differential standing relative to the prevailing hegemony, differential degrees of access to power, and experiencing differential outcomes in consequence.

Hall and Rusher (2004) suggested that policy studies in the context of events might reasonably involve an analysis of the political nature of the event policymaking process. Here, there is an acknowledgement that decisions affecting the hosting of events, the nature of government involvement, the structure of agencies responsible for bidding, developing, managing and marketing events, and the involvement of communities all emerge from a political process. Hall and Rusher (2004) further suggested the need to analyse: public participation in the event planning and policy process; the sources of power in event policymaking; the exercise of choice by public officials in complex policy environments and; perceptions as to the effectiveness of event policies. Increasingly now, there is awareness that policy development for the sector, increasingly dominated by planned events strategically prioritised for place marketing reasons must acknowledge the disparate nature of the sector and the fact that festival and events always require inputs from a variety of stakeholders with diverse orientations. Understanding this diversity can be furthered through use of the literature on the role played by different networks in underpinning festival and event activity. Stokes (2007), for example, has discussed the need to understand the policy and institutional linkages between tourism and cultural development. Getz et al. (2007) have written about the need to understand the efficient management of networks in the interests of managing resource dependency and ultimately of promoting sustainable development in the sector. At times, the policymaking process is hampered by a lack of data detailing the scale and nature of current activity within the sector. In a European context, Ilczuk and Kulikowska (2007: 7) note that statistical data on festivals is lacking for most European countries and conclude that it is impossible to obtain comparable data on a country-by-country basis. This notwithstanding, they state that it is music festivals that represent the dominant type within the international, artistic festival population. Theatre festivals generally take second place, with dance and film festivals coming next in order of prevalence.

A heightened understanding of the diversity of the sector, a diversity that lies, *inter alia*, in the organisational structures, decision-making processes, philosophical approaches, aims and objectives of all its constituent sub-sectors and parts can promote a stronger appreciation of how events can play a variety of societal roles that extend beyond tourism and place marketing. It can also aid the identification of useful synergies and alignments that can develop constituent sub-sectors and their associated policies to mutual benefit.

FURTHER READING

Getz, D. (2009) 'Policy for sustainable and responsible festivals and events: institutionalization of a new paradigm', *Journal of Policy Research in Tourism, Leisure and Events*, 1 (1): 61–78.

Ilczuk, D. and Kulikowska, M. (2007) *Festival Jungle, Policy Desert? Festival Policies of Public Authorities in Europe*. Warsaw: Circle.

Whitford, M. (2004) 'Regional development through domestic and tourist event policies: Gold coast and Brisbane, 1974–2003', *Journal of Hospitality, Tourism and Leisure Science*, 1: 1–24.

Whitford, M. (2009) 'A framework for the development of event public policy: facilitating regional development', *Tourism Management*, 30 (5): 674–82.

22 Power and Politics

> *While the core business of the festival and event sector often revolves around cultural enrichment, celebration, entertainment and fun, these activities are in fact very political in nature. Events and festivals are not 'natural' phenomenon. They do not simply happen. Rather, they are shaped and controlled by a range of agents, each exerting varying degrees of power, in the deliberate pursuit of a range of sometimes conflicting agendas.*

While most planned events and all festivals seek to celebrate, it should be clearly understood that the frivolity that appears to characterise this activity is actually underpinned by a great deal of seriousness. In the process of producing an event, the multiple agents involved strive to achieve a series of objectives that may not be in close alignment. The production that ultimately prevails represents a form of balance between the different actors involved. This balance is variously achieved through consent, coercion, compromise, contestation or negotiation. As

key concepts in event management

Jackson (1989,) put it, politics provide a context in which cultural questions of aesthetics, taste and style cannot be divorced from political questions of power, inequality and oppression. Syme et al. were among the earliest researchers to highlight the fact that 'hallmark events are first and foremost, political events' (1989: 219). At a macro level this is clear from the strong governmental interest shown in bidding for hallmark events and developing event-led urban regeneration and city marketing strategies. Events are key image-builders, intentionally developed to fashion a city or region's image and reputation in certain ways. Powerful stakeholders with vested interests in how policy agendas are shaped variously engage with events in order to further their sectoral interests. This is particularly well recognised in urban studies and geography literatures where a key theme has long been that the reproduction of festivals and events as tourist attractions is strongly shaped by power dynamics.

Events are never 'impromptu or improvised ... and arts festivals in particular, are never spontaneous' (Waterman, 1998: 59). Clearly, the urban studies literature explains how and why powerful stakeholders like city governments and the tourism industry favour the development of events. However, a strong line of enquiry has been to explore both the reproduction of dominant meanings by powerful stakeholders and the resistance that this has evoked in response. Boyle (1997) pointed to the power dynamics involved in their production and argued that events are socially constructed in specific ways by certain groups to promote particular ideas and beliefs. Shin's (2004) case of the Gwangju Biennale, is an example of a study that shows how 'a festival is cultural, but its aim is economic – in advertising the city to tourists and investors – and that its process is immersed in political dynamics that influence potential transformations in the image of a city and urban space' (Shin, 2004: 630). Conceptualising events as key elements in place marketing strategies, Shin highlights the potential tensions and conflicts that can exist between the different stakeholder groups involved. He follows researchers such as Neill (1999) and Sadler (1993), in arguing that the deliberate construction of particular place identities through events can not only promote standardisation but can generate resistance among citizens to the image selected for representation. City authorities in Gwangju chose to introduce a cultural event specifically to alter the city's prevailing image as a 'city of resistance' to a 'city of art'. However, Shin showed how over time, the preferred construction of the Biennale, intended to eradicate old, controversial images of the city was effectively challenged by local citizens who gradually came to reclaim, reinterpret and refashion these images through the event. In similar vein, Hitters' (2000) analysis of Rotterdam as European Cultural Capital 2001 showed this event to be socially and politically contested.

In much of the above literature, mega-events have been the focus. However, festivities also offer insights into how societies work. Festivals have been viewed as demonstrations and celebrations of community power and solidarity (Marston, 1989); as mechanisms of social control (Ekman 1999); and as mechanisms of resistance to social control (Smith, 1995). Researchers have been at pains to demonstrate how the construction of festivals and smaller-scale events is inherently political in nature, involving the elevation of selective cultural details/social positions and community voices to symbolic status and the simultaneous downgrading or silencing of others (De Bres and Davis, 2001; Waterman, 1998). This process unfolds not simply in the interest of constructing a desirable image of place to be represented in the international tourism marketplace, but also more profoundly for the sake of promoting vested interests, maintaining social order and the cultural status quo. Waterman (1998), for example, argues that high-brow arts festivals still explicitly prefer to present themselves as élitist, citing the case of the Israel Festival as one that is unashamedly so. Jamieson's (2004) analysis of the Edinburgh Festival, for example, revealed a festival city that is spatially constructed in ways that privilege visiting audiences, containing them within parts of the city considered 'appropriate' for cultural consumption, while leaving the socially deprived outskirts of the city relatively free of festival activity. Dissecting the multiple layers that make up the Edinburgh festival, Jamieson pointed out that 'behind the animated street scenes, the (city's festival) gaze is influenced by stakeholders, institutions of local government and an expanding service economy ... Although spaces appear as though spontaneously formed ... the city en fête is also the result of painstaking planning by a city administration that seeks to control the ways in which public spaces change' (2004: 65). Historically, the early festival aligned itself with the civilising values of European high culture, although time has attested to the contested territory that festivals represent and since 1958 the festival has incorporated the activities of the high profile fringe. However, Jamieson contends that the revelry of the fringe and indeed of all of Edinburgh's festival zones is a contained revelry.

Power divisions have many, often multiple, bases including social class, race, gender and sexuality. Brown (2011), for example, investigated the gendered embodiments of everyday life at the Michigan Womyn's Music

Festival, an annual women only festival. Waitt (2004) asked questions about the reconstitution of sexuality in Australian national space through an analysis of the Sydney 2002 Gay Games. A key idea is that festivals and other kinds of temporary 'one-off' events may not represent time and space that is 'out of the ordinary' or entirely different to routine societal lifestyles, but that in fact they serve to reinforce existing orderings and workings of ordinary society. Rao (2001), for example, explained how festivals can serve to perpetuate existing societal norms and cultural values. He pointed out how festivals may be celebrated in segregated fashion because of India's caste system. Many widely observed Hindu festivals are private, restricted to family and close friends. As such, they serve to strengthen ties within particular groups and communities, not necessarily across communities. He went on to describe the Jatra, a procession that honours a prominent deity housed in the local temple. This is a type of festival in which all caste groups participate and one which that serves to reify hierarchies within the village. Traditionally, these festivals saw communities being assigned a role appropriate to their caste and occupation. Historically, some were sites of conflict as upwardly mobile groups sometimes tried to renegotiate their place within the village hierarchy. Jeong and Almeida Santos (2004) suggested that festivals can be seen as attempts by dominant political and social groups to exercise hegemony over less powerful groups by supplying the masses with special celebrations that divert attention from 'real' issues. Indeed, they went on to suggest that festivals enable invisible webs of local power networks to be made visible.

This idea that the particular sets of meanings reproduced through events are open to challenge, contestation and disruption from those who disagree or think differently is well accepted in the literature. Boyle and Hughes wrote about local opposition to Glasgow's 1990 City of Culture event, describing the 'discomfort locals have experienced with the willingness of city leaders to forego cultural traditions' (1994: 468). Shin examined how the Gwangju Bienniale in South Korea 'initiated power struggles among promoters who had different goals and images of the city in mind' (2004: 625). Waitt's (2004) analysis of the Sydney 2002 Gay Games discussed the contentiousness, exclusions and resistance fostered by the Games. He found them to be associated with, for example, the fixing of sexual identities in the dualism of homosexual/ heterosexual, the privileging of the culture of masculinity and its imposition onto gay bodies, and the imposition of meanings of togetherness onto people who are materially and socially differentiated.

Hall, C.M. (2006) 'Urban entrepreneurship, corporate interests and sports mega-events: the thin policies of competitiveness within the hard outcomes of neoliberalism', *Sociological Review*, 54: 59–70.

Shin, H. (2004) 'Cultural festivals and regional identities in South Korea', *Environment and Planning D: Society and Space*, 22: 619–32.

Waitt, G. (2004) 'The Sydney 2000 Games and querying Australian national space', *Environment and Planning D: Society and Space*, 20: 167–83.

Waterman, S. (1998) 'Carnival for elites? The cultural politics of arts festivals', *Progress in Human Geography*, 22: 54–74.

23 Regeneration

> *The keen interest shown by local, regional and national governments in bidding for large-scale events is often prompted by the belief that the event will act as catalyst for the long-term regeneration of a location, usually urban, and a local economy, usually struggling to (re)gain a foothold in the global, post-industrial economy.*

key concepts in event management

Regeneration can be thought of in physical terms in the first instance. Physical capital can be understood as equipment, physical infrastructure and property. In the event literature, researchers have long documented the physical capital that has been developed and enhanced through the hosting of events (Balsas, 2004; Eckstein and Delaney, 2002). Since at least 1984, when Ritchie included urban regeneration and the development of infrastructure among the longer-term consequences that large-scale events can yield, city authorities have used events to further the regeneration of local economies and local communities. The regeneration opportunities offered by events, however, have come to range far beyond the physical. Burbank et al. (2002) in their article on mega-events, urban development and public policy traced the emergence of urban policy interest in mega-events from a US perspective. A basic argument they made is that the interest in hosting large-scale events is related to the growth of the global economy and to changes in federal urban policy in the USA. During the 1980s, it became US government policy to encourage cities to be self-reliant, to finance local economic development through entrepreneurial activities and engagement in private-sector partnerships. Ashworth and Voogd (1990) portrayed a similar policy shift in the UK, attributing a proliferation of urban renewal policies (often with an event component) to a market-oriented, public–private partnership approach to urban planning. Within this neo-liberalist, entrepreneurialism framework, inter-city competition greatly intensified in the race to attract footloose capital and international tourists. Investing in bids to host large-scale events quickly came to be viewed as a means of maintaining a leading profile on the international stage (Shoval, 2002). It also became a means of repositioning cities as sites of consumption (Law, 2002). Thus, events came to be valued not only as short-term boosts for local and regional economies but as catalysts for the much longer-term regeneration of city image, community development and destination repositioning.

This changing urban policy dynamic foregrounds the blatantly instrumental approach underpinning cities' interest in hosting large-scale events such as the FIFA World Cup or the **European City of Culture**. Predominant strategic intentions revolve around overhauling identity, revitalising neighbourhoods, infrastructures and economies. One of the ECOC's most frequently discussed in the literature, Glasgow 1990, is widely attributed with having transformed the city's image from a rarely visited, depressed post-industrial city into a lively and attractive city that subsequent to the event increased its inbound tourist flows dramatically. Balsas (2004) has written about the ambitious urban regeneration programme undertaken in Porto, Portugal during its year as ECOC in 2001. The city's plans to upgrade its cultural facilities and to programme an event for the year were less visible than the ambitious urban regeneration plans that involved introducing a new tram system to improve mobility within the city, upgrading the public space within four main squares and their adjacent streets as well as economic and housing programmes. In Cork, the Irish city designated as ECOC in 2005, a twin-track approach was adopted by the local authority. Developing and supporting a cultural programme for the year was one part of this. The other part involved delivering 28 capital projects to do with public infrastructure, community, transport and information technology as well culture, heritage and tourism (Quinn, 2010). Plans for the 2012 London Olympic Games involved urban regeneration on a large scale. The Olympic Park, the largest recreational park built in Europe in the last 150 years, was intended to transform Stratford, an area to the east of the city, with the creation of the largest retail-led, mixed-use regeneration project ever undertaken in the UK (Redwood, 2011). He wrote of the excitement that the hosting of a large-scale sporting event generates among property investors: 'they anticipate that the whole region will be regenerated and property prices will rise at the same time, making it an ideal location in which to invest' (Redwood, 2011: 3). Typically, infrastructural plans and investment on a scale such as this generate a great deal of anticipation in respect of the positive effects that will ensue for property values and for urban renewal.

For some time, however, commentators have been suggesting that such anticipation is misplaced. A number of authors have reported mixed outcomes with several acknowledging negative outcomes (Hall and Hodges, 1996; Hiller, 1998; Roche, 1994). Examples of such negativities include the accumulation of large debts for host communities and the displacement of local residents to make way for infrastructural improvements. Hiller (1998) pointed to the uneven distribution of ensuing impacts, a factor that may be related to the uneven capacity of various stakeholder groups to capitalise on potential opportunities. The displacement of people in order to build new venues and stadia for the event is often a potential issue (Jones, 2001) that leads to lifestyle disruption and damage to social, cultural and business networks of various kinds (Cegielski and Mules, 2002). Empirical evidence questioning the merits of investing in large-scale events continues to emerge with Redwood (2011), for example, marshalling evidence to suggest that the 2010 FIFA World Cup had no impact on house prices in South Africa and that recent Olympic Games have had a similarly negligible effect on host cities. Sadd's (2010) investigation of stakeholders' views on the regeneration plans of the 2012 London Olympic Games suggested that rather than improving the lives of pre-existing businesses and residential communities, the indications were that it would be new residents, with relatively higher incomes, who would benefit from new facilities and housing developments.

It has long been understood that if large-scale events are to have beneficial outcomes that last into the future, then long-term development strategies are needed. The gradual momentum building through these critical perspectives is leading researchers to call for new approaches to event-related regeneration. In particular, the relative merits of deciding to host a series of small-scale events (as distinct from one large-scale event) have been considered (Gibson et al., 2003), perhaps as a way of building capacity that would enhance a location's ability to host a large-scale event in the future (Chalip, 2004; Jago et al., 2003). Mace et al. (2007) suggested that for regeneration to work, it must be for the benefit of existing communities and not for 'new' communities who come to live in the area after the event has taken place. Ziakas and Costa take this further and argue the importance of developing 'a strategic and holistic focus on event portfolios' where the emphasis is on building capacity other time and embedding events into a breadth of policy domains through stakeholder collaboration (2011: 171). A. Smith (2009) investigates how major events can generate benefits for areas beyond the immediate vicinity of the host location. He discusses how benefits can become more spatially diffused through the creation of incidental effects, those that happen automatically without policy intervention. Examples include Leeds' (2008) findings about tourists who avoid event destinations and holiday elsewhere, thus displacing tourist demand and subsequent benefit to other areas. Benefits can also be diffused when parts of an event are 'dislocated' or held at some distance away from the core location. Dislocating events requires an element of foresight and planning as does the use of **leverage** to try to diffuse benefits. A. Smith (2009) points out that a common strategy in this respect is to try to involve other locations as venues for pre-event training. The Scottish city of Aberdeen, for example, hosted the 60-athlete strong Cameroon Olympic squad for the London 2012 Games.

The concept of regeneration is closely related to that of sustainability in that efforts at regeneration clearly aim to enhance the environment (whether physically, socially, politically and so on) long after the event has ceased to be. While some challenge the very possibility of events being sustainable, the developments discussed in the entry on sustainability in this volume suggest that progress is being made, although, undoubtedly more needs to be done. Ponsford's (2011: 194) recent analysis of the Vancouver 2010 Winter Olympics, stressed that 'while event managers are increasingly being equipped with new management frameworks, tools and performance measures to deliver more sustainable events', more experiential knowledge, at an operational level, is needed to advance practice in the field. In conclusion, it is to be noted that the concept of regeneration is now being increasingly discussed within the context of event **leveraging**. Given the growth in awareness of how events can be associated with mixed outcomes, much more importance is being attached to the business of effectively leveraging an event so as to prepare and plan for outcomes that are more closely aligned with the long-term needs of the host city or region.

FURTHER READING

Burbank, M.J., Andranovich, G. and Heying, C.H. (2002) 'Mega-events, urban development and public policy', *Review of Policy Research*, 19 (3): 179–202.
Eckstein, R. and Delaney, K. (2002) 'New sports stadiums, community self-esteem, and community collective conscience', *Journal of Sport and Social Issues*, 26: 236–49.
Ponsford, I.F. (2011) 'Actualising environmental sustainability at Vancouver 2010 venues', *International Journal of Event and Festival Management*, 2 (2): 184–96.
Roche, M. (1994) 'Mega-events and urban policy', *Annals of Tourism Research*, 21: 1 – 19.

24 Regional Development

> Regional development is concerned with developing the potential of regions. It is included as a concept here because in recent decades festivals and events have come to be construed as useful tools of regional development.

To date, it could be argued that there has been an urban bias to the study of festivals and events, a bias which has gone hand-in-hand with a decided preference to study large-scale, hallmark type events as distinct from smaller-scale equivalents (Gibson et al., 2010). There is now a sizeable literature on the role that festivals and events play in urban-based place boosterism and culture-related regeneration strategies in urban centres. This is not the case for events in non-urban, regional contexts. Referring specifically to cultural festivals, Gibson et al. consider this to be an oversight, writing that 'cultural festivals are an under-acknowledged and yet potentially significant component of strategies to develop

key concepts in
event management

grassroots economies' (2010: 281). However, the neglect of events in regional contexts has not been complete and some of the work undertaken in this sphere to date is discussed below. It is, however, an under-researched area, albeit one which has been receiving increasing attention in recent times, especially in Australian contexts.

A useful definition of regional development comes from the Australian Local Government Association (2011), which suggests that it is best viewed as 'a holistic process whereby the environmental, economic, social and cultural resources of a region are harnessed for sustainable progress in ways that reflect the comparative advantages offered by a particular geographic area'. Tourism researchers have long conceived of tourism as a tool for regional development. Following in this tradition, festivals and events have also come to be similarly viewed by policymakers in recent decades. As is the case with tourism, festivals and events represent a mechanism for spreading wealth across an economy and it has been for its wealth generating potential that festivals and events have been most highly prized by policymakers (Getz, 2007). For this reason, a lot of the research on events located in regional, often rural locations has focused on trying to measure economic dimensions. Indeed, as Moscardo (2007) points out, most efforts have limited their analyses to investigating how they contribute to developing tourism within an area as opposed to how they contribute to the development of the region more broadly. While this may not be justifiable, it is understandable. In a tourism context alone, events can contribute by diversifying existing tourism supply and invigorating destinations, tackling seasonality, creating new tourist attractions thus boosting supply in underdeveloped parts of regions and generally contributing to a positive image of place. However, research enquiries are now expanding and there is growing evidence that festivals and events can contribute to regional development in ways that span social, cultural, environmental as well as economic and tourism domains. Furthermore, increasing attention is now being paid to asking 'how' and 'why' events come to be linked into development outcomes, as opposed to simply identifying and calculating 'what' those outcomes might be.

It is now beyond doubt that festivals and events can make significant economic, social and cultural contributions to their host regions (Barr and Dave, 1996). Drawing on earlier work by Fredline et al. (2003), Moscardo (2007) provides a brief summary of the impacts, both negative and positive that the literature has associated with events in regional locations. These include economic (income, employment, multiple effect), tourism (extending season and enhancing destination image) physical (area regeneration and infrastructural development), socio-cultural (improved social networks and enhanced social opportunities for locals), psychological (enhanced sense of community and pride in place), regional community development (enhanced skills base, local and regional linkages, development of partnerships and alliances). In all cases, there are negative corollaries expressed in conflict (psychological, damage of various kinds [environmental, reputation] and loss [economic, cultural]). More recently, Gibson et al. (2010) profiled non-metropolitan cultural festivals in Australia, arguing that they cumulatively create substantial employment and catalyse community activities. Indeed, it may be suggested that relative to their urban counterparts, the contributions made by events in regional contexts may be more important. As evident in the above, the kinds of contributions made by festivals and events are mixed: they do not always constitute assets for their regions. Lade and Jackson (2004) acknowledged this in their investigation of factors contributing to the success of festivals in regional contexts through an analysis of two Australian cases. Their findings suggest that an early market orientation (satisfying customer needs while meeting organisational objectives [Crompton and Lamb, 1986]) is important in becoming successful, although a later adoption of such an orientation within a product-oriented festival may also bring about success, albeit over a longer time period.

A key recent development in the literature has been a growing acknowledgement that any assessment of the regional development potential of events should consider: their capacity to generate **social capital** (González-Reverté and Miralbell-Izard, 2009: 55), the role they play in enhancing local community development capacities, for example, organisational and technical skills, learning and leadership, fostering networking; and their role in contributing to other sectors of the local economy (Lade and Jackson, 2004; Moscardo, 2007). Moscardo's (2007) term 'regional community development', which she labels an event impact, encompassed three constructs: social capital, community capacity and community well-being. She concluded that while 'an event may attract substantial numbers of visitors and generate revenue ... if it does not create community involvement it is unlikely to contribute much to regional development' (2007: 29). According to Moscardo, it is community involvement that enhances social capital and community capacity, two core components of positive regional development.

The **policy** frameworks underpinning the strategic development of festivals and events in regional contexts are, however, very uneven and an evident theme in the literature is the problematic nature of policymaking. At its most basic, relatively little is known about the policy dimensions of festivals and events. Wood has written about the 'generally non-strategic use of events' among local authorities (2006: 167). While a key theme running throughout much of the discussion in this volume alludes to the multi-agency/stakeholder nature of festival and event activity, collaborative approaches to policy development, just as in the tourism area, are uncommon (Dredge and Jenkins, 2007; Whitford, 2009). Reasons as to why this is the case require investigation. In some countries, such as Spain, regional events have been the subject of policy attention for some time. López-Bonilla and López-Bonilla (2010), for example, explained that since 1964, the Spanish government has had a classification scheme whereby festivals can earn an honorary title based on their level of interest to tourists. The title 'Festival of Interest to Tourists' (FITs) can be either a national or an international designation and is granted on the basis of a variety of criteria ranging from age, continuity, extent to which the festival is rooted in the host area, originality and diversity of programming, availability of tourist accommodation and services, and level of tourism promotional activity. To date, there are 273 FITs, many of them over 100 years in age and they can be found in all but 3 of Spain's 50 provinces. López-Bonilla and López-Bonilla (2010) explained how this national policy initiative can be used in the different regional provinces to develop the tourism potential of their regions. The FITs, for example, can be variously promoted as a means of revitalising mature destinations and generating interest in emergent ones. Equally, they can be used to influence demand by season and by location.

González-Reverté and Miralbell-Izard argued that in theory, festivals can be linked to regional development in three ways: 'as providers of wide cultural and social practices, as elements of intercultural interaction' (2009: 62), and because of their complex, multi-functionality across social, artistic, cultural and economic domains. Their analysis of music festivals' contribution to regional development in the Spanish region of Catalonia, however, concluded that their potential to contribute may be constrained by a lack of regional tourism policies, a dearth of event strategic planning and an absence of coordination mechanisms. Gibson et al. (2010) suggested likewise, querying, in the case of cultural festivals, the extent to which their potential is acknowledged and concluding that they tended to be ignored by local planners and regional development policymakers. More recently, Whitford (2009) critiqued event policies for their inconsistency and vagueness, shortcomings that arise from the ad hoc nature of their adoption by various governments. She investigated the situation in South

East Queensland, Australia, where the state has been very proactive in respect of event policymaking. She analysed 219 local government policy documents and found that while support systems to encourage diversity and enterprise were in evidence, the policies were not effectively realising the potential of events in terms of attracting visitors and generating visitor revenue. Whitford's solution is to propose a new framework for developing event public policy that incorporates: the event policy pathway, one that takes an underlying entrepreneurial approach; the event policy community which encompasses the array of stakeholder groups affected and; event development paradigms, the varying development worldviews that can underpin and inform a policy approach.

FURTHER READING

Gibson, C., Waitt, G., Walmsley, J. and Connell, J. (2010) 'Cultural festivals and economic development in nonmetropolitan Australia', *Journal of Planning Education and Research*, 29 (3) 280–93.

González, F.R. and Miralbell, O. (2011) 'The role of social and intangible factors in cultural event planning in Catalonia', *International Journal of Event and Festival Management*, 2 (1): 37–53.

Moscardo, G. (2007) 'Analyzing the role of festivals and events in regional development', *Event Management*, 11: 23–32.

Whitford, M. (2009) 'A framework for the development of event public policy: facilitating regional development', *Tourism Management*, 30 (5): 674–82.

25 Risk Management

Risk has to do with uncertainty. It refers to the possibility that negative consequences might be occasioned from the hosting of an event. Risk management is the business of actively seeking to avoid, prevent, minimise and manage risk.

Risk and the management of risk are matters that have become increasingly important for the event sector (Leopkey and Parent, 2009). Bowdin et al. define risk as 'any future incident that will negatively influence the event' and jeopardise the event organisation's chances of achieving its objectives (2006: 318). Risk management meanwhile, is the process of determining and managing these risks. Until recently, the topic of risk was only infrequently investigated by researchers in the festival and event field and the question of risk management was largely dealt with in textbooks. This is now changing, as the international context within which events, particularly large-scale events, operate have become increasingly risk prone. Indeed, it is likely that issues related to risk and security will become increasingly important in the future (Horne and Manzenreiter, 2006). This section synthesises key developments in the literature on risk and large-scale events, before going on to consider the applied literature on the management of risk.

Laybourn's simple definition of risk is 'a decision in which probabilities are involved' (2004: 291). Sometimes the probabilities are objectively known, other times they are unknown and not easily estimated. The latter situation can be referred to as risk under uncertainty and, in event contexts, the degree of uncertainty increases in line with such factors as the degree of complexity characterising the event and the influential presence of external factors (for example, cost, reliance on the weather, reliance on technology and so on). By definition, the event industry in general is highly susceptible to risk. Its transient, infrequent, 'once-off' nature means little or no time to rehearse, and so little or no room for mistakes, and little time to compensate for disruptions caused by uncontrollable external forces, such as weather, strikes or other unknowns. As Mules (2004) points out, the type of risk associated with events is heightened by the fact that the manager/organiser has only one chance to manage the risk. To an extent, this is positive, as with risk-taking comes innovation, excitement and the extra-ordinariness inherent in events. Simultaneously, however, mis-managed and uncontrolled risk can have devastating consequences. As Boo and Gu (2010) state, risk can directly cause a failed or unsuccessful event.

The industry is increasingly conscious of the fact that large-scale events with high international profiles, carry a large degree of risk in respect of terrorist threats. Usually, it is sports events that are most at risk in this context because these tend to dominate the 'mega-event' scene, have the highest international profile and attract the greatest media attention. Atkinson and Young have written that high profile sporting events have become 'prime targets for terrorism' (2002: 55). Events such as the Olympic Games and the FIFA World Cup represent particular 'terrorism capital' because of their 'high public visibility, global media exposure and symbolic representation' (Taylor and Toohey, 2007). These authors go on to report that over the period 1972 (when the Munich Olympic Games were held) to 2003, sports events have been targeted on 168 different occasions. Thus the threat of terrorism associated with sports events is very real and not surprisingly, has generated research interest on a number of topics including: how events are planned and operationalised in terms of security, screening audiences, controlling entry points; how audiences perceive and react to threats of terrorism; how they may be deterred from attending, or have less than optimal experiences because of the screening checks they must endure because of safety measures adopted by the organisers. Taylor and Toohey (2007), for example, investigated spectators' perceptions of risk at the 2004 Athens Olympic Games, the first Games to be staged in the aftermath of the 9/11 attacks. Their results did not show that a fear of terrorism constituted a deterrent to attending the Games. Indeed a recurring theme in a number of recent studies seems to be that dedicated sport fans will not be deterred from travelling to major sports events by the threat of terrorism (Taylor and Toohey, 2007). However, this finding is not consistent: Neirotti and Hilliard (2006), in a study of attendees at the Athens Olympic Games, found that over one-quarter of respondents knew at least one person who had decided not to attend the Games because of safety concerns. In any case, the cost to event organisers of introducing security measures to safeguard the hosting of the event is staggering and growing all the time. Leopkey and Parent (2009) suggest that the security budget for the 2004 Athens Olympic Games was US$3 billion, while Konstantaki and Wickens (2010) reported that the equivalent budget for the 2012 London Olympic Games will exceed £10 billion.

Leopkey and Parent (2009) argued that while a review of the literature might lead to the assumption that risk management relates only to security and terrorist threats, its application is much broader than that. They detailed 15 risk management issues that cross the breath of event operations from ticketing to site management and media relations. Empirically, they conducted a study into the risk management strategies used by the various stakeholders and organising committees of two major Canadian sporting events. Seven strategies were identified: reduction, avoidance, reallocation, diffusion, prevention, legal and developing relationships.

In the applied event management literature, textbooks dealing with the operational planning and production of events typically include a section detailing the risk management process, with context, identification, evaluation, management and control, and monitoring being the key areas under discussion. Authors are keen to point out that that the importance of effective risk management is such that it is usually subject to legally binding state regulations and legislation. Unfortunately, there are several cases where legislation has been an outcome of a disastrous occurrence at an event. The UK Fire Safety and Safety of Places of Sport Act 1987 was introduced following the Bradford football stadium fire in 1985 when 53 people died. Compliance with relevant legislation and regulations is of the utmost importance for event managers. Defined as the 'act of conforming to a specification, standard or law that has been clearly defined' (Matthews, 2008: 142) compliance is a serious issue in respect of standards, guidelines and regulations in respect of workplace safety and equipment design and use. In the UK, risk management is a legal requirement under the Management of Health and Safely at Work Regulations 1992. In Ireland it is also a legal requirement, with the Code of Practice for Safety at Outdoor Pop Concerts and other Outdoor Musical Events (1990) requiring all events to produce a statement of safety procedures and the Planning and Development (licensing of outdoor events) (2001) requiring all event organisers to produce a safety statement as part of their event licensing process. Silvers' (2008) *Risk Management for Meetings and Events* textbook explains that while the legislation and regulations pertaining to events vary according to jurisdiction, there are a wide variety of laws and codes that typically apply, irrespective of location. She lists 40 of these, including employment, environmental protection, gaming, antidiscrimination and liquor laws; construction, fire safety, public safety, sanitation and special effect codes; as well as noise and traffic/street closure ordinances among others. Legal and ethical compliance in the midst of such requirements is paramount for event organisers and her textbook goes on to deal with the importance of contracts and other legal documents including various licences, leases, orders and agreements.

A key area of risk that events must plan for is crowd management. A key task of the event manager is to control the movement and behaviour patterns of people attending their event. As Silvers wrote: 'attendee management seeks to direct and control the attendee's actions and interactions with the event from arrival through departure' (2008: 289–90). Unfortunately, the festival and event sector has witnessed a number of tragedies in the past, across sporting and cultural arena. At a music festival called the Love Parade held in the German city of Duisburg in 2010, 19 people were trampled to death and 340 were injured while trying to pass through an access tunnel. At the Roskilde Music Festival in Denmark, in 2000, 9 people died and 43 were injured (Paterson, 2010). Silvers (2008) identified a number of typical risks associated with crowds. These include: arrival and departure modes; ineffective registration/ticketing systems; inadequate facilities; inadequate communications; and cross or counter-flow crowd movement. Various other researchers, such as Earl et al. (2004), have written about negative aspects of festival crowds. The risks noted relate to alcohol and drugs, overcrowding, mob behaviour and other public health issues. Different jurisdictions vary in the demands that they place on event organisations in respect of crowd management. In the UK context, for example, the HSE (2000) guide *Managing Crowds Safely* deals with planning, risk assessment, emergency planning, communication and monitoring in its explanation of how to safely manage crowds.

In the minds of event organisers, the concept of risk and the task of risk management are closely associated with that of insurance management. Indeed, insurance coverage and legal liability may be even more uppermost in the mind of the event organiser. Commercial general liability insurance providing coverage for claims made against an individual or company arising from bodily injury or property damage sustained by others is essential for all event organisers. To obtain this a risk management policy is required. In taking decisions about insurance, event organisers need to consider a wide variety of issues which vary depending on factors such as the nature, scale, location, purpose and the involvement of stakeholders including sponsors, vendors and volunteers. Different events are likely to prioritise different aspects: for example, an outdoor event might purchase weather insurance, while a pop music event might wish to insure against non-appearance by key artists. These decisions are taken on the basis of the event organisations seeking to lessen the effects of potential losses, in the context of the vulnerabilities and threats to which their event is exposed.

FURTHER READING

Boo, S. and Gu, H. (2010) 'Risk perception of mega-events', *Journal of Sport & Tourism*, 15 (2): 139-61.

Leopkey, B. and Parent, M.M. (2009) 'Risk management strategies by stakeholders in Canadian major sporting events', *Event Management*, 13: 153–70.

Silvers, J.R. (2008) *Risk Management for Meetings and Events*. Oxford: Butterworth-Heinemann.

Taylor, T. and Toohey, K. (2007) 'Perceptions of terrorism threats at the 2004 Olympic Games: implications for sport events', *Journal of Sport & Tourism*, 12 (2): 99–14.

26 Service Quality

> *Service quality is concerned with meeting standards and expectations. Festivals and events are essentially experiential services, which have both tangible and intangible elements. Satisfying the customer and meeting their needs is a key challenge for the event professional, especially given the often intangible nature of the service at issue and the emotional engagement that it can evoke.*

The question of defining festivals and events is considered and problematised elsewhere in this volume. However, when the issue of quality arises, there is yet a further dimension to consider: the notion of the event/festival as a service. According to O'Neill et al., a festival is 'essentially a service in that it consists of intangible experiences of finite duration within a temporary, managed atmosphere' (1999: 158). The literature on services has always paid great attention to the question of quality. Hyatt (2008) briefly reviewed approaches to defining quality in the event context and suggested that definitions fall into four categories, with quality understood as: conformance to specification; excellence; value; and meeting and/or exceeding customers' expectations. Service quality has to do with a 'global judgment or attitude relating to the superiority of the service' (Parasuraman et al., 1988: 16). The same authors went on to argue that consumer perceptions of service quality are strongly related to the degree of concordance between their expectations and their experiences of service performance. In general, it is agreed that research into service quality at festivals and events helps to identify consumer's preferences or perceptions, which are in turn linked either directly or indirectly to satisfaction and future behaviour (Yuan and Jang, 2008). A useful and simple definition of consumer satisfaction comes from Johnson and Fornell (1991). They see it as a customer's overall evaluation of the performance of an offering to date. A key point about consumer satisfaction noted by researchers is that it is strongly related to customer loyalty (Anderson and Sullivan, 1993; Bolton and Drew, 1991). This in turn is related to profitability (Reichheld and Teal, 1996). Thus, the quality construct is useful in helping to understand the relationship between consumer satisfaction and future purchasing intentions (Kim and Severt, 2011). In recent times, as events come under ever-growing pressure to justify their return-on-investment to a variety of stakeholders, the need to develop ways of measuring the quality of the offering and stakeholder satisfaction with that offering (be it audiences, performers, critics) has become even more urgent.

Researchers generally acknowledge quality to be a complex concept, and the literature approaches it from quite diverse angles. The lack of uniformity, and frequently the intangibility, of the festival and event offering, heightens this complexity. Perhaps because of this, quality in event settings is a relatively under-researched topic (Lee et al., 2009), although research on the topic dates back to at least the early 1990s when attention tended to focus on determining what customers understand and perceive quality to be. As such, the focus has been on programme or product quality. This is experiential, and as Getz (2007) points out, it is open to subjective evaluation by consumers and indeed by all event **stakeholders**. The subjective, experiential dimension of programme/product quality means that it is intimately connected to a number of other concepts, especially consumer perception, consumer satisfaction and consumer loyalty. Consumers perceive that attending an event will yield value in a variety of senses. In simple terms, this value might be relaxation, socialisation, an opportunity to see particular sports persons or musicians in action. Simultaneously, the value yielded may relate to meeting certain socio-psychological needs such as prestige or novelty (Bolton and Drew, 1991). If these perceptions of value are met, then consumer satisfaction is likely to ensue and this in turn has been found to be linked to consumer loyalty and in the case of events, to repeat visitation. Baker and Crompton (2000) investigated four dimensions of festival quality (festival characteristics, specific entertainment features, information sources and comfort amenities) and found that quality was positively related to both satisfaction and repeat-visit intentions. The relationship between quality, satisfaction and consumer loyalty was investigated by Lee et al. (2008) who found that three dimensions of festival quality – food, facility and particularly programme content–indirectly enhanced loyalty through satisfaction. More recently, Lee et al. (2009) compared first-time and repeat visitors. Their findings suggested that for the former, programme, convenient facilities, food and souvenirs all served as value antecedents, but for the latter, only programme and convenient facilities were important. The authors suggest that these findings are of use to festival organisers wishing to improve the efficiency of their festival design.

Operationally, however, researchers seem to agree that current conceptualisations of quality fall short of providing the knowledge that the event manager needs to facilitate quality effectively. As is clear from the above discussion, delivering quality depends on many factors. While the question as to what makes a successful festival is a difficult one to answer, extant research seems clear that service quality is an important contributor to success. Research by Saleh and Ryan (1993) and Thrane (2002) found that music quality was the most important reason explaining attendance at music festivals. However, research suggests that people attend events for multi-dimensional reasons. While event attendance may be motivated by a desire to experience the core product (be it music or football), other reasons including socialising and the opportunity to have out of the ordinary experiences also play a role (Bowen and Daniels, 2005). Thus, it seems that in addition to 'core service elements', 'peripheral aspects' of service provision (Hume, 2008) are also important. O'Neill et al. argued that irrespective of how good a festival may be in terms of its core performance offerings, if 'visitors experience low quality services (such as bad food or unclean toilets) or incompetent service delivery from staff, then future attendance will be in doubt' (1999: 158). Tkaczynski and Stokes (2010) applied SERPERF (a performance only quality measure), and three service quality dimensions (professionalism, core service and environment) to investigate the relationship between service quality, satisfaction and repurchase intention at a jazz and blues festivals in Australia. Professionalism emerged as the dominant factor and thus the authors stressed the importance of the festival staff organising and delivering the festival as service. The quality of the music itself was the second most important factor influencing the service experience of festival attendees. Only the professionalism factor emerged as a useful predictor of both consumer satisfaction and repurchase intention.

In much of the foregoing, discussion has focused on product or programme service. In Tkaczynski and Stokes (2010) can be seen a move to consider organisational quality, that is, the quality of the organisation producing the event. For a discussion of event quality to be complete it must consider the professionalism and competency of the organisers and their practices. In recent years companies and organisations involved in the production of events have come under growing pressure from various statutory and non-statutory agencies to adhere to standardised practices across a variety of domains. Organisations such as the International Organisation for Standardisation (ISO) with its ISO 9000 family of quality management standards, and others such as the European Foundation for Quality Management (EFQM) and Standards UK are influencing the practices of event organisations. Often this has been prompted by the rise of environmental awareness in the sector. Currently, for example, the ISO is working to develop an international standard (ISO 20121) to promote the sustainable management of events and exhibitions. Expected to be finalised by 2012 in time for, and in conjunction with, the London Olympics, the standard will apply to any kind of organisation or individual involved across the broad spectrum of event types. It will require identification of key sustainability issues, such as venue selection, operating procedures, supply-chain management, procurement, communication and transport. The overall intention is to create one standard, internationally recognised framework to implement sustainability and to date some 30 countries have been involved in its development (http://www.eventindustrynews.co.uk/2010/01/sustainable-event-standards-to-be-developed-by-2012.html).

FURTHER READING

Baker, D.A. and Crompton, J.J. (2000) 'Quality, satisfaction and behavioural intentions', *Annals of Tourism Research*, 27 (3): 785–804.

Kim, K. and Severt, D.E. (2011) 'Satisfaction or quality comes first: an empirical analysis', *Journal of Travel and Tourism Marketing*, 28: 81–96.

Lee, J.S., Lee, C.K. and Yoon, Y. (2009) 'Investigating differences in antecedents to value between first-time and repeat festival-goers', *Journal of Travel and Tourism Marketing*, 26: 688–702.

Tkaczynski, A. and Stokes, R. (2010) 'Festperf: a service quality measurement scale for festivals', *Event Management*, 14 (1): 69–82.

27 Social Capital

> *Social capital relates to the social relations between humans and particularly to how the interrelationships between humans lead to the accumulation of certain benefits that are of value both to them individually and to the communities to which they belong.*

Given the inherently communal nature of festival and event activity, and the myriad interrelationships that are vital to the reproduction of this activity, questions about how social capital is implicated are important. Research on social relations within festival and event contexts is plentiful. Some of this research is discussed in this volume's entries on **social impact** and **volunteering** and to a lesser extent in those on **sustainable events** and **evaluation.** Until recently, however, social capital was infrequently used as a theoretical frame of reference, and it remains a small and underdeveloped area of enquiry. It is now receiving increasing attention, largely because of the growing alertness to the wisdom of conceiving of festivals and events in more than economic terms. More broadly, however, it also relates to the growing sense that social capital, recognised as social connections, cooperation, trust, goodwill and reciprocity, and so on is everywhere now on the decline (Cox, 1995; Putnam, 1995). The British Prime Minister's 'Big Society' ideas about rebuilding and empowering local people and communities across the UK is an example of this (http://www.bbc.co.uk/news/uk-politics-12443396 [accessed 26 August 2011]). In this crisis scenario, social practices and settings premised and perpetuated through real-world (as distinct from virtual) social interaction, such as those created through the workings of festivals and events, provide particular insights into the formation and workings of social capital.

As Wilks (2009) noted, social capital is a broad term with many uses and interpretations. A useful starting definition drawn from mainstream sociology conceives of it as 'the capacity of individuals to secure benefits by virtue of their membership in social structures' (Portes, 1998: 6). Interrelationships and connectivity between humans is central to the formation of social capital. Woolcock (1998) defined it as the stocks of social trust, norms and networks that people may access to solve joint problems. Theorising about social capital has focused on both the individual, as member of a social group, as in the seminal work of Bourdieu (2002) as well as on broader groupings of people. In the latter, important indicators of social capital identified include community identity, community pride, social cohesion and enhanced community image. As Coleman (1990) has discussed, social capital brings together several aspects of social theory including social structure, institutional and non-institutional relationships, trust, reciprocity and community networking, into one theory of social action. His theory of social capital concentrated on the idea that strong, healthy community networks are essential for growth and prosperity. Indeed, the basic premise underpinning the idea of social capital is accepted as being that investment in social relations is expected to yield returns in the marketplace (Bourdieu, 1980, 1986; Coleman, 1988, 1990; Portes, 1998; Putnam, 1995).

To date, research into social capital in festival and event contexts has tended to focus on its formation, as opposed to its consequences; festival as opposed to event settings and; either festival attendees or resident communities. Moscardo (2007), for example, wrote about the learning component of festival and event activities (for example, learning through volunteering) and drew on Falk and Kilpatrick (2000) in suggesting that shared participation in learning is a way of building social capital. More recently, the potential that social capital offers to further understanding of the formation, nature and implications of social connections between various actors in festival and event settings is becoming increasingly realised by researchers, such as Misener and Mason (2006), Arcodia and Whitford (2007), Curtis (2010), Finkel (2010) and Quinn and Wilks (2012). In general, social capital theory is used in the literature that tries to measure or evaluate the impacts of festivals and events. Writing in the event context, Misener and Mason (2006) advocated using social capital as a theoretical framework to investigate how events contribute to community development. Suggesting a move away from thinking about how events impact upon society, they envisage that the theoretical lens of social capital offers significant opportunity to unravel the complexity of relationships and power dynamics that characterise communities. Moscardo (2007) argued that one of the key ways in which festivals contribute to regional development is through the building of social capital. Wood (2006) used it to develop a multi-item attitude scale to measure the effect that events have on civic pride. Specifically in festival contexts, social capital has been used by Wilks (2011) as a theoretical framework to investigate the extent to which festival attendees create and deepen social relationships and social bonds. Quinn and Wilks (2012) developed this theme through a comparative study of music festivals in Ireland and the UK. They found that while bonding social capital was prevalent among family and friendship groups (that is, within festival attendees), bridging social capital was generated across different sets of social actors (for example, between attendees and performers, performers and music industry personnel). Arcodia and Whitford (2007) have also explicitly explored the synergies between social capital and festivals, again in the context of festival attendees. They argued that social capital formation is advanced through festival attendance in a number of ways including building social networks, promoting social cohesiveness and facilitating communal celebration. In contrast, Finkel (2010) approached the topic from the perspective of community residents, producing empirical findings supporting the assertion that festivals can be a mechanism for strengthening communities through providing opportunities for shared, collective action and experiences. Mykeletun (2009), meanwhile, approached the problem from the perspective of festival organisers: investigating the workings of a number of forms of capital, including social capital, in a festival in Norway. According to A. Smith (2009: 113), evidence suggests that areas already exhibiting high social capital and a strong sense of community are more likely to benefit from major events. As evidence, he points to a finding of Gursoy and Kendall who concluded that 'residents who expressed a high level of attachment to their communities are more likely to view hosting a mega event as beneficial' (2006: 618). This led him onto the suggestion that social capital, rather than being an outcome of events, is an important prerequisite that influences who benefits. Developing the focus on residents, and by extension the host place, González and Miralbell asserted that events with high levels of social cohesion, integration and participation among local people, and thus with an 'inclusive and socialising character' invariably attract tourists (2011: 39). They argue that two types of factors contribute to the development of social capital in event settings: 'those which generate social cohesion by creating shared motives for celebration and shaping internal networks; and those which foster links with external networks' thereby strengthening the event's external visibility and tourism appeal (2011: 39).

Thus, recently, an increasing interest in social capital and festivals is evident. Festival researchers are drawing on ideas from different social capital theorists and the focus is widening to incorporate the formation and development of social capital within and across an increasing breadth of festival actors or stakeholder groups. It is also beginning to focus more on the mutually formative relationship between place and social capital (Quinn and Wilks, 2012). As Rutten et al. (2010) explain, social capital pertains to the social relations between humans, and since these social relations have a spatial dimension, so too does social capital. Place has long been of interest to festival researchers because festivals are a key mechanism through which people continuously make and re-make collective identities and connections with place. Closely allied to the notion of identity are concepts such as pride in place, kinship and community, all of which are connected to social capital. The role that festivals play in reproducing connections with place is complicated. If they have been noted for their role in perpetuating and reproducing norms and traditions (Ekman, 1999; Lavenda, 1997) they have equally been found to reproduce space in ways that alter or sometimes disrupt local ways of living in, and connecting with, place (Boyle and Hughes, 1994; Misener and Mason, 2006). Consistently, researchers have noted how festivals are socially constructed, never impromptu or improvised (Waterman, 1998) but rather are social practices where dominant meanings are promoted, negotiated and sometimes strongly resisted. Festival spaces, then, are never neutral, and can be characterised by absence as well as presence, resistance as well as acceptance, inclusion as well as exclusion. The specificities of particular places afford them different potentials for forming and developing different types of social capital. This is an assertion that has been considered by a number of researchers, but usually in a way that is more implicit than explicit in its references to social capital theories, and one that remains under-developed (Quinn, 2006, 2009; Sharpe, 2008; Curtis, 2010). While certain areas of study, notably economic geography, have long debated the influence of place on, for example, the successful development of various enterprises, much remains to be done in the study of festivals and events.

FURTHER READING

Arcodia, C. and Whitford, M. (2006) 'Festival attendance and the development of social capital', *Journal of Convention and Event Tourism*, 8 (2): 1–18.

Misener, L. and Mason, D. (2006) 'Creating community networks: can sporting events offer meaningful sources of social capital?', *Managing Leisure*, 11: 39–56.

Putnam, R.D. (1995) 'Bowling alone: America's declining social capital', *Journal of Democracy*, 6 (1): 65–78.

Wilks, L. (2011) 'Bridging and bonding: social capital at music festivals', *Journal of Policy Research in Tourism, Leisure and Events*, 3 (3): 281–97.

It is well understood that the social importance of planned events like festivals goes beyond mere playfulness or entertainment. For decades, theorists have debated the role that they play in sustaining communities of people living in places, serving as vehicles of social control providing both a break from the strictures of routine yet simultaneously reinforcing prevailing societal norms and values.

The marked rise in festivals and events internationally in recent decades has prompted academics such as Manning to exclaim that 'new celebrations are being created and older ones revived on a scale that is surely unmatched in human history' (1983: 4). As already discussed, reasons offered to explain this revival are many, and include both supply- and demand-led factors. From a sociological perspective, their proliferation may be read as a symbolic response to the profound and rapid socio-cultural change being experienced in contemporary society. Not surprisingly, there has been considerable debate in the literature as to the effect that the re-invention of festivities has had on the meanings hitherto generated by what were in the main, relatively localised, community-oriented festivals. Dominant within the debate have been discussions about how festivals serve to legitimate or challenge social order, reproduce social rituals and promote the rise of the spectacle.

According to Handelman (1998, cited in Richards, 2007b), festivals often contain both ritual and spectacle elements. The former are linked to transformation and rites of passage, and are geared towards the transformation of society. Spectacles, alternatively, are more passive forms of celebration that hold up a mirror to society as it is, without any attempt to challenge or contest existing societal norms. The societal importance of festivals lies in the fact that societies and humans more generally define themselves through both ritual and spectacle. Both are premised on collective assembly and on celebrating unity. Since the beginning of recorded history, societies throughout the world have set aside times and spaces for communal celebrations (Turner, 1982). Durkheim argued that secular, routine, daily life leads to a weakening of shared commitments to beliefs and to social bonds and to enhanced centrifugal individualism (Etzioni, 2000). The importance of rituals lies in the fact that they provide an important mechanism through which society can be recreated, as members of society collectively share experiences, thus deepening social bonds.

Carnival, as a form of festivity, has long been of interest to social scientists because it is thought to hold oppositional potential. Carnival originated as a Christian pre-Lenten cultural practice of celebration. It was held in the days preceding Lent, a traditional time of penance and fasting, which in turn leads to Easter. In contemporary times the practice of carnival continues in European countries, such as Italy, but in terms of profile and spectacle it is the carnivals of Latin America, in the Caribbean and in Brazil, that now dominate the popular imagination. As a social practise carnival has evolved over centuries from its original Christian origins. Many of these are in North America and in the other places to which sizeable flows of Caribbean migrants relocated. As discussed elsewhere in this volume, festivals play an important role in identity formation and as Nurse (1999) has frequently discussed: diasporic Caribbean carnivals are hybrid sites where cultural identity is negotiated and affirmed within Caribbean diasporic communities. Some of the largest carnivals today are to be found in places with substantial Caribbean communities. London's Notting Hill Carnival is one example. It dates back to 1959, having been founded in reaction to the racist intimidation and violence from white youths against members of the Caribbean community the previous summer. It takes place annually at the end of August and attracts audiences in excess of 1.5 million (Ferris, 2010).

Burr (2006) suggested that carnival focuses around participation, celebration, spontaneity, and revelry and fits with Nurse's definition of a carnival as: 'a period of celebration of the body, of physical abandon where licentiousness, hedonism, and sexual excess are expressed to music, dancing, masquerading and feasting' (1999: 664). However, most theoretical interpretations of carnival understand its meanings to be dualistic. According to Aching, carnival has been defined as an event that 'frames, stages and foregrounds marginalized and frequently subversive social spaces and identities' (2010: 415). Bakhtin (1978) wrote extensively about the liminal aspect of carnival, whereby temporary legitimacy to cross boundaries and break normal rules is permitted. Equally, though, it is argued that this anarchic foregrounding of subversiveness is socially sanctioned and tightly controlled. As Sharaby wrote 'the anarchistic impulse can be controlled and utilized as a psychological valve that releases pressure by institutionalising it within the framework of formal celebrations, and limiting it to fixed dates' (2008: 587). Aching concurs, explaining that carnival has been viewed 'as a safety valve that contributes to maintaining social order through subversive but controlled acts, or at least, gestures' (2010: 415).

In recent times, as festivals and events have proliferated in response to a wide series of factors, not least of which has been their strategic repositioning in government policies in cities and countries around the world, researchers have debated the relative merits of the rise of the spectacle, the 'festivalisation' of society and the touristification of festivals. Global sporting events are perhaps the ultimate example of the city as tourist spectacle, given their million dollar budgets, world markets and the rapid turn-around of capital (Waitt, 2003). The debate in the literature has tended to develop along dichotomous lines divided as to the extent to which the promotion of the spectacle, which is said to separate actors from spectators, and to involve a 'glossing over' of complex realities in order to heighten appeal, necessitates a loss of meaning for those constituencies who produce the festival. Johansson and Kociatkiewicz (2011) examined festivals in Stockholm and Poland and argued that festivals serve as vehicles for representing simplified, stylised and attractive versions of what are otherwise very heterogeneous and multi-layered cities.

However, drawing on Waterman (1998), Richards argues that classifying festivals as being either ritual or spectacle is fruitless, as in reality, 'each festival tends to include both of these elements to a greater or lesser degree' (2007a: 260). The relative emphasis on either may change over time, and indeed, they may be seen as laying contested claims on the meanings produced through the festival. Handelman earlier distinguished between public events as those that 'present' and those that 'represent': the former are the 'dominant form of occasion that publicly enunciate … statehood, nationhood and civic collectivity' (1990: 42, cited in Richards, 2007b). In contrast, the latter compare and contrast the status quo through playful manifestations of alternative visions of the world. He argued that both of these can provide tremendous spectacles. Nurse's (1999) analysis of Caribbean carnivals found that the substantial tourism and economic dimensions do not overshadow the profound social meanings of these festivities. Meanwhile, Gotham's analysis of the New Orleans Mardi Gras argued that the 'persistence of old Mardi Gras traditions and the creation of new traditions are not just simply residual products of global level changes ... (but) reflect local efforts to resist, absorb and transform the global processes of commodification and standardisation to produce new and locally distinctive cultural traditions' (2005: 312). Azara and Crouch (2006) argued that newly invented and 'touristified' festivals remain expressions of community participation and identity operating within different social and spatial scopes. They used their findings to argue that newly enacted traditions enacted through festival sites, rather than being merely commodified and moments of spectacle geared towards tourist consumption, can instead be 'loci of dialectics where distinctive narratives and ideologies' can be performed.

FURTHER READING

Aching, G. (2010) 'Carnival time versus modern social life: a false distinction', *Social Identities*, 16 (4): 415–25.

Azara, I. and Crouch, D. (2006) 'La cavalcata sarda: performing identities in a contemporary Sardinian festival', in D. Picard and M. Robinson (eds), *Festivals, Tourism and Social Change*. Clevedon: Channel View Publications. pp. 32–45.

Nurse, K. (1999) 'Globalization and Trinidad carnival: diaspora, hybridity and identity in global culture', *Cultural Studies*, 13 (4): 661–690.

Sharaby, R. (2008) 'The holiday of holidays: a triple holiday festival for Christians, Jews and Muslims', *Social Compass*, 55 (4): 581–96.

29 Social Impacts

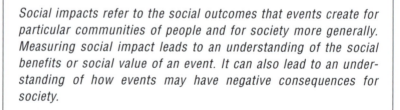

Social impacts refer to the social outcomes that events create for particular communities of people and for society more generally. Measuring social impact leads to an understanding of the social benefits or social value of an event. It can also lead to an understanding of how events may have negative consequences for society.

While impact research in the festivals and events domain was historically dominated by a focus on the economic aspects, researchers have been aware of the social outcomes of festivals and events for at least as long as they have been aware of economic impacts (Ritchie, 1984). Indeed, social benefits have been found to outweigh economic benefits at times. Kim et al. (2006) argued that several researchers have suggested that residents in places that have held sports mega-events can believe the positive social outcomes to be as important as economic outcomes or even more so. Elsewhere, Thomas and Wood (2004) and Wood (2005) indicated that in a UK context, the social benefits of local authority funded events are likely to outweigh the economic benefits. In recent times, Deery and Jago (2010) suggested that understanding the value of the social and environmental impacts of events has become a greater priority for both practitioners and academics.

In a recent review of the social impacts of events literature, Deery and Jago (2010) classified extant research into (1) social impacts of events on communities and (2) social impacts of events on visitors, attendees and other stakeholders. Key preoccupations in both include the development of scales to assess social benefits and costs, with social capital formation being an important focus in the second category and residents' perceptions and support for events being hugely important in the first. Reflecting the tourism literature more broadly, a distinctive body of literature has addressed residents' perceptions of impacts (see review by Gursoy et al., 2004). As Deery and Jago's review of the literature demonstrates, a wide variety of both positive and negative outcomes have been identified in the work investigating impacts on communities (see Table 1). Furthermore, communities have been shown to be comprised of significant internal differences, with resident perceptions being identified as negative, positive and neutral.

The close links between the evolution of tourism studies and festival and event studies is very clear in the context of social impacts. A great deal of the social impact research on events takes its lead in theoretical and methodological terms from social impact research within tourism studies more generally (Fredline et al., 2003; Deery and Jago, 2010). However, the influence of other fields of study, particularly cultural policy, cultural studies, anthropology and sociology are also evident here and will be discussed further on. The widespread use of social exchange theory to investigate residents' perceptions of events has been a notable commonality shared with the wider tourism literature.

Table 1 Positive and negative impacts of events on communities

Positive impacts	Negative impacts
Increased employment opportunities	Rowdy and delinquent behaviour
Increased standard of living	Increased crime levels
Increased entertainment opportunities	Excessive drinking
Economic benefits	Litter
Opportunity to meet new people	Damage to the environment
More interesting things to do	Noise
Enhanced community image	Traffic congestion and parking problems
Community pride	Disruption of normal way of life
Preservation of local culture/heritage	Overcrowding
Increased skill base	Money spent on events, not on community needs
New facilities & infrastructure	Increased cost of living

Source: Henderson et al. (2010) after Fredline et al. (2003).

So too has been the tendency to employ quantitative approaches (usually residents' surveys), and to measure impact from one particular perspective at any given time. In addition, studies have tended to take snapshot 'moment in time' approaches as opposed to longitudinal overviews. Deery and Jago (2010) investigated the consequences of anti-social behaviour using two Australian case studies and demonstrated how positive impacts can come to be overwhelmed by negative effects. A significant line of enquiry in the literature has related to residents perceptions of the social impacts of festivals and events. During the 2000s, a number of researchers (Delamere, 2001; Delamere et al., 2001; Fredline et al., 2003; Small, 2007) developed empirical scales to measure residents' perceptions of festivals and how they impact socially. This literature is discussed in the section on **community festivals** as here the role of community, often residential community support, is of vital importance.

It is useful to note at this point that 'social impact' is not the only concept used in the literature to capture the social ramification of events, at least not when one looks at literature outside of event management. Other concepts identifiable include social cohesion (Crespi-Vallbona and

key concepts in event management

Richards, 2007), social value (Chalip, 2006), social networks (Misener and Mason, 2006) and group identity (De Bres and Davis, 2001). While Deery and Jago (2010) suggested that the social impact literature in particular has come of age, it can be argued that in general, the literatures that deal with the social aspects of events and festivals are quite disparate and uneven in terms of disciplinary underpinnings, theoretical references, research questions and methodological approaches. Some of the terms employed are ill-defined, are employed in different ways or in ways that overlap, and are difficult to apply and operationalise. Acknowledgement of these difficulties has prompted some researchers to search for alternative theoretical frameworks to underpin a comprehensive enquiry into social connections in festival settings. **Social capital** is starting to emerge as a theory that shows real potential and this is discussed elsewhere in this volume.

Social value has also received attention. Writing in the context of cultural policy, McCarthy et al. (2004) talked about social value from two perspectives: public good and private good. 'Intrinsic' benefits are directly related to the artistic product and can provide captivation, pleasure, empathy, cognitive growth, the creation of social networks, and the finding or conveying of community expressions and critiques. 'Instrumental' benefits are those not directly associated with the artistic output, for example, improving learning and academic performance, improving attitude and behaviour. Communitarian theory values participatory leisure activities, such as the arts, very highly because of the social networks and 'shared meanings' they create. As Snowball and Webb (2008: 150) explained, it is not that communal leisure produces unity of voice or widespread consensus, but that participatory leisure enables the development of shared values and goals, so important in developing the 'social self' needed for a healthy society. Crespi-Vallbona and Richards identified perceptions among festival stakeholders that while festivals were important in developing social cohesion and identity they also 'made contradictions evident' (2007: 112). The kind of local cultural events studied here were also seen as a way of incorporating increasing numbers of Spanish immigrants into Catalunya society and an important way of maintaining the region's cultural identity in the face of globalisation. In similar vein, Chalip (2006) linked social value to the celebratory nature of events that can engender a sense of liminality and create a heightened sense of community. He cited numerous studies from anthropology and sociology that attest to the value of festivals and events as occasions and spaces where people re-make social bonds; re-assert and re-shape societal norms and values; and explore and reproduce communal identities. He cited further studies to argue that overall, these processes serve to strengthen social bonds and should be leveraged to ensure that that the effects are not limited to the duration of the actual event itself.

Despite significant advances in the literature, it can still be claimed that much remains to be learnt about how events contribute to social development. Deery and Jago (2010) argued that while many impacts have been identified, little has been done to investigate the consequences of these impacts. A number of researchers have made similar comments. Misener and Mason (2006), focusing specifically on **sports events**, for instance, noted how little is understood about how civic regeneration strategies and tourism development are being used to develop social infrastructure in communities. Yardimci (2007: 2), referring to the Turkish city of Istanbul, wrote of the dynamic impact that festivals have on urban life. She argued that while big cultural events influence the re-shaping of the prevailing intellectual and cultural climate of the city and that 're-integrating marginalised groups within the city is as much a cultural process as an economic one and cultural recognition is as important as material equality' (2007:16), these social and political implications tend to be overlooked. In the mainstream event management literature, Getz (2008) suggested that events should be viewed as 'open-systems' comprising inputs, transforming processes and outcomes. At this point it is well acknowledged that the nature and quality of social impacts is related to the nature of planning involved. However, to date, knowledge of how the first two stages/elements inter-connect to produce the third stage is incomplete. The need to move beyond identifying impacts to develop an understanding of the processes through which outcomes are generated is now becoming increasingly recognised. Until more progress is made in this respect, the body of literature on social impacts can only partially contribute to a comprehensive understanding of the societal role played by festivals and events.

FURTHER READING

Deery, M. and Jago, L. (2010) 'Social impacts of events and the role of anti-social behaviour', *International Journal of Event and Festival Management*, 1 (1): 8–28.

Fredline, L., Jago, L. and Deery, M. (2003) 'The development of a generic scale to measure the social impacts of events', *Event Management*, 8 (1): 23–37.

key concepts in
event management

Gursoy, D., Kim, K. and Uysal, M. (2004) 'Perceived impacts of festivals and special events by organizers: an extension and validation', *Tourism Management*, 25: 171–81.

Misener, L. and Mason, D. (2006) 'Creating community networks: can sporting events offer meaningful sources of social capital?', *Managing Leisure*, 11: 39–56.

30 Sponsorship

> *Event sponsorship involves companies investing funds, or equivalent 'in-kind' goods or services, in event organisations in exchange for the right to be associated with the event in some way.*

The growing commercialisation of leisure and cultural forms, including festivals and events, has received much comment recently. Sponsorship is the most obvious form of this commercialisation (Mason and Cochetel, 2006). Interest in sponsorship rose significantly when several countries moved to ban the advertising of tobacco and alcohol products in broadcast media (Quester and Farrelly, 1998). Event sponsorship is one of the main types of sponsorship, and sports sponsorship in particular is very significant. The commercial success of the Los Angeles Olympic Games is widely noted as having been key in stimulating the growth of corporate event sponsorship. In the event context, the meaning of sponsorship remains unchanged. It is defined by Meenaghan and Shipley as: 'the right to associate with the profile and image of an event and to exploit this association for commercial ends' (1999: 328). According to Pelsmacker et al. (2005), the sponsorship of mega sports events, such as the FIFA World Cup and the **Olympic Games,** two events that count their global television audiences in the billions, can be more effective than advertising in raising brand awareness. At the same time, sponsorship has become a very important stream of revenue for **festival**s and events of varying types. For events that tend not to receive any public funding, such as music festivals, sponsorship is a particularly important supplement to ticket revenue (Getz, 2002). This is particularly true of the growing area of 'popular music' festivals that attract young and relatively homogeneous audiences (Oakes, 2003).

The literature on sponsorship and events is relatively new but it is now sizeable, and has a number of identifiable foci. It is clearly divided into the very applied 'how to get sponsorship' publications, mainly textbooks, aimed specifically at current and prospective event managers; and more academic, research-based papers published in business, marketing and advertising journals. Given the critical role that sponsorship has come to play in determining the financial viability of events, the tasks associated with identifying potential sponsors, preparing sponsorship proposals, evaluating the spin-offs of sponsorships and managing on-going relations with sponsors have become central within the event organisation. The need for event professionals to accumulate expertise in this area has led to a huge volume of publications dealing with the business of effectively developing event sponsorship strategies. The production of event management textbooks has mushroomed in recent times and a chapter on sponsorship is fundamental. Bowdin et al.'s (2006) contribution follows a typical format. Having defined the topic and reviewed recent trends, it gives an overview of the mutual benefits of event sponsorship, the merits of developing a sponsorship policy, the process of developing a sponsorship strategy, of managing and servicing sponsorships and of measuring and evaluating sponsorships.

Within the more research-based material, researchers tend to approach the matter from the perspective of either the sponsoring organisation, asking: What are the returns on sponsorship investment in the immediate and longer term? How is a sponsorship plan developed, implemented and monitored? Or from the perspective of the sponsored event. In the latter case, enquiries address the question of how to secure and maintain sponsorship deals and relationships. In recent decades, as sponsorship has become an important part of brand management strategies, and as festivals and events have become increasingly the focus of sponsorship investment, the question as to why companies sponsor events has stimulated a great deal of research enquiry. Studies have concluded that companies sponsor events for a number of identifiable reasons: to increase or develop product or corporate awareness, to drive sales or to develop market position. Through sponsorship, companies can increase brand awareness, create brand image, re-position the brand/product in customers' minds and increase market share (Pelsmacker et al., 2005). Meenaghan (2001) suggested that sponsorship is more effective than traditional marketing strategies in creating an emotional relationship between products and customers thus positively influencing the latter's attitude and behaviour towards various companies' brands.

In addition, some work has been done on the process of how companies engage in sponsorship. Thjømøe et al.'s (2002) Norwegian study found that companies engaged in what they termed 'a continuum of involvement', ranging from low involvement and limited business-oriented goals to high involvement and mutual goals. Nadva et al. (2010) further investigated this question of how companies choose and evaluate sponsorship, with particular reference to charitable events. They found informal business policies to prevail with respect to event sponsorship and that decisions were often taken on a case-by-case basis.

To date, research has tended to focus on large-scale sports events, however, there are small but growing literatures dealing with other types of events as well. Music festivals are a case in point. Business sponsorship of the arts first developed in the USA in the 1960s but really grew on both sides of the Atlantic in the 1980s. O'Hagan and Harvey (2000), in an investigation into why businesses sponsor arts festivals, identified five key reasons: promotion of company image/name; supply-chain cohesion; corporate entertainment opportunities; non-monetary benefit to managers/owners; and corporate social responsibility. Overall, however, much research has related to impact. Mason and Cochetel's (2006) South African research investigated the residual effect of sponsorship after a sponsor has resigned. They found that 2 years after the cessation of sponsorship, the previous sponsor still maintained high awareness levels among the event audience. The lesson they draw is that new sponsors cannot expect an automatic assumption of 'ownership' of an event. They followed Erdogen and Kitchen (1998) in stressing the importance of 'leveraging other communication methods to cause the old sponsor's residual awareness to decay more rapidly' (Mason and Cochetel, 2006: 139). Rowley and Williams (2008) bemoaned the lack of research into how the practice of sponsoring music festivals effects brand awareness and engagement. They undertook an exploratory study among a sample of UK music festival-goers and found positive results in respect of brand recall and brand values, however, they found little evidence of any impact on brand use. They suggested a number of avenues for future research including the need to develop more sophisticated instruments to measure brand awareness, attitude and use.

The need to develop further understanding both of how companies plan, implement and evaluate their engagement in sponsorship, and about how events and festivals can become more effective at achieving sponsorship are frequently stated in the literature. Masterman (2004), for example, outlined a number of areas that need further work. These included understanding and using target marketing and segmentation; building relationships and exploiting sponsorship rights with supporting marketing activities. More recently, the impact of recession on event sponsorship has begun to emerge as a theme. Current recessionary times have meant a reduction in household disposable income and the competition to attract consumers to events has become increasingly difficult. The need to generate sponsorship revenue has heightened yet, as Wiscombe (2010) noted, the downturn in the global economy post-2007 has made the task of attracting sponsorship more difficult. Businesses now operate in increasingly constrained financial circumstances and companies are becoming more vigilant in ensuring that sponsorship deals yield measureable and acceptable returns on investment. A downturn in event sponsorship investment has implications not only for event organisations but also for the local economies and societies that host events. Wiscombe (2010) made this point in their case study of Lyme Regis, a small seaside resort in the south of England. Lyme Regis hosted 21 events and festivals in 2009. These attracted £398,970 of sponsorship investment from the town's 117 retail outlets in a variety of forms including cash, raffle prizes, advertising, utilities and labour. The impact of the events on the local economy has been estimated to include the generation of £1.9 million income for the retail outlets and the creation of the equivalent of 43 full-time jobs. In timely fashion, Nadav et al. (2010) have stressed the need for a fuller understanding of why companies decide to sponsor events and argue that return on investment is becoming increasingly important. Nadav et al. (2010) pointed to a gap in understanding about how companies plan, implement and monitor their sponsorship programme. In effect they noted that a theoretical framework relating to sponsorship decision making and evaluation is lacking in the literature.

Very recently, however, there are growing signs that companies are re-considering their traditional sponsorship relationships with event organisations. There is evidence that companies, like the international drinks groups Diageo and Red Bull, are beginning to move away from sponsoring event organisations and beginning instead to invest in organising events themselves. Organising events themselves brings them closer to consumers and is very much part of an experiential marketing strategy.

FURTHER READING

Mason, R.B. and Cochetel, F. (2006) 'Residual brand awareness following the termination of a long-term event sponsorship, and the appointment of a new sponsor', *Journal of Marketing Communications*, 12 (2): 125–44.

Nadva, S., Smith, W.W. and Canberg, A. (2010) 'Examining corporate sponsorship of charitable events in the Greater Charleston area', *Event Management*, 14 (3): 239–50.

Pelsmacker, P., Geunes, M. and Van den Bergh, J. (2005) *Foundations of Marketing Communications: a European Perspective*. Harlow: Prentice Hall.

Rowley, J. and Williams, C. (2008) 'The impact of brand sponsorship of music festivals', *Market Intelligence and Planning*, 26 (7): 781–92.

31 Sports Events

> *Sports events have become enormously important in government strategies to develop regenerate economies and stimulate tourism demand. Most of the largest, international events, those referred to as hallmark or mega-events, are sporting in orientation.*

Governments throughout the world recognise the hosting of major sporting events to be an important element in city marketing and tourism stimulation (Gratton and Henry, 2001), and the strategic alignment of events with tourism is most visible in the sports arena. The early appreciation of the economic potential of events encouraged a focus on large-scale events and very often this meant a focus on sports events. According to Doherty (2009), major sports events are one-time or perhaps annual sport competitions, as opposed to leagues. She goes on to say that events are differentiated on the basis of length (maybe a day, a weekend or a week) and profile (an event's profile tends to be higher than its equivalent league[s]). Event sport tourism involves travelling to participate, in whatever capacity, in a sports event. Events range from mega-events (Olympics and FIFA World Cup) to intermediate events (America's Cup) to smaller events. State and municipal governments and public-sector tourism agencies see within large-scale, high-profile sporting events the capacity to attract large numbers of visitors and associated revenue. As Getz states: 'sports as big business is an enduring theme in the literature' (2008: 411) and hallmark events including most notably the Olympic Games but also the FIFA World Cup, the Commonwealth Games and various motor-racing events, have received considerable attention. Much of the literature dealing with sports events adopts a tourism perspective and the literature documenting the relationship between sports events and tourism is now long-standing and extensive.

The literature on sports events and tourism must be set within the broader context of that pertaining to sports and tourism. Literature on sports tourism, defined by Weed and Bull as a 'social, economic and cultural phenomenon arising from unique interactions of activity, people and place' has burgeoned in recent years to such an extent that it now has a dedicated journal (2004: 47). Sports events tourism is clearly part of this broader domain, found at the point where sport, tourism and events overlap (Weed, 2009). Routinely, small-scale sports events attract participants and spectators. The latter will mainly comprise residents. However, in the case of special events, defined by Jago and Shaw (1999) as being of limited duration, infrequent, and out of the ordinary, spectators will also comprise visitors, while very significant numbers of participants in the form of competitors and officials will also be involved. In the case of mega-events, the numbers of people participating, but particularly the number of those travelling to do so, can be very substantial. Thus it is not surprising that the overwhelming focus of sports event research attention has been on mega-events, such as the Olympic Games, International Grand Prix, the FIFA World Cup and other similarly large-scale events. According to Weed (2006), the amount of attention paid to the effects and impacts of these events on tourism is such that sport tourism studies in general, are dominated by sports events studies.

Early work on the area tended to follow the research emphases prevalent within the broader event literature with an overwhelming tendency to study event impacts, and in particular to study economic impacts. It is true to say that much of the development of methodologies to measure the economic impacts of events in general took place in large-scale sports event arenas with early empirical work on events such as Grand Prix (Burgan and Mules, 1989; Burns et al., 1986) being widely cited. The debate on economic impact methodologies has continued to wage over time (see **economic impact** for a fuller discussion) but a great deal of the key contributions have been empirically set in sports events contexts (Dwyer et al., 2005; Lee and Taylor, 2005; Preuss 2007). Much of this work has been undertaken by Australian researchers drawing on Australian events (for example, the Adelaide and Melbourne Grand Prix, and the Sydney 2000 Olympic Games). The outcomes reported have been largely positive although some researchers have argued that large events can generate losses for host city authorities while others have queried their proven ability to contribute to economic development. While it is clear that governments invest in sports events largely to realise economic returns, Misener and Mason (2006) briefly review a number of studies that point either to negative economic impacts or to the over-estimation and over-exaggeration of the economic returns likely to result. Recently, Fourie and Santana-Gallego (2011) took up the debate as to the costs and benefits of mega-events and used a gravity equation model to examine the bilateral tourist flows between 200 countries from 1995 to 2006 in an effort to determine the effect that hosting a mega-event has on tourist arrivals in the host country. They found that the hosting of a mega-event did increase predicted tourism by about 8% in the same year but they cautioned that 'it is not necessarily the most expensive events that yield the most benefits: the type and importantly, timing (seasonality) of the mega-event, and the countries participating in the event all impact on the "success" of these events' (Fourie and Santana-Gallego, 2011: 1369).

Over time, the questions raised by economists have widened to consider other aspects including event leveraging (Chalip, 2006), and the complexities of the event bidding process (Westerbeek et al., 2002; Smith, 2010). The gradual diffusion of sustainability-related concepts has influenced this literature as it has others, and recent years have seen increasing attention being paid to the 'triple bottom line'. As Dansero and Puttilli (2010) pointed out, the literature on the legacy of mega-events has come to highlight the multi-dimensional nature of impacts (sporting, cultural, economic, tourist-related, environmental, architectural, infrastructure). Some of the attention paid to the **social impacts** of sports events is discussed elsewhere in this volume. Equally, the efforts of mega-events, like the **Olympic Games** and the Rugby World Cup, in attending to environmental impacts (see **sustainable events**) and to build legacy in terms of volunteering capacity (see entry **volunteering**) have been cutting edge, relative to the initiatives being undertaken by other events. There has also been a growing understanding that to fully understand event processes and impacts, efforts to research them must view them not as isolated events but as part of complex, multi-layered and complex environments. Kavetsos and Szymanski (2010) made an interesting contribution in this respect in their analysis of national well-being and international sports events. They used life satisfaction data from the Eurobarometer survey series covering 12 European countries to test whether (1) better than expected national athletic performance has an effect on life satisfaction and (2) hosting major sporting events raises reported life satisfaction. While limited support was found for the first hypothesis, significant support was found for the second effect when it came to hosting major football championships.

More commonly, questions have been posed about the role that sports events play in shaping destination image. As Gibson et al. (2008) noted, sports related attributes are important among those that differentiate destinations from one another. Brown et al. (2004) looked at the role that events play in strengthening a destination's brand. Several researchers (Lee et al., 2005; Kaplanidou and Vogt, 2007; Gripsund et al., 2010) have investigated this topic usually in the context of large-scale events. However, more recently, Hallmann and Breuer (2011) investigated the images of small-scale sports events as perceived by spectators and participants. Sports events have also dominated the literature on event **sponsorship**. As noted elsewhere, the commercial success of the Los Angeles Olympic Games has been widely seen as pivotal in stimulating the growth of corporate event sponsorship. Sponsoring events is all about building relationships between a company and its clients. As Allen et al. noted 'creative sponsorship can reach consumers in environments in which they are having a good time and so they are more likely to accept a well-considered marketing message' (2011: 330). As Kahle and Close (2011) put it, as a persuasive tactic, sponsorship reaches fans when they are vulnerable because they are both cognitively overwhelmed and socially committed. The emotional intensity that attends sports fans' consumption of sports events can, however, limit sponsorship effectiveness if emotional arousal overcomes cognitive faculties.

While large-scale sports events have absorbed most research attention, there is also a literature on community sport events. Walo et al. (1996) and Daniels and Norman (2003) have suggested that the economic benefits of smaller events can rival their larger counterparts. Daniels (2007) and Dimmock and Tiyce (2001) have written about the diverse contributions that smaller, community sports events can make. One of these is to provide accessible leisure opportunities for local residents. Spectator retention and audience development is an issue for some lower profile sports events, for example, martial arts. In this context, service quality becomes very important as with high standards of service quality, spectators tend to stay longer, purchase extra services and attract other spectators through word of mouth recommendations (Zeithaml et al., 1996). Some work has been done on perceptions of service quality among spectators at sports events. Ko et al. (2010) for example, found that spectators' pre-existing identification levels with the sport in question, Taekwondo, significantly influenced their quality perceptions of the event. They recommended that event organisations should focus on ensuring service quality in the interest of boosting audience development.

FURTHER READING

Doherty, A. (2009) 'The volunteer legacy of a major sport event', *Journal of Policy Research in Tourism Leisure and Events*, 1 (3): 185–207.
Gibson, H.J., Willming, C. and Holdnak, A. (2003) 'Small-scale event sport tourism: fans as tourists', *Tourism Management*, 24 (2): 181–90.
Misener, L. and Mason, D. (2006) 'Creating community networks: can sporting events offer meaningful sources of social capital?', *Managing Leisure*, 11: 39–56.
Pennington-Gray, L. and Holdnak, A. (2002) 'Out of the stands and into the community: using sorts events to promote a destination', *Event Management*, 7: 177–86.
Weed, M.E. and Bull, C.J. (2004) *Sports Tourism: Participants, Policy and Providers*. Oxford: Elsevier.

32 Stakeholders

Stakeholders are those groups or individuals who can influence, or are influenced by, the workings of an organisation such as a festival or an event. The very nature of festivals and events is such that they are highly dependent on the involvement of multiple and diverse stakeholders.

While it is true to say that all organisations interact, rely and affect stakeholders as defined above, events, in particular are intimately tied into numerous, diverse stakeholder relationships. It is now well recognised that festivals and events require the collaboration of multiple stakeholders that may include government, businesses, not-for-profit organisations as well as employees, volunteers, residents and tourists (Getz, 2008; Getz et al., 2007; Telfer, 2000). These stakeholders can be quite different from each other, with differing degrees of influence and power depending on their importance to the success of the event in question. Furthermore, as Yaghmour and Scott pointed out, each stakeholder is 'influenced by different objectives, complicating goal alignment and cohesion in festival planning and implementation' (2009: 117). Identifying and managing the inter-organisational linkages between these diverse stakeholders is a critical task for event managers (Merrilees et al., 2005), and has generated much attention in the event management literature. It has also attracted much attention from those researchers seeking to unravel the ways in which festivals and events are implicated in the reproduction and expression of group and place **identity**.

The growing interest in investigating the roles and involvement of stakeholders in the sector represents one of the most important recent developments in the festival and event literature as a whole. The academic interest in stakeholders has taken a number of forms. Gursoy et al. (2004), for example, approached the topic with questions about impact in mind. Using a quantitative approach, they developed and tested an instrument to assess organisers' perceptions of the socio-economic impacts of festivals and special events upon their host communities. More recently Getz and Andersson (2010) published exploratory empirical research findings designed to advance the use of stakeholder theory as a useful investigative framework for the festival environment. They contended that it has application in furthering understandings of how festivals 'get started, develop, potentially fail, or become permanent institutions' (2010: 534). They saw a particular usefulness in the attention that it draws to 'the scope and nature of inter-organizational relationships, how they affect the focal organization, and their management in the context of festival viability and long-term sustainability' (2010: 531–2). They linked their exploration of stakeholder theory to that of resource dependency, which according to Donaldson (1996), holds that organisations compete for resources and that those who survive do so by finding an appropriate niche that assures them of continued resources.

Fundamental tenets aired by Getz and Andersson include that 'the most important stakeholders are (often) the ones on which events depend for resources or other types of support' and by extension, 'festival managers must become skilled at managing the relationships that can generate support and resources' (2010: 532). They deduced from their review of extant literature that 'the network of relationships managed by festivals is vital to their creation, stability and long-term survival' (2010: 535). Their empirical work was conducted in Sweden, Norway, the UK and Australia and comprised a sample of 193 festivals. They found four different patterns of stakeholder relationships/dependencies to be evident: paying customers, government, venues and sponsors, all with different management implications. Clear potential avenues for potential research are apparent here.

By definition, the production and delivery of all festivals and events relies on networks of individuals and organisations. Getz et al. wrote about festivals as agencies within an environment 'in which goals and resources for the event are negotiated by multiple parties' (2007: 104). Ebers (1997) suggested that if more than two organisations are linked through networking relationships, such as alliances, outsourcing or other cooperative arrangements, they constitute an inter-organisational network. The application of network theory in the festival and event is beginning to attract attention. Karlsen and Nordström (2009) used Håkansson and Snehota's (2006) network model in their study of festivals in the Barents region of Scandinavia. They found that festivals cooperated with multiple stakeholders who had multiple roles and advocated that in the interest of sustainability, festivals engage in processes of 'giving and taking' that are seen to be mutually beneficial for all parties involved. Gray's (1989) explication of collaboration theory explains why and how stakeholders work together to jointly tackle a problem domain through a process of collaboration. Drawing on both Day and Day (1977) and Gray (1989), Yaghmour and Scott (2009: 118) explain that collaboration is a mechanism for moving from an 'under-organized system in which each stakeholder acts independently, to a negotiated order in which stakeholders continuously reconsider and restructure their relationships through a process that allows them to establish a temporary order for the domain' being negotiated. Organisations engage in collaboration because they want to achieve particular organisational objectives. The outcomes that emerge from collaboration can be said to be explicit, that is, pre-defined at the outset of the collaborative process; or implicit, that is, unplanned or unanticipated outcomes that emerge during the process. Collaboration may result in outcomes at both individual and collaborative levels. Yaghmour and Scott (2009) suggest that the former may include learning, socio-political responsibility, efficiency, risk reduction, legitimacy and resources, while the latter may include goal attainment, social capital, shared meaning, network development and power. These authors employed a qualitative methodology to examine the nature of collaboration in the annual Jeddah Festival in Saudi Arabia.

According to Getz (2002) 'festival viability, effectiveness and long-term sustainability is often questioned in light of the observation that many festivals have stagnated or failed'. In investigating failure among festivals Getz (2002) pointed to the importance of resource dependency theory which holds that successful organisations are those that compete effectively for resources. Stakeholders constitute important gatekeepers through whom resources can be accessed hence building effective relationships with stakeholders may be viewed as fundamental to the sustainability of festival organisations. Reid and Arcodia (2002) classified festival stakeholder as being either 'primary' or 'secondary'. The former included those on whom the festival depended: employees, volunteers, sponsors, suppliers, spectators, attendees and participants. The latter referred to an outer circle that included the host community, media, government, business and tourist organisations and a range of service companies. More recently, Getz et al. (2007) described stakeholders in terms of 'facilitators', 'regulators', 'co-producers', 'allies and collaborators' and those impacted as audiences and the community. They argued that festivals are produced not by stand-alone organisations but by voluntary networks of stakeholders that must be managed effectively by the festival organisation.

Managing stakeholders is clearly an important function. Getz et al.'s (2007) comparative research on Canadian and Swedish cases found a number of different stakeholder management strategies. These included internalizing powerful regulators (for example, getting local authority councillors to sit on boards of directors); getting suppliers to become sponsors; developing longer-term sponsorships; and working closely with independent organisations who have become co-producers. Elsewhere, Andersson and Getz (2009) called for further research to evaluate the long-term efficacy of specific marketing and stakeholder strategies in different cultural and political contexts. This requires understanding the interrelationships between stakeholders and the festival organisation itself. In the context of relationship marketing, Larson (2002) used the political market square concept to analyse the power dynamics evident in a project network of actors marketing a festival. Her analysis identified a series of political processes including gatekeeping, negotiation, coalition building, trust and identity building. Elsewhere, MacKellar (2006) has used a network analysis methodology to study the relationships between organisations staging an event.

Most of the above literature orients itself around the idea that events are first and foremost tourist attractions. Its main priority is to understand how the tourism industry can produce events that attract and satisfy tourists, plus generate a series of beneficial outcomes (tourist expenditure, image enhancement, related investment and so on). However, it is clear that there is now an increasing interest in moving away from a preoccupation with the event as a discrete entity towards a much broader conceptualisation of festivals and events as phenomena embedded in a multiplicity of spatial, socio-cultural, political and environmental contexts. There is further an increasing inclination to problematise the relationships between festivals, events and tourism and to adopt a more critical and reflexive approach.

Beyond the focus on management questions, in the move towards a wider interpretation of event impacts (Hede, 2007) there is growing interest in other stakeholders, including residents. Research into the perceived impacts of events on host communities is well established (Delamere, 2001; Fredline et al., 2003; Gursoy and Kendall, 2006). Social exchange theory underpins a great deal of this research, and studies have tried to assess the extent and manner in which individuals are likely to participate in an exchange if they believe they are likely to gain benefits without incurring unacceptable costs (Homans, 1974, cited in Gursoy and Kendall, 2006: 607). More recently, Crespi-Vallbona and Richards (2007), have called for more nuanced understandings of the relationships between different stakeholders and deeper investigation into shared commonalities, and specifically raise the question of stakeholders in the context of community groups. They point, for example, to the centrality of identity in the discourse about cultural events, yet their analysis of cultural events in the Spanish region of Catalunya demonstrates how the meanings associated with the concept differ. They argue that 'the notion of 'community' is usually treated in an abstract fashion, which obscures rather than clarifies the role of different stakeholders' (Crespi-Vallbona and Richards, 2007: 107).

FURTHER READING

Getz, D., Andersson, T. and Larson, M. (2007) 'Festival stakeholder roles: concepts and case studies', *Event Management*, 10 (2): 103–22.

Getz, D. and Andersson, T. (2010) 'Festival stakeholders: exploring relationships and dependency through a four-country comparison', *Journal of Hospitality and Tourism Research*, 34 (4): 531–56.

Karlsen, S. and Nordström, C.S. (2009) 'Festivals in the Barents region: exploring festival-stakeholder collaboration', *Scandinavian Journal of Hospitality and Tourism*, 9 (2/3): 130–45.

MacKellar, J. (2006) 'An integrated view of innovation emerging from a regional festival', *International Journal of Event Management Research*, 2 (1): 37–48.

33 Sustainable Events

Sustainable events are those that manage to achieve a balance between human activity, resource use and environmental impact. Key areas that event organisations need to focus on to be sustainable include energy; transport; waste management; waste reduction and resource recovery; materials purchasing and procurement.

In event terms, sustainability has implications across economic, environmental, social and cultural domains. The potential for events to contribute to the sustainable development of destinations is manifold: they can extend the season and so spread the visitor load by time; they offer opportunities to build strong and diverse linkages with their host economies; they can offer opportunities to share and co-produce meaningful experiences (in various cultural settings including sports arenas) for both local residents and visiting attendees. Until very recently, there had been a lack of literature on sustainability in festival and event contexts.

This is somewhat surprising, as producing the transient spectacles exemplified by internationally high profile sporting and cultural events can require extraordinary levels of investment and cause serious disruptions to local environments. Evidence to support the latter claim has been available for some time now. De Groote (2005), for example, wrote about the criticism that Australia faced after the 1988 Expo in Brisbane and that the Spanish government encountered in the wake of both the 1992 Expo in Seville and the Olympic Games in Barcelona. A. Smith (2009) concluded that many large-scale events have contributed negatively in terms of social sustainability, tending to dislocate and disadvantage existing community groups as new flows of capital, people, infrastructure and so on, are attracted in by an event in a concentrated period of time. Elsewhere, others have suggested that smaller-scale events may be more sustainable (O'Sullivan and Jackson, 2002), producing outcomes that are less disruptive, and possibly more appropriate to the needs of the host place. It is partly because criticism of this nature has begun to accumulate that sustainability has become increasingly an issue, especially for sports event researchers (Chalip, 2006; Misner and Mason, 2006). When broadly defined, sustainability has to do with meeting the needs of the present generation without compromising the ability of future generations to meet their needs (World Commission on Environment and Development, 1987).

Lawton and Weaver (2010) argued that the literature on event and festival sustainability, being relatively sparse, suggests a later adoption pattern of sustainability-related innovation. Until recently, relatively few researchers considered environmental sustainability practices in the sector, however, environmental issues are now beginning to receive much more attention. Upham et al.'s (2009) research into carbon emissions related to an international arts festival and Collins and Flynn's (2007) research into the ecological footprint of a UK FA Cup Final are two examples. Lawton and Weaver (2010) surveyed 135 North American birding festivals to investigate the nature of extant sustainable ancillary resource management (SARM) practices, that is, practices not directly linked to the core activity of bird watching but rather related to ancillary activities like waste minimisation, recycling and energy conservation. They identified a modest level of SARM practices which they described in terms of the 'superficial environmentalism' which they argue can be found across the tourism and hospitality sectors more generally.

Among practitioners, there is growing acknowledgment of the need to ensure that festival and event activities are planned and operationalised in a sustainable manner. According to Heitmann and David (2010), event organisations in countries that are signatories to the 1992 Rio Declaration on sustainability are being encouraged to be cognisant of their responsibilities in this regard, and some of the world's largest events have begun to demonstrate leadership. The Olympic Games is a case in point. In 2007, the organising committee of the 2012 London Games produced *The London 2012 Sustainability Plan* covering the following key areas.

1 Climate change: minimising greenhouse gas emissions and ensuring legacy facilities are able to cope with the impacts of climate change.
2 Waste: minimising waste at every stage of the project, ensuring no waste is sent to landfill during Games time, and encouraging the development of new waste processing infrastructure in East London.
3 Biodiversity: minimising the impact of the Games on wildlife and their habitats in and around Games venues, leaving a legacy of enhanced habitats where we can, for example, the Olympic Park.
4 Inclusion: promoting access for all and celebrating the diversity of London and the UK, creating new employment, training and business opportunities.
5 Healthy living: inspiring people across the country to take up sport and develop active, healthy and sustainable lifestyles. (London 2012 Olympic Games Organising Committee, 2007)

In this, the London Games committee is actively seeking to comply with the British Standard for Sustainable Events, introduced in 2007. As noted elsewhere in the **Olympic Games** section of this volume, however, when the new government came to power in the UK in 2010 priorities shifted and the updated 2010 document (DCMS, 2010) appears to place lesser emphasis on sustainability. The UK is not the only jurisdiction where standards, guides and certification now exist to foster sustainable practices in the event sector. Heitmann and David (2010) listed a series of guidelines, produced by public and private agents in recent years to promote sustainability in the events sector in the UK, Germany, Canada and the USA. Several national tourism development agencies, such as Tourism Australia and Fáilte Ireland, the Irish National Tourism Development Authority, have produced guides and fact sheets on green events. The latter produced *A Guide to Running Green Meetings and Events* (Fáilte Ireland, 2010: 5) in response to the 'growing international requirement by businesses for a more sustainable supply chain ... a definable demand from consumers for greater environmental standards … a growing belief that businesses cannot avoid these issues'. Increasingly, support agencies are producing guidelines and supports to encourage and assist events to become more environmentally conscious of their activities. The ICARUS Foundation, a Canadian not-for-profit organisation that advocates sustainable tourism, for example, has produced a *Greening Your Festivals and Events Guide* (Graci and Dodds, 2008). Industry players are also taking action: the Perth Convention Bureau, the largest event and exhibition facility in Western Australia, for example, has recently developed an environmental policy (Tourism Western Australia, 2012).

Encouraged by the initiatives of governments, government agencies and environmental advocacy groups, cognisant of a growing environmental awareness among consumers and sometimes inspired by a desire to cultivate a reputation for being 'green', event organisations are increasingly adopting environmentally friendly practices. The Glastonbury festival is one example: 'Glastonbury has a global reputation for great music, good times, carnivalesque debauchery but what differentiates it from other festivals of the same scale is an attempt to give space to progressive green issues' (Smith, K., 2009). It has introduced a series of initiatives and policies to minimise their impact on the environment. A headline grabbing development in 2010 was its solar panel initiative. Glastonbury became the largest private solar energy station in the UK when it installed more than 1000 solar panels to power some of the numerous generators needed to operate the festival. Roskilde Festival in Denmark is another event that has been active on the environmental front. It has developed a 'Green Footsteps programme', which includes a wide variety of sustainability initiatives including recycling incentives, supporting Fair Trade products and rewarding attendees who limit their carbon footprint while travelling to the festival. Elsewhere, industry newsletter and media fora, like http://www.eventindustrynews.co.uk, continuously report on the event sector's growing engagement with sustainability practices.

The upsurge of activity among policymakers and practitioners is being mirrored in event management textbooks, where there is an increased focus on the 'greening' of events. According to Goldblatt 'greener events' can be defined as 'special events that continually endeavour to provide superior experiences in environmentally friendly strategies' (2011: 191). Implicit here, as Goldblatt sees it, are three core values: innovation, conservation and education. His *Special Event: A New Generation and the Next Frontier* describes a series of steps that event managers can take to begin adopting environmentally friendly practices. Jones' (2010) *Sustainable Event Management* is entirely devoted to the concept of sustainability. It is designed as a practical guide for organisers seeking to make their event environmentally sound. It takes readers through what it identifies as the key sustainability indicators: energy and emissions, transport, water, waste and purchasing and resource use. It also considers the importance of developing a marketing and communications strategy to alert and engage event attendees with the greening practices being advocated and applied through the operationalisation of the event. Throughout, it uses event case studies to highlight effective practices already in place.

While the above are signs that the event sector has begun to come to grips with the task of reflecting on and managing the ways in which its activities impact upon the environment, the challenges remain onerous. As BOP Consulting acknowledges 'while the awareness of climate change in particular is now widespread, being able to take steps to implement change to existing business practices and business models is far harder' (2011: 27). Its attempt to capture the breadth of impacts generated by 11 festivals held annually in Edinburgh incorporates an environmental dimension. In so doing, the researchers who produced the report worked closely with Festivals Edinburgh Environmental Working Group with the primary aim of improving the festivals' self-assessment of their environmental impact. The Carbon Trust's Mapping method was used to try to calculate environmental values for the festivals' operations. So too were a set of online tools designed to track emissions and waste, and to promote sustainability practices in the music and cultural sector. The study produces a figure equating to the CO_2 emissions of all the festivals in 2010 in absolute terms, as well as to the amount equating to individual tickets sold in relative terms. It concluded that audience travel to and from the city accounted for 95% of all emissions. However, because of missing data, it stresses that the emissions identified represent a very significant under-estimation of Edinburgh Festivals' actual omissions.

The specific question of climate change, and the implications that it may have for event activity is one that has received very little attention. Mair (2011) took up this topic from an Australian perspective. She outlined some of the bio-physical (sea-level rise, bushfire, water quality) and socio-economic impacts (settlement damage, impact on demand) associated with climate change that could affect the event sector. Furthermore, she went on to consider some of the mitigation and adaptation approaches that event organisations are employing to manage their vulnerability to climate change. She argued that while a number of Australian events are developing mitigation measures (for example, using alternative energy sources) a great deal remains to be done.

FURTHER READING

BOP Consulting (2011) 'Edinburgh Festivals impact study', technical report. Available at: www.bop.co.uk (accessed 3 November 2011).

Mair, J. (2011) 'Events and climate change: an Australian perspective', *International Journal of Event and Festival Management*, 2 (1): 245–53.

Ponsford, I.F. (2011) 'Actualizing environmental sustainability at Vancouver 2010 venues', *International Journal of Event and Festival Management*, 2 (2): 184–96.

Smith, A. (2009) 'Theorising the relationship between major sport events and social sustainability', *Journal of Sport & Tourism*, 14 (2–3): 109–20.

World Commission on Environment and Development (1987) *Our Common Future*. Oxford: Oxford University Press.

34 Tourism

> *The development and promotion of planned events and festivals for the purpose of enhancing the tourism attractiveness of places.*

Event tourism is described by Getz (1991) as the systematic development and marketing of events as tourism attractions. More recently, he described it as the set of interrelationships that underpin 'the marketing of events to tourists, and the development and marketing of events for tourism and economic development purposes' (2008: 406). Festival tourism, meanwhile, has been defined by O'Sullivan and Jackson as 'a phenomenon in which people from outside a festival locale visit during the festival period' (2002: 355). Today, even the most cursory analysis of any number of national tourism strategies shows how strongly festivals and events have come to feature in destination development and marketing initiatives. The rise in the number of dedicated event development and marketing agencies in cities throughout the world and the close relationship between event tourism activities and the work of destination marketing organisations is equally telling. In the academic literature, festivals and events are conceptualised as broadly positive phenomena. Very frequently, research papers open with introductory paragraphs emphasising the important roles that festivals and events play in developing destinations, attracting visitors, extending the season, generating wealth and fostering community spirit.

The relationship between events and tourism is not new. Historical research demonstrates that festivals and events have a long history of acting as tourist attractions and of effecting the reproduction of places as tourism destinations. Gold and Gold (2005: 268), for example, described how the recognition of Greenwich as the fulcrum of the earth's time zones in 1884 inspired the hosting of a year-long festival intended to boost international tourism to the city. Adams (1986) discussed how, as long ago as 1859, the Handel Centenary Festival held in London's Crystal Palace was marketed as a tourist attraction with the organisers distributing 50,000 prospectuses in the European offices of the railway companies serving the Crystal Palace. The relationship between events and tourism has, however, deepened, become more widespread, more strategic and more complex in recent decades. The phenomenon of 'event tourism' has proliferated since the late 1980s. It is one manifestation of the growing emphasis on entrepreneurialism and public-private partnerships in the increasingly neoliberal urban and regional policies of advanced capitalist economies (Ashworth and Voogd, 1990; Burbank et al., 2002; Hall, 2006). Capturing internationally mobile flows of tourist investment, capital, revenue and arrivals is a key driver of consumption-oriented societies and events are prized because they have the potential to: signal place distinctiveness in the highly competitive global marketplace; extend the visitor season; animate static attractions; and generally enhance the attractiveness and product range of any given locale. From a consumer perspective, events also offer visitors opportunities to socialise, to actively engage with the destination they are visiting, to access meaningful experiences, and to temporarily transcend the banality of everyday life.

A very sizeable literature now conceptualises events and festivals solely or predominantly as tourism entities. This literature provides analysis and commentary on the dramatic rise in interest that communities of varying natures, in towns, cities, regions and countries have exhibited in hosting events in recent decades. It is interested in investigating the contribution that events make to destinations in a variety of ways, from place marketing and branding destinations, to generating revenue and contributing to economic development, to creating visitor experiences and realising visitor motivations. From a tourism industry perspective, festivals and special events function as attractions. Attractions, of course, are vital for the tourism industry. Frequently, it is they that motivate the travel that sets up demand for key tourism services like transport, accommodation and hospitality more generally (Andersson and Getz, 2009). They also serve to generate 'new' income for a region by specifically drawing visitors from outside the area and by perhaps encouraging them to stay longer while there. Being human-made attractions, they offer tremendous potential for a place to strategically invent or re-invent itself as a destination. Furthermore, they can be used to extend the tourist season and to attract visitors at relatively quiet times of the year. In the mid-1990s, Dublin, and more recently, other Irish cities, such as Cork (since 2005), have successfully re-invented the 17 March national holiday, St Patrick's Day, into several day-long St Patrick's Festivals. This has significantly increased visitor arrivals and effectively brought forward the start of the tourist season.

Clearly, festivals and events offer attractive possibilities for branding or repositioning a destination in the increasingly competitive international marketplace (Jago et al., 2003). The case of Edinburgh and its long-standing Edinburgh International Festival is often cited as an excellent example of how events can be effectively leveraged to successfully brand a destination. Less dramatically, events of all descriptions can be used to complement, supplement and re-invigorate a destination's promotional efforts more generally. Events can also be construed as mechanisms for heightening visitor experiences, adding new points of interest and new activities, thereby sustaining visitor interest in a destination and increasing the latter's capacity to attract and hold visitors for longer periods of time (Getz, 2005). Often, events are used to animate static attractions and to promote the diverse agenda at issue. At Fota House, in Cork, for example, the Irish Heritage Trust has initiated an events programme to engage and encourage active visitor participation in understanding and interpreting the various histories of the house and demesne.

Tourism destinations have become increasingly concerned to strategically exploit the resources represented by festivals and events of all descriptions and to incorporate them into tourism development and marketing strategies. Policy thinking, both at national and international levels has encouraged this development. The UNWTO, for example, produced a Practical Guide to Tourism Destination Management (WTO, 2007) in which it discusses the tourism potential of events under a number of headings including: brand builders, generators of business growth, tactical levers and vehicles for local pride and community building. Countless national tourism agencies, in countries as diverse as Australia, Canada, Dubai and Ireland, have shown strategic intent in the development of event activity by producing a series of incentives and schemes to encourage event tourism. Many events are now highly dependent on tourism. All of those classified as 'mega' or 'hallmark' come into this category because by definition they depend on inward flows of not only attendees but also producers, performers, suppliers, sponsors, media and others. However, tourism is increasingly dependent on event activity and it is becoming ever more difficult to unravel the proliferation and multiplication of event types from the proliferation of tourist activity. The food and beverage area is a case in point. It has become increasingly important in the drive to develop cultural tourism, particularly in rural regions (Hall and Mitchell, 2001), and what is now variously described as gourmet, gastronomic or culinary tourism frequently relies on festivals and events to develop markets and raise the profile of both products and destinations. While very high profile hallmark events, such as the FIFA World Cup, tend to capture a majority of media attention and a sizeable amount of research attention, the fact that a multitude of small communities regularly host events, often with a strategic tourism intent has not gone unnoticed in the literature. The role that small-scale events, often found in rural areas, play in enhancing destination attractiveness and profile, and attracting tourist revenue is widely discussed. Goldblatt (1997: 361) suggested that small and large communities invest in festivals because they see in them the opportunity to earn 'tourism dollars'. Walo et al. (1996) similarly point out that all levels of government use them to promote tourism while regional tourism agencies use them as part of their marketing strategies (Getz, 1989).

In terms of devising strategic management approaches for event tourism, the overall goal is to ensure efficiency in terms of resource use, effectiveness and competitiveness in terms of delivering quality services to participants, attendees and stakeholders of various kinds (Soteriades and Dimou, 2011). Network analysis is becoming increasingly advocated as a useful approach (Larson, 2009a, 2009b; Mackellar, 2006).

The process and practice of event tourism involves many stakeholders, multiple interactions and different organisational structures within any given destination. Network analysis acknowledges this and provides a framework for investigating how stakeholders interrelate, and for identifying where the resource inter-dependencies are.

By and large, the tenor of the event tourism literature suggests that the event tourism relationship is a mutually beneficial one, however, the role that tourism plays in effecting cultural change in festival settings has long been of enormous interest to researchers. Greenwood's (1972) analysis of a Basque festival initiated a still ongoing debate about tourism and commoditisation. Following Marx, Greenwood argued that the Spanish Ministry of Tourism's involvement in the *Fuenterrabia* transformed the festival from an authentic, locally embedded and meaningful cultural practice into a public spectacle for outsiders. The intervention, he argued, led to a decline of local interest and a loss of meaning such that 'the ritual has become a performance for money. The meaning is gone' (Greenwood, 1972: 78). As Sofield and Li note, his commoditisation thesis was a very attractive one, and it became 'one of the most powerful indictments of the corrosive effects of tourism' (1998: 270). It also quickly became one of the most frequently cited, strengthened by its inclusion in Cohen's (1988) paper on **authenticity** and commoditisation in tourism. Greenwood's interpretation, however, has been subsequently critiqued and the usefulness of his commoditisation thesis hotly debated ever since. Originally, the core question was whether the commoditisation of festivals and events through tourism resulted in a reduction in the authenticity or meaningfulness of these cultural practices. Recently, however, Shepherd (2002: 195) has argued that commodification within the sphere of culture is a social fact, and suggests that discussion should now focus less on what has been commodified and more on how authenticity becomes constructed and decided.

As mentioned elsewhere, the development of scholarship and research in the event field is closely related to that in the tourism domain. There are multiple instances where conceptual and methodological progresses made in the latter have been transferred and applied in the former. Understanding host community perceptions of, and engagement in, festivals and events would be one example. The long established literature on motivation would be another, in that it shares similar theoretical underpinnings with research on tourist motivations.

FURTHER READING

Getz, D. (2008) 'Event tourism: definition, evolution and research', *Tourism Management*, 29: 403–28.

Hall, C.M. and Mitchell, R. (2001) 'Wine and food tourism', in N. Douglas and R. Derrett (eds), *Special Interest Tourism: Context and Cases*. Brisbane: John Wiley & Sons. pp. 307–29.

Hjalager, A.M. (2009) 'Cultural tourism innovation systems – the Roskilde festival', *Scandinavian Journal of Hospitality and Tourism*, 9 (2–3): 266–87.

Jago, L., Chalip, L., Brown, G. and Ali, S. (2003) 'Building events into destination branding: insights from experts', *Event Management*, 8 (1): 3–14.

35 Volunteering

> *Volunteering, the practice of giving one's services freely without requiring compensation, has always been widespread in the festival and event sector. Festival and event organisations everywhere, irrespective of size, type or location, tend to have a marked reliance on volunteers.*

Human capital refers to the skills, abilities and training of individuals (Coleman, 1990). In the event literature, a sizeable body of work on volunteering investigates how human capital is fostered through the hosting of festivals and events. The practice of volunteering is widespread within the sector and countless small-scale planned events of all description prosper on the strength of voluntary endeavours. Getz (1993) was among the earliest researchers to write about the valuable role that festivals and events play in the lives of local, place-based communities. As he and others began to note, festival and events do not require extensive capital investment or sizeable infrastructural development but rather prosper on the base of local enthusiasm and local voluntary energies (Turko and Kelsey, 1992; Getz, 1993; Janiskee, 1994). Yet even in the global, hallmark sports event arena, the critical role played by voluntarism is very evident. At this level, the scale of volunteerism can be staggering. The 2000 Sydney and 2004 Athens Olympic Games, for example, both relied on over 40,000 volunteers (Cuskelly et al., 2006) while according to Yan and Chen 2008, the Beijing Games in 2008 involved 100,000. Currently, the London 2012 Olympic Games are recruiting up to 70,000 volunteers, or 'Games Makers' (London 2012 Olympic Games Organising Committee, 2012). In Brazil, host to the 2016 Games, 15,000 people had already registered to be volunteers soon after the official designation was announced in October 2009 (de Jong, 2009). As Doherty (2009) discusses, the economic contribution of such extensive involvement is very considerable. She has discussed the case of the 2004 Sydney Olympic Games which used 45,000 volunteers who contributed an average of 100 hours each. Had the Games been required to pay an equivalent number of staff, it may well have amounted to AUS$45 million. A sizeable literature investigating various aspects of volunteering now exists.

An important question in the literature has been what motivates people to voluntarily involve themselves in the running of events. Green and Chalip (2004) pointed out that from an understanding of what motivates volunteers come effective recruitment and retention strategies. Bang and Ross (2005) identified seven different motivations: career orientation, love of sport, community involvement, extrinsic rewards, interpersonal contacts, expression of values and personal growth. Bang (2009) suggested that the extent to which volunteers are satisfied by their volunteering experience will influence their decision to volunteer again in the future. Furthermore, drawing on brand management research, Bang (2009) investigated the extent to which the reputation of a sporting event impacts upon volunteer commitment and presents empirical evidence to argue that an event's reputation (in this case a sports event) influences both volunteer commitment and volunteer satisfaction. A key argument made in the literature in general, is that given the size of the resource that volunteers represent in terms of labour, vital expertise, skill and knowledge (Dorsch et al., 2002), event organisations have a vested interest in actively developing volunteer commitment.

A key topic of discussion has been the value generated by events in fostering voluntary involvement. This value has been understood to be multi-dimensional. From the perspective of the event organisation and its stakeholders, the economic value of this voluntary involvement is clearly immense, but so too is its social value. This social value may become apparent in the likelihood of volunteers continuing to volunteer their services when further opportunities arise after any given event is over (Doherty, 2009) and in the opportunities that volunteering presents for people to obtain training and to upskill themselves (Smith and Fox, 2007). High levels of satisfaction with the experience of volunteering at events have been noted (Elstad, 1996). Benefits identified include an enhanced sense of community, opportunities to develop personal networks, and acknowledgement of their contribution.

Quite a lot of research on volunteers has focused on sports event. In this context, Solberg et al. investigated the 'value' of volunteers at the 1999 World Ice Hockey Championship and found that a large number of the volunteers at that event 'received so-called psychological returns from [their participation]' and that 'more than 80% would do the job over again' (2002: 26). Manzenreiter and Horne have argued that mega-sporting events can produce 'emotionally powerful and shared experiences' (2005: 30). Meanwhile, Doherty (2009) pointed out that because volunteers are often the 'face of the Games', their enthusiasm and support for the Games acts as a symbol for the positive values that they espouse.

Generally speaking, much of the literature has focused on the management of volunteers in operational contexts. The management of volunteers in turn, has tended to focus on recruiting, allocating, training, planning work-flow and handling volunteers such that they contribute effectively to a successful event (Gladden et al., 2005). Clearly, while volunteers can be the life force of a festival or event, a reliance on voluntarism is not unproblematic. Hede and Rentschler (2008) discuss a volunteer mentoring scheme, devised by two regional arts organisations in Australia for festival volunteer-managers. It was found to offer a form of professional development difficult to access in regional locations. In general, a good deal of practitioners' attention focuses on recruiting volunteers. Clearly this is important, but the literature seems agreed on the simultaneous need to put greater effort into managing volunteers. Ensuring that volunteers are satisfied with their involvement and that they are gaining some rewards for their efforts is critical to maintaining volunteer support. Martinez and McMullin (2004), for example, found that when appreciation is shown to volunteers (thank you notes, volunteer parties), satisfaction levels are higher.

More recently, Doherty (2009) has asked questions about volunteering and future legacy. Given the increasingly important role played by voluntarism in contemporary society, she suggested that it is important to examine the role that events play in introducing people to volunteering, and the manner in which their experiences may translate into future volunteering activity either at another event or in a more routine setting. Previously, Downward and Ralson (2006) undertook a survey of volunteers 1 year after they had been involved in the 2002 Commonwealth Games. They found that the personal development volunteers' experienced was a consistent predictor of their intention to volunteer both in general, and for another event. Doherty (2009) used social exchange theory to investigate which aspects of volunteers' experiences with the 2001 Canada Games were most likely to impact on their future volunteering decisions. They found that virtually all participants indicated an interest in volunteering for another event. Among volunteers involved in planning the event, the opportunity to make a difference in the community was a significant determinant of future intent to volunteer, while the experience of being over-burdened and inconvenienced by the experience had the opposite effect. Meanwhile, for volunteers involved on-site, personal interactions, making a difference to one's community and developing one's skills while doing something different meant that they were positively inclined to volunteer for another event in the future.

In recent times, the challenge of building legacies from event volunteering has come to be viewed more strategically by key facilitating stakeholders. In Canada, a not-for-profit organisation called 2010 Legacies Now (2012) was created in 2000 'to build support for Vancouver's bid for the 2010 Olympic and Paralympic Winter Games and to ensure a stronger sport system for British Columbia'. In 2011, the organisation continues to work with over 4000 organisations and groups with the continued aim of strengthening not only voluntarism, but also sport and recreation, healthy living, literacy and accessibility. In July 2010, in similar vein, New Zealand Major Events, a unit within the New Zealand government's Ministry of Economic Development, established VolunteerNet, a website that connects people looking for volunteering opportunities with event organisers looking for volunteers. The 2011 Rugby World Cup is the largest sporting event ever hosted in New Zealand and VolunteerNet is a legacy initiative that 'aims to leverage off the interest in volunteering for (the 2011 event) … to build a network of experienced and enthusiastic volunteers'. Its aims are to: enhance the volunteer recruitment and management process for event organisers; increase the network of skilled volunteers available to the events sector; make event-related volunteering opportunities more accessible to all New Zealanders; proactively connect volunteers with opportunities that match their skills and experience; help promote volunteering in New Zealand in general (VolunteerNet, 2011)

Policy initiatives such as these reflect a real shift in thinking about the contribution that events can make to developing not only economic but also social and human capital. They reflect a more holistic approach to the strategic use of events and a move to thinking about the processes that underpin the kinds of value and beneficial impacts that events can generate. They capture the idea that if intelligently resourced and supported, events can have a strong developmental role, encouraging change in particular directions, as envisaged in long-term planning strategies.

FURTHER READING

Bang, H. (2009) 'The direct and indirect influences of sporting event organization's reputation on volunteer commitment', *Event Management*, 13: 139–52.

Cuskelly, G., Hoye, R. and Auld, C. (2006) *Working with Volunteers in Sport*. London: Routledge.

Doherty, A. (2009) 'The volunteer legacy of a major sport event', *Journal of Policy Research in Tourism Leisure and Events*, 1 (3): 185–207.

Downward, P. and Ralston, R. (2006) 'The sports development potential of sport event volunteering: insights from the XVII Manchester Commonwealth Games', *European Sport Management Quarterly*, 6: 333–51.

conclusion

This book has tried to bring together a number of the concepts that might reasonably be considered as central to the study of festival and event management. Part of the challenge was to identify how knowledge has been developing over time and to capture and synthesise, in an accessible way, key directions of change. Undoubtedly there are omissions both in this text and in the literature itself. In this conclusion, the intention is to point to some of the omissions noted in the literature and by extension, to point to areas where further research would prove fruitful. The level of research being done in the festival and event field is now extensive, very substantial in terms of size and breadth, and it shows no signs of abating in terms of output. The breadth of knowledge being generated is extending all the time and in ways that are closely and timely attuned to developments in the sector.

The effect of recession on the health of the sector is an example of a topic that has begun to excite interest recently. Contrary to what might have been expected, the music festival sector in the UK has continued to do well in recession (Warman, 2010). One stimulating factor has been the rise of the 'staycation' with an increase in the number of people incorporating a festival into their annual holiday. Showing admirable adaptability to changing economic circumstances, many festivals have responded by providing increasingly diverse and sophisticated accommodation (usually camping) options as part of their product offering. However, more generally, as was to be expected, the downturn in the global economy, that began in 2007, has taken its toll on the event sector. Webber et al. (2010) highlighted the negative impact that recession has on the discretionary spending upon which festivals and events depend for survival. Lee and Goldblatt (2012) surveyed members of the International Festival and Events Association to investigate the impact of the recession on the sector currently and into the future. They found that organisations experienced a decline in their profit margins because of decreased sponsorship, the general effect of the recession on all revenue sources and an increase in product/service costs. In terms of moving forward post-recession, securing more sponsorships and diversifying various revenue sources were the strategies that event organisations were planning to use to overcome the challenges posed by the challenging economic environment. As Devine and Devine (2012) pointed out, the immediate post-recession period brings new sets of challenges as governments introduce austerity measures and reduce public spending on sectors including culture and sports. Devine et al. (2012) examined the impact of recession and austerity measures on an event in Northern Ireland, arguing that straightened economic times require event organisations to think 'outside the box' to address challenges and to work closely with their stakeholders to generate innovative ideas and processes to generate new sources of financing. For the growing number of festivals and events funded by public and local authorities, budget over-runs will meet growing intolerance, as the need for greater accountability and 'value' in terms of delivery becomes paramount. In this context, some festivals are ceasing to operate, and will continue to cease operating, especially when consumer spending is tempered by economic uncertainties.

To date, the generation of both theoretical and applied understandings of festival and event activities has relied heavily on empirical investigations in the Western world. Andersson and Getz (2009) reminded us that almost all extant literature pertains to festival management in a small number of Western developed nations. The reality of the sports event industry now is that this seems set to change: the world's emergent economies are increasingly viewing the sector through strategic lens. The academic literature needs to keep pace by investigating environments that clearly embody significant ethnic, cultural, religious, linguistic as well as substantial economic differences in emerging and non-Western nations, as well as in the West. The international spotlight that will shift to South America and to Brazil, in particular, as it hosts two enormous sporting events – the FIFA World Cup (2014) and the Olympic Games (2016) in the near future, will undoubtedly prompt a great deal of event-related research in emerging economy contexts.

When international events are at issue, then the interest in managing risk will be ever-present. This will undoubtedly continue into the future so long as political and economic uncertainties continue to prevail. As the cost of staging events continues to rise, and as the associated economic risks increase in tandem, it seems certain that research into forecasting, identifying and managing risk will continue to grow to address current gaps in knowledge. This includes the need for more research into the prediction and monitoring of the costs associated with hosting events. According to Flyvbjerg and Stewart (2012) indications are that the London Olympics will be the most expensive to date with a projected cost of £8.4 billion in real terms, a figure that is 101% over budget. For cities preparing bids in the future, Flyvbjerg and Stewart (2012) recommended that 'reference class forecasting', where costings for previous Games form the basis for future Games budgets, be used. Transferring knowledge from the IOC (International Olympic Committee) and from one host city to the next is critical in assisting organising committees, which, by definition, are embarking on a mega-project for the very first time.

Significant shifts in aspects of event marketing constitute another dynamic that will in all likelihood attract growing research attention in the future. Motivated by the need to understand their customer base, companies are displaying tendencies to move from simply sponsoring events to becoming involved in organising them themselves. This is a development with ramifications that remain to be uncovered: what effects will it have on event and festival organisations' funding structures? How will the unfettered, relaxed 'get away from it all' ambiance traditionally associated with festivals negotiate the commercial ethos that can only strengthen with such a shift? The extraordinary rise of social media and what this means for event activities is another topic that will attract increasing research interest in coming years.

At several points throughout the text, reference was made to the close relationship evident between the evolution of tourism research and enquiries into festivals and events. Often, shortcomings in the former are also evidenced in the latter and when development occurs in the former, its effects soon spill over. At present, issues pertaining to disability and wider questions of access are well discussed within the leisure sphere and also seem to be rising up the research agenda within tourism studies. In the latter, an increase in publications and even special journal issues (for example, *Current Issues in Tourism*, 2011) on the topic can be noted. Accordingly, the notion that societal groups experience differential access to both leisure and holidaying practices is becoming more pronounced, and there is a growing interest in investigating the type of factors that constrain participation and limit consumer experiences. In contrast, the topic of disability and access remains very under-researched in the festival and event field. This is surprising, given the growth in events organised and supported by public authorities, and the fact that these very often have social and cultural agendas pertaining to inclusion and participation. Darcy and Harris (2003) acknowledge this deficit in the literature and seek to redress it from an Australian perspective through a review of relevant legislation, event disability planning and a best practice case study.

These and many, many other issues will continue to preoccupy the interest of a growing number of researchers as they seek to monitor, problematise and critically comment on the meanings, nature and value of the event sector. As the vast literature on festivals and events documents, this is a dynamic sector that continues to grow and develop throughout the world. As it does, it will continue to: function as a complicated set of social practices replete with meaning for communities and individuals the world over; create valuable experiences for participants, spectators and other stakeholders alike; generate valuable outcomes for economies and societies from local through to international domains and; offer abundant opportunity to continuously inspire and captivate the human imagination.

references

Andersson, T.D., Armbrecht, J. and Lundberg, E. (2008) 'Impact of mega-events on the economy', *Asian Business & Management*, 7: 163–79.

Aching, G. (2010) 'Carnival time versus modern social life: a false distinction', *Social Identities*, 16 (4): 415–25.

Adams, R. (1986) *A Book of British Music Festivals*. London: Robert Royce.

Aldskogius, H. (1993) 'Festivals and meets: the place of music in 'summer Sweden'', *Geografiska Annaler Series B*, 75: 55–72.

Allen, J., O'Toole, W., McDonnell, I. and Harris, R. (1999) *Festivals and Special Event Management*. Milton, Queensland: John Wiley & Sons Australia.

Allen, J., O'Toole, W., McDonnell, I. and Harris, R. (2002) *Festival and Special Event Management*, 4th edn. London: Wiley.

Allen, J., O'Toole, W., Harris, R. and McDonnell, I. (2011) *Festivals & Special Event Management*, 5th edn. Milton, Queensland: John Wiley & Sons Australia.

Anderson, E.W. and Sullivan, M.W. (1993) 'The antecedents and consequences of customer satisfaction for firms', *Marketing Science*, 12 (2): 125–43.

Andersson, T. and Getz, D. (2009) 'Tourism as a mixed industry: differences between private, public and not-for-profit festivals', *Tourism Management*, 30: 847–56.

Anwar, S. and Sohail, M. (2004) 'Festival tourism in the United Arab Emirates: first-time versus repeat visitor perceptions', *Journal of Vacation Marketing*, 10 (2): 161–70.

Ap, J. (1992) 'Residents' perceptions on tourism impacts', *Annals of Tourism Research*, 19 (4): 665–90.

Arcodia, C. and McKinnon, S. (2004) 'Public liability insurance: its impact on Australian rural festivals', *Journal of Convention & Event Tourism*, 6 (3): 101–10.

Arcodia, C. and Whitford, M. (2006) 'Festival attendance and the development of social capital', *Journal of Convention and Event Tourism*, 8 (2): 1–18.

Arnold, N. (2000) 'Festival tourism: recognizing the challenges; linking multiple pathways between global villages of the new century', in B. Faulkner, G. Moscardo and E. Laws (eds), *Tourism in the 21st Century. Reflections on Experience*. New York: Continuum.

Ashworth, G.J. and Voogd, H. (1990) *Selling the City: Marketing Approaches in Public Sector Planning*. London: Belhaven Press.

Atkinson, M. and Young, K. (2002) 'Terror games: media treatment of security issues at the 2002 winter Olympic Games', *Olympika: The International Journal of Olympic Studies*, 11: 53–78.

Australian Government (2012) About Australia. Available at: http://australia.gov.au/about-australia/australian-story/festivals-in-australia (accessed 30 July 2012).

Australian Local Government Association (2011) Available at: http://www.alga.asn.au/policy/regdev/ (accessed 11 February 2011).

Autissier, A.M. (2009) *The Europe of Festivals: from Zagreb to Edinburgh. Intersecting Viewpoints*. Toulouse: Culture Europe International.

Axelsen, M. and Swan, T. (2010) 'Designing festival experiences to influence visitor perceptions: the case of a wine and food festival', *Journal of Travel Research*, 49 (4): 436–50.

Azara, I. and Crouch, D. (2006) 'La cavalcata sarda: performing identities in a contemporary Sardinian festival', in D. Picard and M. Robinson, (eds), *Festivals, Tourism and Social Change*. Clevedon: Channel View Publications. pp. 32–45.

Bakhtin, M. (1968) *Rabelais and his World*, trans. H. Iswolsky. Cambridge, MA: MIT Press.

Bakhtin, M. (1978) *The Question of Dostoyevsky's Poetics*. Tel-Aviv: Hakibbutz Haarzi (in Hebrew).

Bailey, B.A. and Davidson, J.W. (2005) 'Effects of group singing and performance for marginalized and middle-class singers', *Psychology of Music*, 33 (3): 269–303.

Bailey, C., Miles, S. and Stark, P. (2004) 'Culture-led urban regeneration and the revitalisation of identities in Newcastle, Gateshead and the North East of England', *International Journal of Cultural Policy*, 10 (1): 4–65.

Baker, D.A. and Crompton, J. J. (2000) 'Quality, satisfaction and behavioural intentions', *Annals of Tourism Research*, 27 (3): 785–804.

Baloglu, S. and Love, C. (2005) 'Association meeting planners' perceptions and intentions for five major US convention cities: the structured and unstructured images', *Tourism Management*, 26 (5): 743–52.

Balsas, C.J.L. (2004) 'City centre regeneration in the context of the 2001 European capital of culture in Porto, Portugal', *Local Economy*, 19 (4): 396–410.

Bang, H. (2009) 'The direct and indirect influences of sporting event organization's reputation on volunteer commitment', *Event Management*, 13: 139–52.

Bang, H. (2010) 'Motivation to volunteer for special sporting events: differences between first-time and veteran volunteers', *Event Management*, 13 (Supplement 1, International Conference on Festivals and Events Research): S26–S28.

Bang, H. and Ross, S. (2005) 'Measuring volunteer motivation at the Twin Cities Marathon', paper presented at the Conference of the North American Society for Sport Management, Regina, Saskatchewan, Canada.

Baptista Alves, H.M., Campón Cerro, A.M. and Ferreira Martins, A.V. (2010) 'Impacts of small tourism events on rural places', *Journal of Place Management and Development*, 3 (1): 22–37.

Barr, P. and Dave, D. (1996) 'Expanding regional economies through community festivals: a study in South Carolina, United States', *International Journal of Management*, 13 (3): 323–31.

BBC (2011) 'News at Ten', 8 August 2011.

Beaulieu, A.F. and Love, C. (2005) 'Characteristics of a meeting planner', *Journal of Convention & Event Tourism*, 6 (4): 95–124.

Beavens, Z. and Laws, C. (2004) Principles and applications in ticketing and reservations management, in I. Yeoman, M. Robertson, J. Ali-Knight, S. Drummond and U. McMahon-Beattie (eds.), *Festival and Events Management*. Oxford: Elservier Butterworth-Heinemann. pp. 183–201.

Beavens, Z. and Laws, C. (2008) "Never let me down again': loyal customer attitudes towards ticket distribution channels for live music events: a netnographic exploration of the US leg of the Depeche Mode 2005–2996 world tour', in M. Robertson and E. Frew (eds), *Events and Festivals*. Abingdon: Routledge. pp. 19–41.

Benedict, B. (1983) *The Anthropology of World's Fairs: San Francisco's Panama Pacific International Exposition of 1915*. Berkeley, CA: Lowie Museum of Anthropology.

Benneworth, P. and Dauncey, H. (2010) 'International urban festivals as a catalyst for governance capacity building', *Environment and Planning C: Government and Policy*, 28 (6): 1083–100.

Bengry Howell (2010) 'How commerce is tainting the festival experience'. Available at: http://www.bps.org.uk/news/how-commerce-tainting-festival-experience (accessed 16 March 2012).

Bergmann, B. (1999) 'Introduction: the art of ancient spectacle', in B. Bergman and C. Kondoleon (eds), *The Art of Ancient Spectacle*. Washington D.C.: National Gallery of Art. pp. 9–35.

Berridge, G. (2006) *Event Design and Experience*. Oxford: Butterworth-Heinemann.

Black, D. (2007) 'The symbolic politics of sport mega-events: 2010, in comparative perspective', *Politikon*, 34 (3): 261–76.

Blau, J. (1996) 'The toggle switch of institutions: religion and art in the US in the nineteenth and early twentieth centuries', *Social Forces*, 74: 1159–77.

Blau, P.M. (1975) *Approaches to the Study of Social Structure*. New York: Free Press.

Boissevain, J. (ed.) (1992) *Revitalizing European Rituals*. London: Routledge.

Bojanic, D.C. and Warnick, R.B. (2012) 'The role of purchase decision involvement in a special event', *Journal of Travel Research*, 51 (3): 357–66.

Bolton, R.N. and Drew, J.H. (1991) 'A longitudinal analysis of the impact of service changes on customer attitudes', *Journal of Marketing Research*, 55 (1): 1–9.

Boo, S. and Busser, J.A. (2006) 'Impact analysis of a tourism festival on tourists destination images', *Event management*, 9 (4): 223–37.

Boo, S. and Gu, H. (2010) 'Risk perception of mega-events', *Journal of Sport & Tourism*, 15 (2): 139—61.

Boo, H., Ghiselli, R. and Almanza, B. (2000) 'Consumer perceptions and concerns about the healthfulness and safety of food served at fairs and festivals', *Event Management*, 6 (2): 85–92.

BOP Consulting (2011) 'Edinburgh Festivals impact study', technical report. Available at: http://www.bop.co.uk. Accessed 18/11/11.

Bourdieu, P. (1980) 'Le capital social, note provisoire', *Actes de la Recherche Science Sociales*, 31: 2–3.

Bourdieu, P. (1986) *Distinction*. London: Routledge.

Bourdieu, P. (2002) 'The forms of capital', in N.W. Biggart (ed.), *Readings in Economic Sociology*. Malen, MA: Blackwell. pp. 280–91.

Bowdin, G., Allen, J., O'Toole, W., Harris, R. and McDonnell, I. (2006) *Events Management*, 2nd edn. Oxford: Butterworth-Heinemann.

Bowen, H.E. and Daniels, M. (2005) 'Does the music matter? Motivations for attending a music festival', *Event Management*, 9 (3): 155–64.

Boyko, C.T. (2008) 'Are you being served? The impacts of a tourist hallmark event on the place meanings of residents', *Event Management*, 11 (4): 161–77.

Boyle, M. (1997) 'Civic boosterism in the politics of local economic development', *Environment and Planning A*, 29 (11): 1975–97.

Boyle, M. and Hughes, G. (1994) 'The politics of urban entrepreneurialism in Glasgow', *Geoforum*, 25: 453–70.

Brennan-Horley, C., Connell, J. and Gibson, C. (2007) 'The Parkes Elvis revival festival: economic development and contested place identities in rural Australia', *Geographical Research*, 45 (1): 71–84.

Brewster, M., Connell, J. and Page, S.J. (2009) 'The Scottish Highland Games: evolution, development and role as a community event', *Current Issues in Tourism*, 12 (3): 271–93.

Britton, S. (1991) 'Tourism, capital and place: towards a critical geography of tourism', *Environment & Planning: Society and Space*, 9: 451–78.

Brown, K. (2011) 'Beyond rural idylls: imperfect lesbian utopias at Michigan Womyn's Music Festival', *Journal of Rural Studies*, 27 (1): 13–23.

Brown, G., Chalip, L., Jago, L. and Mules, T. (2004) 'Developing brand Australia: examining the role of events', in N. Morgan, A. Pritchard and R. Pride (eds), *Destination Branding: Creating the Unique Selling Proposition*. Oxford: Elsevier Butterworth-Heinemann. pp. 279–305.

Brown, J. (2009) 'IOC swayed by Rio's samba style as Windy City is blown away', *Independent*, 03 October 2009. Available at: http://www.independent.co.uk/sport/olympics/ioc-swayed-by-rios-samba-style-as-windy-city-is-blown-away-1797001.html (accessed 30 July 2012).

Bruner, E.M. (1994) 'Abraham Lincoln as authentic reproduction: a critique of post-modernism', *American Anthropologist*, 96 (2): 397–415.

Burbank, M.J., Andranovich, G. and Heying, C.H. (2002) 'Mega-events, urban development and public policy', *Review of Policy Research*, 19 (3): 179–202.

Burland, K. and Pitts, S.E. (2010) 'Understanding jazz audiences: listening and learning at the Edinburgh jazz and blues festival', *Journal of New Music Research*, Special Issue: Understanding Audience Experience, 39 (2): 125–34.

Burns, J.P.A. and Mules, T.L. (1989) 'An economic evaluation of the Adelaide Grand Prix', in G. Syme, B. Shaw, M. Fenton and W. Mueller (eds), *The Planning and Evaluation of Hallmark Events*. Aldershot: Gower. pp. 172–85.

Burns, J., Hatch, J. and Mules, T. (eds) (1989) *The Adelaide Grand Prix: The Impact of a Special Event*. Adelaide: The Centre for South Australian Economic Studies.

Burns, J.P.A. and Mules, T.L. (1986) 'A framework for the analysis of major special events', in J.P.A. Burns, J.H. Hatch and T.L. Mules (eds), *The Adelaide Grand Prix: The Impact of a Special Event*. Adelaide: The Centre for South Australian Economic Studies. pp. 5–38.

Burr, A. (2006) 'The 'freedom of the slaves to walk the streets'. Celebration. Spontaneity and revelry versus logistics at the Notting Hill carnival', in D. Picard and M. Robinson (eds), *Festivals, Tourism and Social Change*. Clevedon: Channel View Publications. pp. 84–98.

Bush, J. (2000) 'The granite state consumer, strengthening the sense of community'. University of New Hampshire. Available at: http://www.ceinfo.unh.edu (accessed 12 September 2011).

Camden Council (2012) 'Legacy projects'. Available at: http://www.camden.gov.uk/ccm/navigation/leisure/camden-in-2012/legacy-projects/ (accessed 01 June 2012).

Carlsen, J., Getz, D. and Soutar, G. (2000) 'Event evaluation research', *Event Management*, 6: 247–57.

Carlsen, J., Andersson, T.D., Ali-Knight, J., Jaeger, K. and Taylor, R. (2010) 'Festival management innovation and failure', *International Journal of Event and Festival Management*, 1 (2): 120–31.

Carlsen, J. and Andersson, T.D. (2011) 'Strategic SWOT analysis of public, private and not-for-profit festival organisations', *International Journal of Event and Festival Management*, 2 (1): 83–97.

Carlsen, J., Ali-Knight, J. and Robertson, M. (2007) 'Access: a research agenda for Edinburgh festivals', *Event Management*, 11(1/2): 3–11.

Carlson, A.B. (2010) 'Calabar carnival. A Trinidadian tradition returns to Africa', *African Arts*, Winter: 42–59.

Carrell, S. (2009) 'Edinburgh festival: marketing campaign unites city's celebrations', *Guardian*, 24 March 2009. Available at: http://www.guardian.com.uk/culture/2009/mar/24/edinburgh-festival-marketing-campaign (accessed 20 March 2012).

Carter, H. (2010) 'Liverpool profited from year as capital of culture', *Guardian*, 11 March 2010. Available at: http://www.guardian.co.uk/travel/2010/mar/11/liverpool-profited-from-being-culture-capital (accessed 01 August 2012).

Caust, J. (2003) 'Putting the "art" back into "arts policy making": how arts policy has been captured by the economics and the marketers', *International Journal of Cultural Policy*, 9 (1): 51–63.

Cegielski, M. and Mules T. (2002) 'Aspects of residents' perceptions of the GMC 400 – Canberra's V8 supercar race', *Current Issues in Tourism*, 5 (1): 54–70.

Çela, A., Knowles-Lankford, J. and Lankford, S. (2007) 'Local food festivals in Northeast Iowa communities: a visitor and economic impact study', *Managing Leisure*, 12 (2–3): 171–86.

Chacko, H. and Schaffer, J. (1993) 'The evolution of a festival: Creole Christmas in New Orleans', *Tourism Management*, 14 (4): 475–82.

Chalip, L. (2004) 'Beyond impact: a general model for sport event leverage', in B.W Ritchie and D. Adair (eds), *Sport Tourism: Interrelationships, Impacts and Issues*. Clevedon: Channel View Publications. pp. 226–52.

Chalip, L. (2006) 'The buzz of big events. Is it worth bottling?'. Available at: http://www.deakin.edu.au/buslaw/management-marketing/aem/fairfax-fellows/docs/chalip-2006.pdf (accessed 17 May 2012).

Chang, J. (2006) 'Segmenting tourists to aboriginal cultural festivals: an example in the Rukai tribal area, Taiwan', *Tourism Management*, 27 (6): 1224–34.

Chaudhuri, A. (2006) *Emotion and Reason in Consumer Behaviour*. Oxford: Butterworth-Heinemann.

Chwe, M.S.Y. (1998) 'Culture, circles and commercials. Publicity, common knowledge and social coordination', *Rationality and Society*, 10: 47–75.

Cogliandro, G. (2001) *European Cities of Culture for the year 2000: A Wealth Of Urban Cultures For Celebrating The Turn Of The Century*. Strasbourg: Association of the European Cities of Culture of the year 2000, AECC/AVEC.

Cohen, A. (1986) 'Of symbols and boundaries, or does Eartie's greatcoat hold the key?', in A. Cohen (ed.), *Symbolising Boundaries: Identity and Diversity in British Cultures*. Manchester: Manchester University Press. pp. 1–19.

Cohen, E. (1988) 'Authenticity and commoditization in tourism', *Annals of Tourism Research*, 15 (3): 371–86.

Coleman, J.S. (1988) 'Social capital in the creation of human capital', *American Journal of Sociology*, 94: 95–120.

references

Coleman, J.S. (1990) *Foundations of Social Theory*. Cambridge: Cambridge University Press.

Collins, A. and Flynn, A. (2007) Assessing the environmental consequences of major sporting events: the 2003/04 FA Cup Final', *Urban Studies*, 44 (3): 457–76.

Connell, J. and Page, S.J. (2005) 'Evaluating the economic and spatial effects of an event: the case of the world medical and health games', *Tourism Geographies*, 7 (1): 63–85.

Convention Industry Council (n.d.) Available at: http://www.conventionindustry.org/glossary/main.asp (accessed 18 February 2011).

Cornelissena, S. (2008) 'Scripting the nation: sport, mega-events, foreign policy and state-building in post-apartheid South Africa', *Sport in Society*, 11 (4): 481–93.

Costa, X. (2001) 'Festivity: tradition and modern forms of sociability', *Social Compass*, 48 (4): 541–8.

Cote, T.R., Convery, H., Robinson, D., Ries, A., Barrett, T., Frank, L., Furlong, W., Horan, J. and Dwyer, D. (1995) 'Typhoid fever in the park: epidemiology of an outbreak at a cultural interface', *Journal of Community Health*, 29 (6): 789–806.

Cox, K. (1993) 'The local and the global in the new urban politics', *Environment and Planning D: Society and Space*, 11: 433–48.

Cox, E. (1995) *A Truly Civil Society. The 1995 Boyer Lectures*. Sydney: ABC.

Crespi-Vallbona, M.A. and Richards, G. (2007) 'The meaning of cultural festivals. Stakeholder perspectives in Catalunya', *International Journal of Cultural Policy*, 13 (1): 103–22.

Crompton, J.L. (1999) *Measuring the Economic Impact of Visitors to Sports Tournaments and Special Events*. Ashburn, VA: National Recreation and Park Association.

Crompton, J.L. and McKay, S.L. (1994) 'Measuring the economic impacts of festivals and events. Some myths, misapplications and ethical dilemmas', *Festival Management & Event Tourism*, 2 (1): 33–43.

Crompton, J.L. and McKay, S.L. (1997) 'Motives of visitors attending festival events', *Annals of Tourism Research*, 24 (2): 425–39.

Crompton, T. and Lamb, C. (1986) *Marketing Government and Social Services*. New York: John Wiley & Sons.

Curtis, R.A. (2010) 'Australia's capital of jazz? The (re)creation of place, music and community at the Wangaratta Jazz Festival', *Australian Geographer*, 41 (1): 101–116.

Cuskelly, G., Hoye, R. and Auld, C. (2006) *Working with Volunteers in Sport*. London: Routledge.

Daniels, M.J. (2007) 'Central place theory and sport tourism impacts', *Annals of Tourism Research*, 32 (20): 332–47.

Daniels, M.J. and Norman, W. C. (2003) 'Estimating the economic impacts of seven regular sport tourism events', *Journal of Sports Tourism*, 8 (4): 214–22.

Dansero, E. and Puttilli, M. (2010) 'Mega-event tourism legacies: the case of the Torino 2006 Winter Olympic Games – a territorialisation approach', *Leisure Studies*, 29 (3): 321–41.

Darcy, S. and Harris, R. (2006) 'Inclusive and accessible special event planning: an Australian perspective', *Event Management*, 8: 39–47.

key concepts in
event management

Davidson, R. (2011) 'Web 2.0 as a marketing tool for conference centres', *International Journal of Event and Festival Management*, 2 (2): 117–38.

Day, R. and Day, J. (1977) 'A review of the current state of negotiated order theory: an appreciation and a critique', *Sociological Quarterly*, 18 (1): 126–42.

DCMS (2010) *Plans for the Legacy from the 2012 Olympic and Paralympic Games*. London: DCMS.

De Bres, K. and Davis, J. (2001) 'Celebrating group and place identity: a case study of a new regional festival', *Tourism Geographies*, 3 (3): 326–37.

De Groote, P. (2005) 'Economic and tourism aspects of the Olympic Games', *Tourism Review*, 60 (3): 20–8.

Debord, G. (1994) *The Society of the Spectacle*. New York: Zone.

Decco, C. and Baloglu, S. (2002) 'Non-host community resident reactions to the 2002 Winter Olympics: the spillover impacts', *Journal of Travel Research*, 41 (1): 46–56.

Deery, M. and Jago, L. (2010) 'Social impacts of events and the role of anti-social behaviour', *International Journal of Event and Festival Management*, 1 (1): 8–28.

Deffner, A.M. and Labrianidis, L. (2005) 'Planning culture and time in a mega-event: Thessaloniki as the European City of Culture in 1997', *International Planning Studies*, 10 (3–4): 241–64.

De Jong, J. (2009) 'Chasing the Olympic dream'. Available at: http://www.majoreventsint. com/pub/news.php?mscID=779 (accessed 5 August 2012).

Delamere, T.A. (2001) 'Development of a scale to measure resident attitudes toward the social impacts of community festivals, part ii: verification of the scale', *Event Management*, 7: 25–38.

Delamere, T.A., Wankel, L.M. and Hinch, T.D. (2001) 'Development of a scale to measure resident attitudes toward the social impacts of community festivals, part 1: item generation and purification of the measure', *Event Management*, 7 (1): 11–24.

Department for Media, Culture and Sport (2001) 'Building on PAT 10: progress report on social inclusion'. Available at: http://www.sportdevelopment.org.uk/index. php?option=com_contentsandview=articleandid=67:report-of-the-policy-action-team-10-the-contribution-of-sport-and-the-artsandcatid=48:policyanditemid=65 (accessed 4 July 2012).

Department for Media, Culture and Sport (2010) 'What we do: arts and communities'. Available at: http://www.culture.gov.uk/what_we_do/arts/3206.aspx (accessed 17 May 2011).

Derrett, R. (2003) 'Making sense of how festivals demonstrate a community's sense of place', *Event Management*, 8: 49–58.

Devine, A. and Devine, F. (2012) 'The challenge and opportunities for an event organiser during an economic recession', *International Journal of Event and Festival Management*, 3 (2): 122–36.

Di Giovine, M.A. (2009) 'Revitalization and counter-revitalization: tourism, heritage and the lantern festival as catalysts for regeneration in Hôi An, Viêt Nam', *Journal of Policy Research in Tourism, Leisure and Events*, 1 (3): 208–30.

Dimmock, K. and Tiyce, M. (2001) 'Festivals and events: celebrating special interest tourism', in N. Douglas and R. Derrett (eds), *Special Interest Tourism*. Brisbane: John Wiley & Sons. pp. 355–83.

DiPietro, R.B., Breiter, D., Rompf, P. and Godlewska, M. (2008) 'An exploratory study of differences among meeting and exhibition planners in their destination selection criteria', *Journal of Convention & Event Tourism*, 9 (4): 258–76.

Doherty, A. (2009) 'The volunteer legacy of a major sport event', *Journal of Policy Research in Tourism Leisure and Events*, 1 (3): 185–207.

Donaldson, L. (1996) 'The normal science of structural contingency theory', in S. Clegg, C. Hardy and W. Nord (eds), *Handbook of Organizational Studies*. London: Sage. pp. 57–77.

Dorsch, K.D., Riemer, H.A., Sluth, V., Paskevich, D.M. and Chelladurai, P. (2002) *What Affects a Volunteer's Commitment?* Toronto: Canadian Centre for Philanthrophy.

Douglas, N., Douglas, N. and Derrett, R. (2001) *Special Interest Tourism*. Milton, Australia: John Wiley & Sons Australia.

Downward, P. and Ralston, R. (2006) 'The sports development potential of sport event volunteering: insights from the XVII Manchester commonwealth games', *European Sport Management Quarterly*, 6: 333–51.

Dredge, D. and Jenkins, K. (2007) *Tourism Policy and Planning*. Brisbane: John Wiley.

Drengner, J., Gaus, H. and Jahn, S. (2008) 'Does flow influence the brand image in event marketing?', *Journal of Advertising Research*, 48 (1): 138–47.

Duncan, T. (2002) *IMC: Using Advertising and Promotion to Build Brands*. Boston, MA: McGraw-Hill.

Dunstan, G. (1994) *Becoming Coastwise, the Path of Festivals and Cultural Tourism. Landscape and Lifestyle Choices for the Northern Rivers of NSW*. Lismore: Southern Cross University.

Durkheim, E. (1912) *The Elementary Forms of Religious Life*. New York: Oxford University Press.

Duvignaud, J. (1976) 'Festivals: a sociological approach', *Cultures*, 1: 13–25.

Duyves, M. (1995) 'Framing preferences, framing differences: inventing Amsterdam as gay capital', in R. Parker and J. Gagnon (eds), *Conceiving Sexuality: Approaches to Sex Research in a Post-Modern World*. London: Routledge. pp. 51–66.

Dwyer, L., Forsyth, P. and Spurr, R. (2005) 'Estimating the impacts of special events on an economy', *Journal of Travel Research*, 43: 351–9.

Dwyer, L., Mellor, R., Misillis, N. and Mules, T. (2000) 'Forecasting the economic impact of events and conventions', *Event Management*, 6 (3): 191–204.

Dwyer, L., Forsyth, P., Madden, J. and Spurr, R. (2000) 'Economic impacts of inbound tourism under different assumptions regarding the macroeconomy', *Current Issues in Tourism*, 3 (4): 325–63.

Earl, C., Parker, E., Tatrai, A. and Capra, M. (2004) 'Influences on crowd behaviour at outdoor music festivals', *Environmental Health*, 4 (2): 55–62.

Earl, C., Parker, E. and Capra, M. (2005) 'The management of crowds and other risks at outdoor music festivals: an international study', *Environmental Health*, 5 (1): 37–49.

Ebers, M. (1997) *The Formation of Inter-Organisational Networks*. Oxford: Oxford University Press.

Eckstein, R. and Delaney, K. (2002) 'New sports stadiums, community self-esteem, and community collective conscience', *Journal of Sport and Social Issues*, 26: 236–49.

Edinburgh Festivals (2011) Available at: http://www.eif.co.uk/visiting-edinburgh/edinburghs-festivals/edinburghs-festivals (accessed 5 October 2011).

Edinburgh Festivals (2012) 'Environmental policy'. Available at: http://www.edbookfest.co.uk/about-us/going-green/environmental-policy (accessed 5 October 2011).

Eisinger, P. (2000) 'The politics of bread and circuses. Building the city for the visitor class', *Urban Affairs Review*, 35 (3): 316–33.

Ekman, A.K. (1999) 'The revival of cultural celebrations in regional Sweden: aspects of tradition and transition', *Sociologia Ruralis*, 39 (3): 280–93.

Elstad, B. (1996) 'Volunteer perceptions of learning and satisfaction in a mega-event: the case study of the XVII olympic winter games in Lillehammer', *Festival Management and Event Tourism*, 4: 75–83.

European Major Exhibition Centres Association (EMECA) (2012) 'About us'. Available at: http://www.emeca.eu (accessed 17 February 2012).

Emery, P.R. (2002) 'Bidding to host a major sports event: the local organising committee perspective', *International Journal of Public Sector Management*, 1: 316–35.

Emery, P. (2003) 'Sports event management', in L. Trenberth (ed.), *Managing the Business of Sport*. Palmerston North: Dunmore Press. pp. 269–92.

Erdogen, B.Z. and Kitchen, P.J. (1998) 'Managerial mindsets and the symbiotic relationship between sponsorship and advertising', *Marketing Intelligence and Planning*, 16 (6): 369–74.

Etzioni, A. (2000) 'Toward a theory of public ritual', *Sociological Theory*, 18 (1): 44–59.

Evans, G. and Shaw, P. (2004) *The Contribution of Culture to Regeneration in the UK: A Report to the DCMS*. London: London Metropolitan University.

Event Industry News (2012) Available at: http://www.eventindustrynews.co.uk/2010/02/liverpool-convention-bureau-launches-new-branding-and-strategy.html (accessed 2 January 2012).

Fáilte Ireland (2010) *A Guide to Running Green Meetings and Events*. Dublin: Fáilte Ireland. Available at: http://www.meetinireland.com/Trade/Support/Green-Meetings-and-Events.aspx (accessed 18 June 2011).

Falassi, A. (1987) *Time out of Time: Essays on the Festival*. Albuquerque, NM: University of New Mexico.

Falk, I. and Kilpatrick, S. (2000) 'What is social capital? A study of interaction in a rural community', *Sociologia Ruralis*, 40 (1): 87–110.

Fallon, P. and Schofield, P. (2004) 'First-time and repeat visitors to Orlando, Florida: a comparative analysis of destination satisfaction', in G.I. Crouch, R.R. Perdue, H.J.P. Timmermans and M. Uysal (eds), *Consumer Psychology of Tourism, Hospitality and Leisure*. Wallingford: CABI Publishing. pp. 203–14.

Faulkner, B., Chalip, L., Brown, G., Jago, L., March, R. and Woodside, A. (2001) 'Monitoring the tourism impacts of the Sydney 2000 Olympics', *Event Management*, 6: 231–46.

Féile an Phobail (2012) 'About us'. Available at: http://www.feilebelfast.com/about-us/ (accessed 30 May 2012).

Felenstein, D. and Fleischer, A. (2009) 'Local festivals and tourism promotion: the role of public assistance and visitor expenditure', *Journal of Travel Research*, 41: 385–92.

Ferrari, S. and Resciniti, R. (2007) 'La gestione degli eventi turistico-culturali nella prospettiva esperienziale', *Annali della Facoltà di Economia di Benevento*, 12: 257–84.

Ferris, L. (2010) 'Incremental art: negotiating the route of London's Notting Hill carnival', *Social Identities*, 16 (4): 519–36.

Festivalslab (2012) Available at: http:/festivalslab.com (accessed 17 February 2012).

Finkel, R. (2009) 'A picture of the contemporary combined arts festival landscape', *Cultural Trends*, 18 (1): 3–21.

Finkel, R. (2010) "Dancing around the ring of fire': social capital, tourism resistance, and gender dichotomies at up helly Aa in Lerwick, Shetland', *Event Management*, 14 (4): 275–85.

Florek, M. and Insch, A. (2011) 'When fit matters: leveraging destination and event image congruence', *Journal of Hospitality Marketing & Management*, 20 (3–4): 265–86.

Flyvbjerg, B. and Stewart, B. (2012) *London Olympics over Budget*. Oxford: Said Business School, University of Oxford.

Foley, P. (1991) 'The impact of the WSG on Sheffield', *Environment and Planning* C, 9: 65–78.

Foley, M., McGillivray, D. and McPherson, G. (2012a) *Event Policy. From Theory to Strategy*. Oxon: Routledge.

Foley, M., McGillivray, D. and McPherson, G. (2012b) 'Policy pragmatism: Qatar and the global events circuit', *International Journal of Event and Festival Management*, 3 (1): 101–15.

Formica, S. (1998) 'The development of festivals and special events studies', *Festival Management and Event Tourism*, 5 (3): 131–7.

Formica, S. and Uysal, M. (1998) 'Market Segmentation of an international cultural-historical event in Italy', *Journal of Travel Research*, 36 (4): 16–24.

Fourie, J. and Santana-Gallego, M. (2011) 'The impact of mega-events on tourist arrivals', *Tourism Management*, 32 (6): 1364–70.

Fowler, H.W., Fowler, F.G. and Murray, J.A.H. (1964) *The Concise Oxford Dictionary of Current English*. Oxford: Clarendon Press.

Fredline, E. (2006) 'Host and guest relations and sport tourism', in H. Gibson (ed.), *Sport Tourism: Concepts and Theories*. New York: Routledge. pp. 131–47.

Fredline, L. and Faulkner, B. (2000) 'Host community reactions: a cluster analysis', *Annals of Tourism Research*, 27 (3): 763–84.

Fredline, L., Jago, L. and Deery, M. (2003) 'The development of a generic scale to measure the social impacts of events', *Event Management* 8 (1): 23–37.

Fredline, E., Raybould, R., Jago, L. and Deery, M. (2005) 'Triple bottom line event evaluation: a proposed framework for holistic event evaluation', paper presented at the International Event Research Conference, Sydney.

Freeman, E.R. (1984) *Strategic Management: a Stakeholder Approach*. Boston: MA: Pitman.

Freire-Gibb, L.C. (2011) 'A platform for local entrepreneurship: the case of the lighting festival of Frederikshavn', *Local Economy*, 26 (3): 157–69.

Frew, E. and Ali-Knight, J. (2009) 'Independent theatres and the creation of a fringe atmosphere', *International Journal of Culture, Tourism and Hospitality Research*, 3 (3): 211–27.

Frey, B. (1994) 'The economics of music festivals', *Journal of Cultural Economics*, 18 (1): 29–39.

Fuller, C.J. (1992) *The Camphor Flame: Popular Hinduism and Society in India*. Princeton, NJ: Princeton University Press.

García, B. (2001) 'Enhancing sport marketing through cultural and arts programs: lessons from the Sydney 2000 Olympic Arts Festivals', *Sport Management Review*, 4: 193–219.

García, B. (2004) 'Cultural policy in European cities: lessons from experience, prospects for the future', *Local Economy*, 19 (4): 312–26.

García, B. (2005) 'De-constructing the city of culture: the long term cultural legacies of Glasgow 1990', *Urban Studies*, 42(5–6): 1–28.

Gauthier, J. (2009) 'Selling Alberta at the mall: the representation of a Canadian province at the 2006 Smithsonian folklore festival', *International Journal of Cultural Studies*, 12 (6) 639–59.

Geertz, C. (1993) *The Interpretation of Cultures*. London: Fontana Press.

Getz, D. (1989) 'Special events, defining the product', *International Journal of Tourism Management*, 10 (2): 125–37.

Getz, D. (1991) *Festivals, Special Events and Tourism*. New York: Van Nostrand Reinhold New York.

Getz, D. (1993) 'Festivals and special events', in M.A. Khan, M.D. Olsen and T. Var (eds), *Encyclopedia of Hospitality and Tourism*. New York: Van Nostrand Reinhold. pp. 789–810.

Getz, D. (1997) *Event Management and Event Tourism*. New York: Cognizant Communication Corporation.

Getz, D. (1998) 'Information sharing among festival managers', *Festival Management & Event Tourism*, 5 (1/2): 33–50.

Getz, D. (2000) 'Developing a research agenda for the event management field', in J. Allen, R. Harris, L.K. Jago and A.J. Veal (eds), *Events Beyond 2000: Setting the Agenda, Proceedings of the Conference on Event Evaluation, Research and Education*. Sydney: Australian Centre for Event Management, University of Technology. pp. 10–21.

Getz, D. (2002) 'Why festivals fail', *Event Management*, 7 (4): 209–19.

Getz, D. (2005) *Event Management and Event Tourism*. New York: Cognizant Communication.

Getz, D. (2007) *Event Studies. Theory, Research and Policy for Planned Events*. Oxford: Butterworth-Heinemann.

Getz, D. (2008) 'Event tourism: definition, evolution and research', *Tourism Management*, 29 (3): 403–28.

Getz, D. (2009) 'Policy of sustainable and responsible festivals and events, institutionalization of a new paradigm', *Journal of Policy Research in Tourism, Leisure and Events*, 1 (1): 61–78.

Getz, D. and Andersson, T. (2010) 'Festival stakeholders: exploring relationships and dependency through a four-country comparison', *Journal of Hospitality and Tourism Research*, 34 (4): 531–56.

Getz, D. and J. Cheyne (1997) 'Special event motivations and behavior', in C. Ryan (ed.), *The Tourist Experience*. London: Cassell. pp. 136–54.

Getz, D. and Frisby, W. (1988) 'Evaluating management effectiveness in community-run festivals', *Journal of Travel Research*, 27 (1): 22–7.

Getz, D., Andersson, T. and Larson, M. (2007) 'Festival stakeholder roles: concepts and case studies', *Event Management*, 10 (2): 103–122.

Getz, D., Andersson, T. and Carlsen, J. (2010) 'Festival management studies: Developing a framework and priorities for comparative and cross-cultural research', *International Journal of Event and Festival Management*, 1 (1): 29–59.

Gelder, G. and Robinson, P (2009) 'Critical comparative study of visitor motivations for attending music festivals: a case study of Glastonbury and V festival', *Event Management*, 13: 181–96.

Gibson, C. and Davidson, D. (2004) 'Tamworth, Australia's 'country music capital': place marketing, rurality, and resident reactions', *Journal of Rural Studies*, 20 (4): 387–404.

Gibson, C., Waitt, G., Walmsley, J. and Connell, J. (2010) 'Cultural festivals and economic development in nonmetropolitan Australia', *Journal of Planning Education and Research*, 29 (3): 280–93.

Gibson, H. (1998) 'Sport tourism: A critical analysis of research', *Sport Management Review*, 1: 45–76.

Gibson, H. (2006) *Sport Tourism: Concepts and Theories*. London: Routledge.

Gibson, H., Willming, C. and Holdnak, A. (2003) 'Small-scale event sport tourism: fans as tourists', *Tourism Management*, 24 (2): 181–90.

Gibson, H., Qi, C.X. and Zhang, J.J. (2008) 'Destination image and intent to visit China and the Beijing Olympic Games', *Journal of Sport Management*, 22: 427–50.

Girginov, V. and Parry, J. (2005) *The Olympic Games Explained*. London: Routledge.

Gladden, J.M., McDonald, M.A. and Barr, C.A. (2005) 'Event management', in L.P. Masteralesic, C.A. Barr and M.A. Hums (eds), *Principles and Practice of Sport Management*, 2nd edn. Sudbury, MA: Jones and Bartlett. pp. 272–94.

Gnoth, J. and Anwar, S.A. (2000) 'New Zealand bets on event tourism', *Cornell Hotel and Restaurant Administration Quarterly*, August: 72–83.

Goffman, E. (1959) *The Presentation of Self in Everyday Life*. New York: Anchor.

Gold, J.R. and Gold, M.M. (2005) *Cities of Culture: Staging International Festivals and the Urban Agenda, 1851–2000*. Aldershot: Ashgate.

Goldblatt, J. (1997) *Special Events: Best Practices in Modern Events Management*. New York: Van Nostrand Reinhold.

Goldblatt, J. (2002) *Special Events: Twenty-First Century Global Event Management*, 3rd edn. The Wiley Management Series. New York: Wiley.

Goldblatt, J. (2011) *A New Generation and the Next Frontier*, 6th edn. New York: Wiley.

Goldblatt, J. and Supovitz, F. (1999) *Dollars and Events: How to Succeed in the Special Events Business*. New York: John Wiley & Sons.

Goldblatt, J.J. (2004) *Special Events: Event Leadership for a New World*. New York: Wiley.

Goldblatt, J.J. (2005) *Special Events: Event Leadership for a New World*, 4th edn. Hoboken, NJ: John Wiley & Sons.

González-Reverté, F. and Miralbell, O. (2011) 'The role of social and intangible factors in cultural event planning in Catalonia', *International Journal of Event and Festival Management*, 2 (1): 37–53.

González-Reverté, F. and Miralbell-Izard, O. (2009) 'Managing music festivals for tourism purposes in Catalonia (Spain)', *Tourism Review*, 64 (4): 53–65.

Gotham, F.K. (2005) 'Tourism from above and below: globalization, localization and New Orlean's Mardi Gras', *International Journal of Urban and Regional Research*, 29 (2): 309–26.

Graci, S. and Dodds, R. (2008) *The ICARUS Foundation's Greening Your Festivals and Events Guide*. Toronto: ICARUS Foundation. Available at: http://www.theicarus foundation.com/index.html (accessed 5 August 2012).

Grappi, S. and Montanari, F. (2011) 'The role of social identification and hedonism in affecting tourist re-patronising behaviours: the case of an Italian festival', *Tourism Management*, 32 (5): 1128–40.

Gration, D., Raciti, M. and Arcodia, C. (2011) 'The role of consumer self-concept in marketing festivals', *Journal of Travel & Tourism Marketing*, 28 (6): 644–55.

Gratton, C. and Henry, I. (eds) (2001) *Economics of Sport and Recreation*. London: Taylor and Francis.

Gray, B. (1989) *Collaborating: Finding Common Ground for Multiparty Problems*. San Francisco, CA: Jossey-Bass.

Green, C. and Chalip, L. (2004) 'Pathways to volunteer commitment: lessons from the Sydney olympic games', in R. Stebbins and M. Graham (eds), *Volunteering as Leisure/ Leisure as Volunteering: An International Assessment*. Wallingford: CABI. pp. 49–68.

Greenwood, D. (1972) 'Tourism as an agent of change: a Spanish Basque case study', *Ethnology*, 11: 80–91.

Griffiths, R. (2006) 'City/culture discourses: evidence from the competition to select the European Capital of Culture 2008', *European Planning Studies*, 14 (4) 415–30.

Grimes, G. (1994) 'Volunteers: stars of every event', *Fundraising Management*, 25 (8): 12.

Gripsund, G., Nes, E.B. and Olsson, U.H. (2010) 'Effects of hosting a mega-sport event on country image', *Event Management*, 14: 193–204.

Grunwell, S. and Ha, I. (2008) 'Film festivals: an empirical study of factors for success', *Event Management*, 11: 201–10.

Gursoy, D. and Kendall, K.W. (2006) 'Hosting mega events: modeling locals' support', *Annals of Tourism Research*, 33 (3): 603–623.

Gursoy, D., Kim, K. and Uysal, M. (2004) 'Perceived impacts of festivals and special events by organizers: an extension and validation', *Tourism Management*, 25: 171–81.

Gyimóthy, S. (2009) 'Casual observers, connoisseurs and experimentalists: a conceptual exploration of niche festival visitors', *Scandinavian Journal of Hospitality and Tourism*, 9 (2–3): 177–205.

Håkansson, H. and Snehota, I. (2006) 'No business is an island: the network concept of business strategy', *Scandinavian Journal of Management*, 22 (3): 256–70.

Hall, C.M.(1989) 'The definition and analysis of hallmark tourist events', *Geojounal*, 19 (3): 263–68.

Hall, C.M. (1992) *Hallmark Tourist Events. Impacts, Management & Planning*. London: Belhaven Press.

Hall, C.M. (1997) *Hallmark Tourist Events – Impacts, Management and Planning*. London: Wiley.

Hall, C.M. (2006) 'Urban entrepreneurship, corporate interests and sports mega-events: the thin policies of competitiveness within the hard outcomes of neoliberal-ism', *Sociological Review*, 54: 59–70.

Hallmann, K. and Breuer, C. (2011) 'Images of rural destinations hosting small-scale sport events', *International Journal of Event and Festival Management*, 2 (3): 218–44.

Hall, C.M. and Hodges, J. (1996) 'The party's great, but what about the hangover?: the housing and social impacts of mega-events with special reference to the 2000 Sydney Olympics', *Festival Management and Event Tourism*, 4 (1–2): 13–20.

Hall, C.M. and Mitchell, R. (2001) 'Wine and food tourism', in N. Douglas and R. Derrett (eds), *Special Interest Tourism: Context and Cases*. Brisbane: John Wiley & Sons. pp. 307–29.

Hall, C.M. and Rusher, K. (2004) 'Politics, public policy and the destination', in I. Yeoman, M. Robertson, J. Ali-Knight, S. Drummond and U. McMahon-Beattie (eds), *Festival and Events Management: An International Arts and Culture Perspective*. Oxford: Elsevier. pp 217–231.

Hall, C.M. and Sharples, L. (2008) *Food and Wine Festivals and Events Around the World*. Oxford: Butterworth-Heinemann.

Hanchett, S. (1972) 'Festivals and social relations in a Mysore village: mechanics of two processions', *Economic and Political Weekly*, 7: 31–3.

Harris, R., Jago, L., Allen, J. and Huyskens, M. (2001) 'Towards an Australian event research agenda: first steps', *Event Management*, 6 (4): 213–21.

Havitz, M.E. and Dimanche, F. (1997) 'Leisure involvement revisited: conceptual conundrums and measurement advances', *Journal of Leisure Research*, 29 (3): 245–78.

Havitz, M.E. and Dimanche, F. (1999) 'Leisure involvement revisited: drive properties and paradoxes', *Journal of Leisure Research*, 31 (2): 122–49.

Hede, A. (2005) 'Sports-events, tourism and destination marketing strategies: an Australian case study of Athens 2004 and its media telecast', *Journal of Sport Tourism*, 10 (3): 187–200.

Hede, A. (2007) 'Managing special events in the new era of the triple bottom line', *Event Management*, 11: 13–22.

Hede, A. and Rentschler, R. (2008) 'Mentoring volunteer festival managers: evaluation of a pilot scheme in regional Australia', in M. Robertson, and E. Frew (eds), *Events and Festivals*. Abingdon: Routledge. pp. 56–69.

Heitmann, S. and David, L. (2010) 'Sustainability and events management', in P. Robinson, D. Wale and G. Dickson (eds), *Events Management*. Wallingford: CABI. pp. 181–200.

Henderson, J.C., Foo, K., Lim, H. and Yip, S. (2010) 'Sports events and tourism: the Singapore formula one grand prix', *International Journal of Event and Festival Management*, 1 (1): 60–73.

Herrero, L.C., Sanz, J.A., Devesa, M., Bedate, A. and Del Barrio, M.J. (2006) 'The economic impact of cultural events: a case study of Salamanca 2002, European capital of culture', *European Urban and Regional Studies*, 13 (1): 41–57.

Hiller, H.H. (1998) 'Assessing the impact of mega-events: a linkage model', *Current Issues in Tourism*, 1 (1): 47–57.

Hitters, E. (2000) 'The social and political construction of a European cultural capital: Rotterdam 2000', *International Journal of Cultural Policy*, 6 (2): 183–99.

Hjalager, A.M. (2009) 'Cultural tourism innovation systems – the Roskilde festival', *Scandinavian Journal of Hospitality and Tourism*, 9 (2–3): 266–87.

Hjalager, A. and Richards, G. (eds) (2002) *Tourism and Gastronomy*. London: Routledge.

Holloway, I., Brown, L. and Shipway, R. (2010) 'Meaning not measurement. Using ethnography to bring a deeper understanding to the participant experience of festivals and events', *International Journal of Event and Festival Management*, 1 (1): 74–85.

Homans, G (1974) *Social Behavior: Its Elementary Forms*, (Revised ed.) New York: Harcourt Brace Jovanovich.

Homans, G.C. and Stein, P.P. (1974) *Social Behavior: The Elements of Form*, trans S. Samuels. New York: Harcourt Brace Jovanovich.

Horne, J. and Manzenreiter, W. (2006) 'An introduction to the sociology of sports mega-events', *Sociological Review*, 54(Supplement s2): 1–24.

Houghton, M. (2008) 'Classifying wine festival customers: comparing an inductive typology with Hall's wine tourist classification', *International Journal of Culture, Tourism and Hospitality Research*, 2 (1): 67–76.

HSE (Health Services Executive) (2000) *Managing Crowds Safely: A Guide for Organisers at Events and Venues*. London: HMSO.

Hughes, H.L. (eds) (2006) 'Gay and lesbian festivals: tourism in the change from politics to party', in D. Picard and M. Robinson (eds), *Festivals, Tourism and Social Change. Remaking Worlds*. Clevedon: Channelview Publications. pp. 238–54.

Hultkrantz, J. (1998) 'Mega-event displacement of visitors: the world championship in athletics, Göteborg 1995', *Festival Management & Event Tourism*, 5 (1): 1–8.

Hume, M. (2008) 'Understanding core and peripheral service quality in customer repurchase of the performing arts', *Managing Service Quality*, 18 (4): 349–369.

Hyatt, C. (2008) 'Facilitating quality in event management', in C. Mallen and L.J. Adams (eds), *Sport, Recreation and Tourism Event Management. Theoretical and Practical Dimensions*. Oxford: Elsevier/Butterworth-Heinemann. pp. 165–78.

Ilczuk, D. and Kulikowska, M. (2007) *Festival Jungle, Policy Desert? Festival Policies of Pubilc Authorities in Europe*. Warsaw: Circle.

International Congress and Convention Association (2012) Available at: http://www.icca.com (accessed 17 February 2012).

Isar, R.F. (1976) 'Culture and the arts festival of the twentieth century', *Cultures*, 3: 125–45.

Iso-Ahola, S. (1980) *The Social Psychology of Leisure and Recreation*. Dubuque, IA: Brown.

Iso-Ahola, S. (1983) 'Towards a social psychology of recreational travel', *Leisure Studies*, 2 (1): 45–57.

Jackson, J., Houghton, M., Russell, R. and Triandos, P. (2005) 'Innovations in measuring economic impacts of regional festivals: a do-it-yourself kit', *Journal of Travel Research*, 43 (4): 360–7.

Jackson, P. (1989) *Maps of Meaning*. London: Unwin Hyman.

Jago, L. and Dwyer, L. (2006) *Economic Evaluation of Special Events: A Practitioner's Guide*. Altona, Victoria: Common Ground Publishing.

Jago, L.K. and Shaw, R.N. (1998) 'Special events: a conceptual and definitional framework', *Festival Management & Event Tourism*, 5 (1): 21–32.

Jago, L. and Shaw, R. (1999) 'Consumer perceptions of special events: a multi-stimulus validation', *Journal of Travel and Tourism Marketing*, 8 (4): 1–24.

Jago, L., Chalip, L., Brown, G. and Ali, S. (2003) 'Building events into destination branding: insights from experts', *Event Management*, 8 (1): 3–14.

Jago, L., Chalip, L., Brown, G., Mules, T. and Ali, S. (2002) 'The role of events in helping to brand a destination', in J. Jago, M. Deery, R. Harris, A. Hede and J. Allen (eds) *Events and Place-making: Proceedings of an International Research Conference 2002.* Sydney. Sydney: Australian Centre for Event Management.

Jago, L., Dwyer, L., Lipman, G., van Lill, D. and Vorster, S. (2010) 'Optimising the potential of mega-events: an overview', *International Journal of Event and Festival Management*, 1 (3): 220–37.

Jamieson, K. (2004) 'Edinburgh: the festival gaze and its boundaries', *Space and Culture*, 7 (1): 64–75.

Janiskee, R. (1994) 'Some macroscale growth trends in America's community festival industry', *Festival Management and Event Tourism*, 2 (1): 10–14.

Janiskee, R. (1996) 'The temporal distribution of America's community festivals', *Festival Management & Event Tourism*, 5: 51–58.

Jenkins, C.L. (2010) 'Book review: the Sage handbook of tourism studies', *Annals of Tourism Research*, 37: 1190–216.

Jeong, S. and Almeida Santos, C. (2004) 'Cultural politics and contested place identity', *Annals of Tourism Research*, 31 (3): 640–56.

Jeong, S.O. and Park, S.H. (1997) 'A cross-cultural application of the novelty scale', *Annals of Tourism Research*, 24 (1): 238–40.

Jóhannesson, G.T. (2010) 'Emergent vikings: the social ordering of tourism innovation', *Event Management*, 14: 261–74.

Johnson, M.D. and Fornell, C. (1991) 'A framework for comparing customer satisfaction across individuals and product categories', *Journal of Economic Psychology*, 12 (2): 267–86.

Johansson, M. and Kociatkiewicz, J. (2011) 'City festivals: creativity and control in staged urban experiences', *European and Regional Studies*, 18 (4): 392–405.

Johnson, G., Scholes, K. and Whittington, R. (2008) *Exploring Corporate Strategy. Text and Cases.* Harlow: Pearson Education.

Jones, C. (2001) 'Mega-events and host region impacts: determining the true worth of the 1999 rugby world cup', *International Journal of Tourism Research*, 3 (3): 241–51.

Jones, C. (2008) 'Assessing the environmental impact of a major sporting event', *Tourism Economics*, 14: 343–360.

Jones, C. (2012) 'Festivals and events in emergent economies: a sea change, and for whom?', *International Journal of Event and Festival Management*, 3 (1): 9–11.

Jones, M. (2010) *Sustainable Event Management: A Practical Guide.* London: Earthscan.

Judd, D.R. and Fainstein, S.S. (eds) (1999) *The Tourist City.* New Haven, CT: Yale University Press.

Kahle, L.R. and Close, A.G. (eds) (2011) *Consumer Behavior Knowledge for Effective Sports and Event Marketing.* New York: Routledge.

Kang, M., Suh, S. and Jo, D. (2005) 'The competitiveness of international meeting destinations in Asia. Meeting planners' versus buying centers' perceptions', *Journal of Convention & Event Tourism*, 7 (2): 57–85.

Kaplan, A.M. and Haenlein, M. (2009) 'Consumer use and business potential of virtual worlds: the case of second life', *The International Journal on Media Management*, 11 (3/4): 93–101.

Kaplanidou, K. and Vogt, C. (2007) 'The interrelationship between sport event and destination image and sport tourists' behaviours', *Journal of Sport Tourism*, 12 (3/4): 183–206.

Karadakis, K., Kaplanidou, K. and Karlis, G. (2010) 'Event leveraging of mega sport events: a swot analysis approach', *International Journal of Event and Festival Management*, 1 (3): 170–85.

Karlsen, S. and Nordström, C.S. (2009) 'Festivals in the Barents region: exploring festival-stakeholder collaboration', *Scandinavian Journal of Hospitality and Tourism*, 9 (2/3): 130–45.

Kates, S.M. and Belk, R.W. (2001) 'The meanings of leisure and gay pride day: resistance through consumption and resistence to consumption', *Journal of Contemporary Ethnography*, 30 (4) 392–429.

Kavetsos, G. and Szymanski, S. (2010) 'National well-being and international sports events', *Journal of Economic Psychology*, 31 (2): 158–71.

Kellett, P., Hede, A. and Chalip, L. (2008) 'Social policy for sport events: leveraging (relationships with) teams from other nations for community benefit', *European Sport Management Quarterly*, 8 (2): 101–21.

Kim, H. and Jamal, T. (2007) 'Touristic quest for existential authenticity', *Annals of Tourism Research*, 34(1): 181–201.

Kim, H., Cheng, C.K. and O'Leary, J.T. (2007) 'Understanding participation patterns and trends in tourism cultural attractions', *Tourism Management*, 28: 1366–371.

Kim, H.J., Gursoy, D. and Lee, S.B. (2006) 'The impact of the 2002 world cup on South Korea: comparison of pre-and post-games', *Tourism Management*, 27: 86–96.

Kim, K. and Severt, D.E. (2011) 'Satisfaction or quality comes first: an empirical analysis', *Journal of Travel and Tourism Marketing*, 28: 81–96.

Kim, S.S., Park, J. and Lee, J. (2010) 'Predicted economic impact analysis of a mega-convention using multiplier effects', *Journal of Convention & Event Tourism*, 11 (1): 42–61.

Kim. S.S., Yoon, S. and Kim, Y. (2011) 'Competitive positioning among international convention cities in the East Asian region', *Journal of Convention & Event Tourism*, 12 (2): 86–105.

Klamer, A. (2002) 'Accounting for social and cultural values', *De Economist*, 150 (4): 453–73.

Knox, K. (2004) 'Implications and use of information technology within events', in I. Yeoma, M. Robertson, J. Ali-Knight, S. Drummond and U. McMahon-Beattie (eds), *Festival and Events Management: An International Arts and Culture Perspective*. Oxford: Elsevier Butterworth-Heinemann. pp. 97–111.

Ko, Y., Kim, M.K., Kim, Y.K., Lee, J.H. and Cattani, K. (2010) 'Consumer satisfaction and event quality perception: a case of US open taekwondo championship', *Event Management*, 14 (3): 205–14.

Kong, L. (2000) 'Cultural policy in Singapore: negotiating economic and socio-cultural agendas', *Geoforum*, 31 (4): 385–90.

Konstantaki, M. and Wickens, E. (2010) 'Residents' perceptions of environmental and security issues at the 2012 London Olympic Games', *Journal of Sport & Tourism*, 15 (4): 337–57.

Kurin, R. (2001) 'Why we do the festival', in F. Proschan (ed.), *Smithsonian Festival of American Folklore Program Book*. Washington, DC: Smithsonian Institution.

Kurin, R. (2006) 'We are very much still here', in F. Proschan (ed.), *Smithsonian Folklore Festival Program Book*. Washington, DC: Center for Folklore and Cultural Heritage.

Kuzgun, E., Göksel, T., Özalp, D., Somer, B. and Alvarez, M.D. (2010) 'Perceptions of local people regarding Istanbul as a European capital of culture', *European Planning Studies*, 8 (3): 1173–186.

Lade, C. and Jackson, J. (2004) 'Key success factors in regional festivals: some Australian experiences', *Event Management*, 9 (1): 1–11.

Lamberti, L., Noci, G., Guo, J. and Zhu, S. (2011) 'Mega-events as drivers of community participation in developing countries: the case of Shanghai world expo', *Tourism Management*, 32: 1474–483.

Langen, F. and García, B. (2009) *Measuring the Impacts of Large Scale Cultural Events: a Literature Review*. Liverpool: Impacts 08, European Capital of Culture Research Programme.

Lankford, S.V. and Howard, D. (1994) 'Development of a tourism impact attitude scale', *Annals of tourism Research*, 21: 121–39.

Larson, M. (2002) 'A political approach to relationship marketing: case study of the Storsjöyran festival', *International Journal of Tourism Research*, 4 (2): 119–43.

Larson, M. (2009a) 'Festival innovation: complex and dynamic network interaction', *Scandinavian Journal of Hospitality and Tourism*, 9 (2–3): 288–307.

Larson, M. (2009b) 'Joint event production in the jungle, the park and the garden: metaphors of event networks', *Tourism Management*, 30: 393–9.

Larson, M. (2011) 'Innovation and creativity in festival organisations', *Journal of Hospitality Marketing & Management*, 20 (3/4): 287–310.

Lavenda, R.H. (1997) *Corn Fests and Water Carnivals: Celebrating Community in Minnesota*. Washington: Smithsonian Institution Press.

Law, C. (2002) *Urban Tourism*. London: Continuum.

Lawton, L.J. (2009) 'Birding festivals, sustainability and ecotourism: an ambiguous relationship', *Journal of Travel Research*, 48 (2): 259–67.

Lawton, L.J. and Weaver, D.B. (2010) 'Normative and innovative sustainable resource management at birding festivals', *Tourism Management*, 31: 527–36.

Laybourn, P. (2004) 'Risk and decision making in event management', in I. Yeoman, J. Ali-Knight, S. Drummond and U. McMahon-Beattie (eds), *Festival and Events Management: An International Arts and Culture Perspective*. Oxford: Elsevier Butterworth Heinemann.

Lee, C. and Taylor, T. (2005) 'Critical reflections on the economic impact assessment of a mega-event: the case of 2002 FIFA World Cup', *Tourism Management*, 26 (4): 595–603.

Lee, C.K. (2000) 'A comparative study of Caucasian and Asian visitors to a cultural expo in an Asian setting', *Tourism Management*, 21: 169–76.

Lee, C.K. and Kim, J.H. (1998) 'International tourism demand for the 2002 World Cup Korea a combined forecasting technique', *Pacific Tourism Review*, 2 (2): 1–10.

Lee, C.K., Lee, Y.K. and Lee, B. (2005) 'Korea's destination image formed by the 2002 World Cup', *Annals of Tourism Research*, 32 (4): 839–58.

Lee, C.K., Lee, Y. and Wicks, B.E. (2004) 'Segmentation of festival motivation by nationality and satisfaction', *Tourism Management*, 25: 61–70.

Lee, J. and Kyle, G. (2012) 'Recollection accuracy of festival consumption emotions', *Journal of Travel Research*, 51 (2): 178–190.

Lee, J.S., Lee, C.K. and Yoon, Y. (2009) 'Investigating differences in antecedents to value between first-time and repeat festival-goers', *Journal of Travel and Tourism Marketing*, 26: 688–702.

Lee, J., Almanza, B.A. and Nelson, D.C. (2010) 'Food safety at fairs and festivals: vendor knowledge and violations at a regional festival', *Event Management*, 14: 215–23.

Lee, M.J. and Black, K.J. (2005) 'A review of economic value drivers in convention and meeting management research', *International Journal of Contemporary Hospitality Management*, 17 (4/5): 409–20.

Lee, S. and Goldblatt, J. (2012) 'The current and future impacts of the 2007–2009 economic recession on the festival and event industry', *International Journal of Event and Festival Management*, 3 (2): 137–148.

Lee, T.J. (2009) 'The successful conference venue: perceptions of conference organisers and hotel managers', *Event Management*, 13: 171–80.

Lee, T.J. (2010) 'The successful conference venue: perceptions of conference organisers and hotel managers', *Event Management*, 13: 223–32.

Lee, Y.K., Lee, C.K., Lee, S.K. and Babin, B.J. (2008) 'Festivalscapes and patrons' emotions, satisfaction, and loyalty', *Journal of Business Research*, 61: 56–64.

Leeds, M.A. (2008) 'Do good Olympics make good neighbours?', *Contemporary Economic Policy*, 26 (3): 460–67.

Legacies Now (2012) http://www.2010legaciesnow.com/about-us/ (accessed 20 November 2012).

Leopkey, B. and Parent, M.M. (2009) 'Risk management strategies by stakeholders in Canadian major sporting events', *Event Management*, 13: 153–70.

Lewis, C. and Pile, S. (1996) 'Woman, body, space: rio carnival and the politics of performance', *Gender, Place and Culture*, 3 (1): 23–41.

Li, M., Huang, Z. and Cai, L.A. (2009) 'Benefit segmentation of visitors to a rural community-based festival', *Journal of Travel & Tourism Marketing*, 26(5): 585–98.

Li, R. and Petrick, J. (2006) 'A review of festival and event motivation studies', *Event Management*, 9 (4): 239–45.

Liao, H. and Pitts, A. (2006) 'A brief historical review of Olympic urbanization', *The International Journal of the History of Sport*, 23 (7): 1232–52.

Lin, K., Stein, P. and Goldblatt, J. (2011) 'New investment: an exploratory case study of three mature Edinburgh festivals and their future funding opportunities', *Event Management*, 15 (2): 179–95.

Litvin, S.W. and Fetter, E. (2006) 'Can a festival be too successful? A review of Spoleto, USA', *International Journal of Contemporary Hospitality Management*, 18: (1): 41–9.

Liverpool Convention Bureau (2012) 'News'. Available at: http://www.liverpool conventionbureau.com/press/news/liverpool-launches-bidding-tool/ (accessed 31 July 2012).

Loftman, P. and Nevil, B. (1996) 'Going for growth: prestige projects in three British cities', *Urban Studies*, 33: 991–1020.

London 2012 Olympic Games Organising Committee (2007) *The London 2012 Sustainability Plan*. Available at: http://www.london2012.com/mm/Document/ Publications/Sustainability/01/25/66/62/One-planet-olympics-2005_Neutral.pdf (accessed 18 June 2011).

London 2012 Olympic Games Organising Committee (2012) Available at: http:// www.london2012.com/get-involved/volunteer/london-2012-games-makers/ (accessed 5 September 2011).

López-Bonilla, J.M. and López-Bonilla, L.M. (2010) 'Designated public festivals of interest to tourists', *European Planning Studies*, 18 (3): 435–47.

MacCannell, D. (1976) *The Tourist. A New Theory of the Leisure Class*. New York: Schocken Books.

Mace, A., Hall, P. and Gallent, N. (2007) 'New East Manchester: urban renaissance or urban opportunism', *European Planning Studies*, 15 (1): 51–65.

MacKellar, J. (2006) 'An integrated view of innovation emerging from a regional festival', *International Journal of Event Management Research*, 2 (1): 37–48.

Madden, J.R. (2002) 'The economic consequences of the Sydney Olympics: the CREA/Arthur Andersen study', *Current Issues in Tourism*, 5 (1): 7–2.

Magdalinski, T. and Nauright, J. (2004) 'Commercialization of the modern Olympic games', in T. Slack (ed.), *The Commercialization of Sport*. London: Routledge. pp. 185–204.

Mair, J. (2011) 'Events and climate change: an Australian perspective', *International Journal of Event and Festival Management*, 2 (1): 245–53.

Mallen, C. and Adams, L. (2008) *Sport, Recreation and Tourism Event Management: Theoretical and Practical Dimensions*. New York: Butterworth-Heinmann.

Manning, F.E. (1983) 'Cosmos and chaos: celebrating the modern world', in F.E. Manning (ed.), *The Celebration of Society: Perspectives on Contemporary Cultural Performances*. Bowling Green, OH: Bowling Green University Press. pp. 3–30.

Manzenreiter, W. and Horne, J. (2005) 'Public policy, sports investments and regional development initiatives in Japan', in, J. Nauright and S. Schimmel (eds), *The Political Economy of Sport*. London: Palgrave MacMillan. pp. 152–82.

Mark, M. (2002) 'The first nations of Taiwan: a special report on Taiwan's indigenous peoples', *Cultural Survival Quarterly*, 26 (2): 1–4.

Markwell, K. and Waitt, G. (2009) 'Festivals, space and sexuality: gay pride in Australia', *Tourism Geographies*, 11 (2): 143–68.

Marris, T. (1987) 'The role and impact of mega-events and attractions on regional and national tourism development resolutions', *Tourism Review*, 42 (4): 3–12.

Marston, S.A. (1989) 'Public rituals and community power: St. Patrick's day parades in Lowell, Massachusetts, 1841–1874', *Political Geography Quarterly*, 8 (3): 255–69.

key concepts in event management

Marston, S.A. (2002) 'Making difference: conflict over Irish identity in the New York city St. Patrick's Day parade', *Political Geography*, 21 (3): 373–92.

Martensen, A., Grønholdt, Bendtsen, L. and Jensen, M.J. (2007) 'Application of a model for the effectiveness of event marketing', *Journal of Advertising Research*, September: 283–301.

Martinez, T.A. and McMullin, S.L. (2004) 'Factors affecting decisions to volunteer in nongovernmental organizations', *Environment & Behavior*, 36 (1): 112–26.

Mason, R.B. and Cochetel, F. (2006) 'Residual brand awareness following the termination of a long-term event sponsorship and the appointment of a new sponsor', *Journal of Marketing Communications*, 12 (2): 125–44.

Masterman, G.R. (2004) 'A strategic approach for the use of sponsorship in the events industry: in search of a return on investment', in I. Yeoman, M. Robertson and J. Ali-Knight (2004) (eds), *Festivals and Events Management: An International Arts and Culture Perspective*. Elsevier: Oxford. pp. 260–72.

Matheson, C.M. (2005) 'Festivity and sociability: a study of a celtic music festival', *Tourism Culture & Communication*, 5: 149–163.

Matthews, D. (2008) *Special Event Production: The Process*. Oxford: Butterworth-Heinemann.

Matthews-Salazar, P.M. (2006) 'Becoming all Indian: Gauchos, Pachamama Queends and tourists in the remaking of an Andean festival', in D. Picard and M. Robinson (eds), *Festivals, Tourism and Social Change*. Clevedon: Channel View Publications. pp. 71–83.

Mayfield, T. and Crompton, J. (1995) 'The status of the marketing concept among festival organisers', *Journal of Travel Research*, 33: 14–22.

McCarthy, J. (2005) 'Promoting image and identity in 'cultural quarters': the case of Dundee', *Local Economy*, 20 (3): 280–293.

McCarthy, K.F., Heneghan Ondaatje, E., Zakaras, L. and Brooks, A. (2004) *Gifts of the Muse: Reframing the Debate about the Benefits of the Arts*. Santa Monica: Rand Corporation. Available at: http://www.rang.org (accessed 18 February 2011).

McCartney, G. and Osti, L. (2007) 'From cultural events to sport events: a case study of cultural authenticity in the dragon boat races', *Journal of Sport & Tourism*, 12 (1): 25–40.

McClinchey, K. (2008) 'Urban ethnic festivals, neighbourhoods and the multiple realities of marketing place', *Journal of Travel and Tourism Marketing*, 25 (3): 251–64.

McDowall, S. (2010) 'A comparison between Thai residents and non-residents in their motivations, performance evaluations and overall satisfaction with a domestic festival', *Journal of Vacation Marketing*, 16 (3): 217–33.

McKercher, B., Mei, W.S. and Tse, T.S.M. (2006) 'Are short duration cultural festivals tourist attractions?', *Journal of Sustainable Tourism*, 14 (1): 55–6.

Meenaghan, T. and Shipley, D. (1999) 'Media effect in commercial sponsorship', *European Journal of Marketing*, 33 (3/4): 328–48.

Meenaghan, T. (2001) 'Understanding sponsorship effects', *Psychology and Marketing*, 18 (2): 95–122.

Merrilees, B., Getz, D. and O'Brien, D. (2005) 'Marketing stakeholder analysis: branding the Brisbane Goodwill Games', *European Journal of Marketing*, 39(9/10): 1060–77.

Misener, L. and Mason, D. (2006) 'Creating community networks: can sporting events offer meaningful sources of social capital?', *Managing Leisure*, 11: 39–56.

Mohr, K., Backman K.F., Gahan, L.W. and Backman S.J. (1993) 'An investigation of festival motivations and events satisfaction by visitor type', *Festival Management & Event Tourism*, 1 (3): 89–97.

Molloy, J. (2002) 'Regional festivals: a look at community support, the isolation factor and funding sources', *Journal of Tourism Studies*, 13 (2): 2–15.

Molotch, H. (1976) 'The city as a growth machine: towards a political economy of place', *American Journal of Sociology*, 82 (2): 309–32.

Morgan, M. (2008) 'What makes a good festival? Understanding the event experience', *Event Management*, 12 (2): 81–93.

Moscardo, G. (2007) 'Analyzing the role of festivals and events in regional development', *Event Management*, 11: 23–32.

Mossberg, L. (ed.) (2000) *Evaluation of Events: Scandinavian Experiences*. New York: Cognizant Communication Corporation.

Mossberg, L. and Hallberg, A. (1999) 'The presence of a mega-event: effects of destination image and product country images', *Pacific Tourism Review*, 3: 213–25.

Müller, D.K. and Pettersson, R. (2005) 'What and where is the indigenous at an indigenous festival? – Observations from the winter festival in Jokkmokk, Sweden', in C. Ryan and M. Aicken (eds), *Indigenous Tourism: The Commodification and Management of Culture*. Elsevier.

Mules, T. (2004) 'Evolution in event management: the God Coast's Wintersun festival', *Event Management*, 9: 95–101.

Muñoz, F. (2006) 'Olympic urbanism and Olympic villages: planning strategies in Olympic host cities, London 1908 to London 2012', *The Sociological Review*, 54 (s2): 175–87.

Mykletun, R. (2009) 'Celebration of extreme playfulness: Ekstremsportveko at Voss', *Scandinavian Journal of Hospitality and Tourism*, 9 (2–3): 146–76.

Mykeletun, R.J. and Jaeger, K. (2009) 'The Festivalscape of Finnmark', *Scandinavian Journal of Hospitality and Tourism*, 9 (2–3): 327–48.

Nadav, S., Smith, W.W. and Canberg, A. (2010) 'Examining corporate sponsorship of charitable events in the Greater Charleston area', *Event Management*, 14 (3): 239–50.

Nagle, J. (2005) 'Everybody is Irish on St Paddy's: ambivalence and alterity at London's St Patrick's Day 2002', *Identities: Global Studies in Culture and Power*, 12 (4): 563–83.

Narayan, D. and Pritchett, L. (1999) 'Cents and sociability: household income and social capital in rural Tanzania', *Economic Development and Cultural Change*, 47 (4): 871–97.

Nebenzahl, I.D. and Jaffe, E.D. (1991) 'The effectiveness of sponsored events in promoting a country's image', *International Journal of Advertising*, 10: 223–37.

Neill, W.J.V. (1993) 'Physical planning and image enhancement: recent developments in Belfast', *International Journal of Urban and Regional Research*, 17(4): 595–609.

Neirotti, L. and Hilliard, T. (2006) 'Impact of Olympic spectator safety perception and security concerns on travel decisions', *Tourism Review International*, 10: 269–284.

Nicholson, R.E. and Pearce, D.G. (2001) 'Why do people attend events: a comparative analysis of visitor motivations at four South Island events', *Journal of Travel Research*, 39 (4): 449–60.

Nielson (2008) 'Beijing Olympics draw largest ever global TV audience', Nielsen Wire. Available at: http://blog.nielsen.com/ nielsenwire/media entertainment/beijing-olympics-draw-largest-ever-global-tv-audience/ (accessed 22 January 2013).

Nordfors, D. (2009) 'What is innovation?'. Available at: http://www.america.gov/st/ scitech-english/2009/November/20091109105608ebyessedo0.6893579.html (accessed 4 March 2011).

Nurse, K. (1999) 'Globalization and Trinidad carnival: diaspora, hybridity and identity in global culture', *Cultural Studies*, 13 (4): 661–90.

O'Brien, D. (2006) 'Event business leveraging the Sydney 2000 Olympic games', *Annals of Tourism Research*, 33 (1): 240–61.

O'Brien, D. and Chalip, L. (2007) 'Executive training exercise in sport event leverage', *International Journal of Culture, Tourism and Hospitality Research*, 1 (4): 296–304.

O'Callaghan, C. and Linehan, D. (2007) 'Identity, politics and conflict in dockland development in Cork, Ireland: European capital of culture 2005', *Cities*, 24 (4): 311–23.

O'Hagan, J. and Harvey, D. (2000) 'Why do companies sponsor arts events? Some evidence and a proposed classification', *Journal of Cultural Economy*, 24 (3): 205–24.

O'Neill, M., Getz, D. and Carlsen, J. (1999) 'Evaluation of service quality at events: the 1998 Coca-Cola masters surfing event at Margaret River, Western Australia', *Managing Service Quality*, 9 (3): 158–166.

O'Sullivan, D. and Jackson, M. (2002) 'Festival tourism: a contributor to sustainable local economic development?', *Journal of Sustainable Tourism*, 10 (4): 325–42.

O'Sullivan, D., Pickernell, D. and J. Senyard (2009) 'Public sector evaluation of festivals and special events', *Journal of Policy Research in Tourism, Leisure and Events*, 1 (1): 19–36.

Oakes, S. (2003) 'Demographic and sponsorship considerations for jazz and classical music festivals', *The Service Industries Journal*, 23 (3): 165–78.

Okech, R.N. (2011) 'Promoting sustainable festival events tourism: a case study of Lamu Kenya', *Worldwide Hospitality and Tourism Themes*, 3 (3): 193–202.

O'Leary Analytics (2011) 'Oxegen 2011 – a case study on social media and festivals'. Available at: http://olearyanalytics.com/901/oxegen-2011-a-case-study-on-social-media-and-festivals/ (accessed 2 August 2012).

Olsen, K. (2002) 'Authenticity as a concept in tourism research: the social organization of the experience of authenticity', *Tourist Studies*, 2 (2): 159–82.

Oppermann, M. (1996) 'Convention destination images: analysis of association meeting planners' perceptions', *Tourism Management*, 17 (3): 175–82.

Oppermann, M. and Chon, K.S. (1997) 'Convention participation decision-making process', *Annals of Tourism Research*, 21 (1): 178–91.

Ostor, A. (1980) *The Play of the Gods: Locality, Ideology, Structure and Time in the Festivals of a Bengali Town*. Chicago, IL: The University of Chicago Press.

O'Sullivan, D. and Jackson, M.J. (2002) 'Festival tourism: a contributor to sustainable local economic development?', *Journal of Sustainable Tourism*, 10 (4): 325–342.

Owen, K. (2002) 'The Sydney olympics and urban entrepreneurialism', *Australian Geographical Studies*, 40 (3): 323–36.

Packer, J. and Ballantyne, J. (2010) 'The impact of music festival attendance on young people's psychological and social well-being', *Psychology of Music*, 39 (2): 164–81.

Palmer/Rae Associates (2004) *Study on European Cities and Capitals of Culture 1995–2004*. Belgium: European Commission.

Papagiannopoulos, P., Xenikos, D. and Vouddas, P. (2009) 'Event management and group communications: the case of the 2004 Olympic games in Athens', *Event Management*, 13 (2): 103–16.

Parasuraman, A., Zeithaml, V.A. and Berry, L.L. (1988) 'SERVQUAL: a multiple-item scale for measuring consumer perceptions of service quality', *Journal of Retailing*, 64: 12–40.

Pasanen, K., Taskinen, H. and Mikkonen, J. (2009) 'Impacts of cultural events in Eastern Finland – development of a Finnish event evaluation tool', *Scandinavian Journal of Hospitality and Tourism*, 9 (2–3): 112–29.

Paterson, T. (2010) 'Love parade tragedy: "I'll never forget the sight of all those twisted bodies"', *Independent*, 26 July 2010. Available at: http://www.independent.co.uk/news/world/europe/love-parade-tragedy-ill-never-forget-the-sight-of-all-those-twisted-bodies-2035410.html (accessed 10 June 2011).

Pegg, S. and Patterson, I. (2010) 'Rethinking music festivals as a staged event: gaining insights from understanding visitor motivations and the experiences they seek', *Journal of Convention & Event Tourism*, 11: 85–99.

Pelsmacker, P., Geunes, M. and Van den Bergh, J. (2005) *Foundations of Marketing Communications: A European Perspective*. Harlow: Prentice Hall.

Pine, B.J. and Gilmore, J.H. (1999) *The Experience Economy. Work is Theatre & Every Business a Stage*. Boston, MA: Harvard Business School Press.

Ponsford, I.F. (2011) 'Actualizing environmental sustainability at Vancouver 2010 venues', *International Journal of Event and Festival Management*, 2 (2): 184–96.

Portes, A. (1998) 'Social capital: its origins and applications in modern sociology', *Annual Review of Sociology*, 24: 1–24.

Prentice, R. and Andersen, V. (2003) 'Festival as creative destination', *Annals of Tourism Research*, 30 (1): 7–30.

Preuss, H. (2007) 'The conceptualisation and measurement of mega sport event legacies', *Journal of Sport and Tourism*, 12 (3/4): 207–27.

PriceWaterhouseCoopers (2010) *Shining the light on Successful Sponsorships. An Assessment of Ulster Bank's Festival Sponsorships*. Dublin: PriceWaterhouseCoopers.

Pugh, C. and Wood, E. (2004) 'The strategic use of events within local government: a study of London borough councils', *Event Management*, 9 (1): 61–71.

Putnam, R.D. (1995) 'Bowling alone: America's declining social capital', *Journal of Democracy*, 6 (1): 65–78.

Quester, P. and Farrelly, F. (1998) 'Brand association and memory decay effects of sponsorship: the case of the Australian formula one grand prix', *Journal of Product and Brand Management*, (6): 539–56.

Quinn, B. (2003) 'Symbols, practices and myth-making: cultural perspectives on the Wexford Festival Opera', *Tourism Geographies*, 5 (3): 329–49.

Quinn, B. (2005a) 'Arts festivals and the city', *Urban Studies*, 42 (5–6): 927–43.

Quinn, B. (2005b) 'Changing festival places: insights from Galway', *Social and Cultural Geography*, 6 (2): 237–252.

Quinn, B. (2006) 'Problematising 'festival tourism': arts festivals and sustainable development in Ireland', *Journal of Sustainable Tourism*, 14 (3): 288–306.

Quinn, B. (2009a) 'Festivals, events and tourism', in T. Jamal and M. Robinson (eds), *The Sage Handbook of Tourism Studies*. London: Sage. pp. 483–503.

Quinn, B. (2009b) 'The European capital of culture initiative and cultural legacy: an analysis of the cultural sector in the aftermath of Cork 2005', *Event Management*, 13: 249–64.

Quinn, B. (2010) 'Arts festivals, urban tourism and cultural policy', *Journal of Policy Research in Tourism, Leisure and Events*, 2 (3): 264–79.

Quinn, B. and Wilks, L. (2012) 'Festival connections: people, place and social capital', in G. Richards, M. De Brito and L. Wilks (eds), (forthcoming, 2013) *Exploring the Social Impact of Events*. Abingdon: Routledge.

Raffestin, C. (1980) *Pour une Géographie du Pouvoir*. Paris: Litec.

Ralston, L. and Crompton J.L. (1988) *Motivation and Emotions*. Englewood Cliffs, NJ: Prentice-Hall.

Rao, V. (2001) 'Celebrations as social investments: festival expenditures, unit price variation and social status in rural India', *Journal of Development Studies*, 38 (1): 71–97.

Reason, M. and García, B. (2007) 'Approaches to the newspaper archive: content analysis and press coverage of Glasgow's year of culture', *Media, Culture and Society*, 29 (2): 305–32.

Red Bull (2011) 'What is flugtag?'. Available at: http://www.redbull.ie/cs/Satellite/en_IE/What-is-Flugtag/001242941926673 (accessed 24 January 2012).

Redmond, P. (2010) 'Derry/Londonderry named UK City of Culture'. Available at: http://www.culture.gov.uk/news/media_releases/7252.aspx (accessed 1 August 2012).

Redwood, F. (2011) 'Gold rush', *Financial Times*, 20/21 August 2011: 3.

Reichheld, F.F. and Teal, T. (1996) *The Loyalty Effect*. Boston, MA: Harvard Business School Press.

Reid, S. and Arcodia, C. (2002) 'Understanding the role of the stakeholder in event management', paper presented at Events and Place Making. UTS Business: Event research conference, UTS Australian Centre for Event Management, UTS Sydney.

Richards, G. (2000) 'The European cultural capital event: strategic weapon in the cultural arms race?', *International Journal of Cultural Policy*, 6 (2): 159–81.

Richards, G. (2007a) 'The meaning of cultural festivals', *International Journal of Cultural Policy*, 13 (1): 103–22.

Richards, G. (2007b) 'Culture and authenticity in a traditional event: the views of producers, residents and visitors in Barcelona', *Event Management*, 11: 33–44.

Richards, G. and Wilson, J. (2004) 'The impact of cultural events on city image: Rotterdam, cultural capital of Europe 2001', *Urban Studies*, 41 (10): 1931–51.

Richards, G. and Wilson, J. (2006) 'Developing creativity in tourist experiences: a solution to the serial reproduction of culture', *Tourism Management*, 27(6): 1209–23.

Richards, G., Hitters, E. and Fernandes, C. (2002) *Rotterdam and Porto: Cultural Capitals 2001: Visitor Research*. Arheim, NY: ATLAS.

references

Ritchie, J.R.B. (1984) 'Assessing the impacts of hallmark events: conceptual and research issues', *Journal of Travel Research*, 23 (1): 2–11.

Ritchie, J.R.B. and Smith, B.H. (1991) 'The impact of a mega-event on host region awareness: a longitudinal study', *Journal of Travel Research*, 30 (1): 3–10.

Richins, M.L. (1997) 'Measuring emotions in the consumption experience', *Journal of Consumer Research*, 24 (2): 127–46.

Rittichainuwat, B.N., Jeffrey A., Beck, J.A. and Lalopa, J. (2001) 'Understanding motivations, inhibitors, and facilitators of association members in attending international conferences', *Journal of Convention & Exhibition Management*, 3 (3): 45–62.

Robinson, P., Wale, D. and Dickson, G. (eds) (2010) *Events Management*. Wallingford: CABI.

Roche, M. (1994) 'Mega-events and urban policy', *Annals of Tourism Research*, 21: 1–19.

Roche, M. (2000) *Mega-events and Modernity: Olympics and Expos in the Growth of Global Culture*. London: Routledge.

Rogers, P. and Anastasiadou, C. (2011) 'Community involvement in festivals: exploring ways of increasing local participation', *Event Management*, 15 (4): 387–99.

Rogers, T. (2003) *Conferences and Conventions: A Global Industry*. Oxford: Butterworth-Heinemann.

Rolfe, H. (1992) *Arts Festivals in the UK*. London: Policy Studies Institute.

Rothschild, P.C. (2011) 'Social media use in sports and entertainment venues', *International Journal of Event and Festival Management*, 2 (2): 139–50.

Rowley, J. and Williams, C. (2008) 'The impact of brand sponsorship of music festivals', *Market Intelligence & Planning*, 26 (7): 781–92.

Rutten, R., Westlund, H. and Boekema, F. (2010) 'The spatial dimension of social capital', *European Planning Studies*, 18 (6): 863–71.

Sacco, P.L. and Blessi, G.T. (2007) 'European culture capitals and local development strategies: comparing the Genoa and Lille 2004 cases', *Homo Oeconomicus*, 24 (1): 111–41.

Sadd, D. (2010) 'What is event-led regeneration? – are we confusing terminology? A case study of previous Olympic-related regeneration projects', *Event Management*, 13 (Supplement 1, International Conference on Festivals and Events Research): S20–S22.

Sadler, D. (1993) 'Place-marketing, competitive places and the construction of hegemony in Britain in the 1980s', in G. Kearns and C. Philo (eds), *Selling Places: The City as Cultural Capital, Past and Present*. Oxford: Pergamon Press. pp. 175–192.

Saleh, F. and C. Ryan (1993) 'Jazz and knitwear: factors that attract tourists to festivals', *Tourism Management*, 14 (4): 289–97.

Santos, M.L.L., Dos, Gomes, R.T. and Neves, J.S. (2003) *Públicos do Porto 2001*. Lisbon: Observatório das Actividades Culturais.

Schmitt, B.H. (1999) *Experiential Marketing*. New York: The Free Press.

Schneider, I.E. and Backman, S.J. (1996) 'Cross-cultural equivalence of festival motivations: a study in Jordan', *Festival Management and Event Tourism*, 4 (3–4): 139–44.

Schumpeter, J.A. (1954) *History of Economic Analysis*. London: Allen and Unwin.

Schuster, J.M. (2001) 'Ephemera, temporary urbanism and imaging', in L.J. Vale and S.B Warner (eds), *Imaging the City—Continuing Struggles and New Directions*. New Brunswick, NJ: CUPR Books. pp. 361–96.

Scott, D. (1996) 'A comparison of visitors' motivations to attend three urban festivals', *Festival Management & Event Tourism*, 3: 121–8.

Sharaby, R. (2008) 'The holiday of holidays: a triple holiday festival for Christians, Jews and Muslims', *Social Compass*, 55 (4): 581–96.

Sharpe, E. (2008) 'Festivals and social change: intersections of pleasure and politics at a community music festival, leisure sciences', 30 (3): 217–34.

Shaw, C.A. (2008) *Five Ring Circus: Myths and Realities of the Olympic Games*. Gabriola Island, BC: New Society Publishers.

Shepherd, R. (2002) 'Commodification, culture and tourism', *Tourist Studies*, 2 (2): 183–201.

Shimp, T. (2003) *Advertising, Promotion and Supplemental Aspects of Integrated Marketing Communication*, 6th edn. Mason, OH: Thomson.

Shin, H. (2004) 'Cultural festivals and regional identities in South Korea', *Environment and Planning D: Society and Space*, 22: 619–32.

Shone, A. and Parry, B. (2004) *Successful Event Management: A Practical Handbook*. London: Thomson.

Shoval, N. (2002) 'A new phase in the competition for the Olympic gold: the London and New York bids for the 2012 Games', *Journal of Urban Affairs*, 24 (5): 583–99.

Shukla, S. (1997) 'Building diaspora and nation: the 1991 "cultural festival of India"', *Cultural Studies*, 11 (2): 296–315.

Silvers, J.R. (2008) *Risk Management for Meetings and Events*. Oxford: Butterworth-Heinemann.

Simeon, M.I. and Buonincontri, P. (2011) 'Cultural event as a territorial marketing tool: the case of the Ravello Festial on the Italian Amalfi coast', *Journal of Hospitality Marketing and Management*, 20: 385–406.

Sjøholt, P. (1999) 'Culture as a strategic development device: the role of 'European cities of culture,' with particular reference to Bergen', *European Urban and Regional Studies*, 6 (4): 339–47.

Small, K. (2007) 'Social dimensions of community festivals: an application of factor analysis in the development of the social impact perception (sip) scale', *Event Management*, 11: 45–55.

Small, K., Edwards, D. and Sheridan, L. (2005) 'A flexible framework for evaluating the socio-cultural impacts of a (small) festival', *International Journal of Event Management Research*, 1 (1): 66–77.

Smith, A. (2009) 'Theorising the relationship between major sport events and social sustainability', *Journal of Sport & Tourism*, 14 (2–3): 109–20.

Smith, A. (2010) 'Leveraging benefits from major events: maximising opportunities for peripheral urban areas', *Managing Leisure*, 15 (3): 161–80.

Smith, A. and Fox, T. (2007) 'From "event-led" to "event-themed" regeneration: the 2002 commonwealth games legacy scheme', *Urban Studies*, 44 (5–6): 1125–43.

Smith, K. (2009) 'Glastonbury festival welcomes The Camp for Climate Action', *The Ecologist*. Available at: http://www.theecologist.org/green_green_living/out_and_about_/271602/glastonbury_festival_welcomes_the_camp_for_climate_action.html (accessed 5 August 2012).

Smith, M., Macleod, N. and Hart Robinson, M. (2010) *Key Concepts in Tourist Studies*. London: Sage.

Smith, S. (1995) 'Where to draw the line: a geography of popular festivity', in A. Rogers and S. Vertovec (eds), *The Urban Context*. Oxford: Berg. pp. 141–64.

Snowball, J.D. and Webb, A.C.M. (2008) 'Breaking into the conversation: cultural value and the role of the South African national arts festival from apartheid to democracy', *International Journal of Cultural Policy*, 14 (2): 149–64.

Snowball, J.D. and Willis, K.G. (2006) 'Building cultural capital: transforming the South African national arts festival', *South African Journal of Economics*, 74 (1): 20–33.

Society of Incentive Travel Executives (SITE) (2012) 'History'. Available at: http://www.siteglobal.com (accessed 17 February 2012).

Sofield, T. and Li, F. (1998) 'Historical methodology and sustainability: an 800-year-old festival from China', *Journal of Sustainable Tourism*, 6 (4): 267–92.

Solberg, H.A. (2003) 'Major sporting events: assessing the value of volunteers' work', *Managing Leisure*, 8: 17–27.

Solberg, H.A. and Preuss, H. (2007) 'Major sport events and long-term tourism impacts', *Journal of Sport Management*, 2: 213–34.

Solberg, H.A., Anderson, T.D. and Shibli, S. (2002) 'An exploration of the direct impacts from business travellers at world championships', *Event Management*, 7 (3): 151–64.

Sonder, M. (2004) *Event Entertainment and Production*. Hoboken, NJ: Wiley.

Soteriades, M.D. and Dimou, I. (2011) 'Special events: a framework for efficient management', *Journal of Hospitality Marketing & Management*, 20 (3–4): 329–46.

Stokes, R. (2007) 'Relationships and networks for shaping events tourism: an Australian study', *Event Management*, 10 (2): 145–58.

Syme, G., Shaw, B., Fenton, D. and Mueller, W. (eds) (1989) *The Planning and Evaluation of Hallmark Events*. Aldershot: Avebury.

Taks, M., Chalip, L., Green, B.C., Kesanne, S. and Martyn, S. (2009) 'Factors affecting repeat visitation and flow-on tourism as sources of event strategy sustainability', *Journal of Sport & Tourism*, 14 (2–3): 121–42.

Taylor, R. (2001) 'Product, service, experience: what differentiates event visitors from everyday tourism visitors?', *Touristics*, 17 (1): 16–19.

Taylor, R. and Shanka, T. (2002) 'Attributes for staging successful wine festivals', *Event Management*, 7 (3): 165–75.

Taylor, T. and Toohey, K. (2007) 'Perceptions of terrorism threats at the 2004 Olympic games: implications for sport events', *Journal of Sport & Tourism*, 12 (2): 99–114.

Telfer, D. (2000) 'Tastes of Niagara: building strategic alliances between tourism and agriculture', *International Journal of Hospitality and Tourism Administration*, 1 (1): 71–88.

Thjømøe, H.M., Olson, E. and Brønn, P.S. (2002) 'Decision-making processes surrounding sponsorship activities', *Journal of Advertising Research*, November-December: 6–15.

Thomas, R. and Wood, E. (2004) 'Event-based tourism: a survey of local authority strategies in the UK', *Local Governance*, 29 (2): 127–36.

Thrane, C. (2002) 'Jazz festival visitors and their expenditures: linking spending patterns to musical interest', *Journal of Travel Research*, 40 (3): 281–86.

Throsby, D. (1999) 'Cultural capital', *Journal of Cultural Economics*, 23 (3): 3–12.

key concepts in
event management

Throsby, D. (2001) *Economics and Culture*. Cambridge: Cambridge University Press.

TIA (Travel Industry Association of America) (2004) 'Dometsic trip activity by US travellers'. Available at: http://www.tia.org/resources/images/charts/domestic_tip_activity_2004.gif (accessed 10 July 2006).

Timothy, D.J. and Boyd, S. (2003) *Heritage Tourism*. Harlow: Longman.

Tkaczynski, A. and Rundle-Thiele, S.R. (2011) 'Event segmentation: a review and research agenda', *Tourism Management*, 32: 426–34.

Tkaczynski, A. and Stokes, R. (2010) 'Festperf: a service quality measurement scale for festivals', *Event Management*, 14 (1): 69–82.

Tomlijenovic, R., Larsson, M. and Faulkner, H. (2001) 'Predictors of satisfaction with festival attendance: a case of Storsjöyran rock festival', *Tourism*, 49 (2): 123–32.

Toohey, K. (2008) 'The Sydney Olympics: striving for legacies – failed expectations for regional economic development', *The International Journal of the History of Sport*, 25 (14): 1953–71.

Toohey, K. and Taylor, K. (2006) 'Security, perceived safety and event attendee enjoyment at the 2003 Rugby World Cup', *Tourism Review International*, 11 (4): 257–67.

Toohey, K., Taylor, K. and Choong-Ki, L. (2003) 'The FIFA World Cup 2002: the effects of terrorism on sport tourists', *Journal of Sport & Tourism*, 8 (3): 167–85.

Torche, F. and Valenzuela, E. (2011) 'Trust and reciprocity: a theoretical distinction of the sources of social capital', *European Journal of Social Theory*, 14 (2): 181–98.

Tourism Western Australia (2012) 'Green events'. Available at: http://www.tourism.wa.gov.au/Policies_Plans_Strategies/Climate_Change/Pages/Green_Events.aspx (accessed 5 August 2012).

Trott, P. (2002) *Innovation Management and New Product Development*. Harlow: Prentice Hall.

Tum, J., Norton, P. and Wright, J. (2006) *Management of Event Operations*. Oxford: Butterworth-Heinemann/Elsevier.

Turko, D.M. and Kelsey, C.W. (1992) *Determining the Economic Impact of Recreation Special Events*. Alexandria, VA: National Recreation and Park Association.

Turner, V. (1982) *From Ritual to Theatre: The Human Seriousness of Play*. New York: Performing Arts Journal Publications.

Tyrrell, T. and Johnston, T. (2001) 'A framework for assessing direct economic impacts of tourist events. Distinguishing origins, destinations, and causes of expenditures', *Journal of Travel Research*, 40 (1): 94–100.

Ulrich, D. (1998) 'Six practices for creating communities of value, not proximity', in F. Hesselbein, M. Goldsmith, R. Beckhard and R.F. Schubert (eds), *The Community of the Future*. San Francisco, CA: Jossey-Bass. pp. 155–66.

UNWTO (2012) 'Tourism highlights 2011'. Available at: www.unwto.org/facts (accessed 2 February 2012).

Upham, P., Boucher, P. and Hemment, D. (2009) 'Piloting a carbon emissions audit for an international arts festival under tight resource constraints', *Sustainable Tourism Futures: Perspectives on Systems, Restructuring and Innovations*. London: Taylor & Francis. pp. 152–168.

references

Uysal, M., Gahan, L. and Martin, B. (1993) 'An examination of event motivations: a case study', *Festival Management & Event Tourism*, 1 (1): 5–10.

Uysal, M. and Gitelson, R. (1994) 'Assessment of economic impacts: festivals and special events', *Festival Management and Event Tourism*, 2 (1): 3–9.

Van der Wagen, L. (2005) *Event Management for Tourism, Cultural, Business and Sporting Events*, 2nd edn. Frenchs Forest, NSW: Pearson Education Australia.

Van Niekerk, M. and Coetzee, W.L.J. (2011) 'Utilizing the VICE model for the sustainable development of the Innibos arts festival', *Journal of Hospitality Marketing & Management*, 20 (3–4): 347–65.

Van Winkle, C.M. and Backman, K. (2009) 'Examining visitor mindfulness at a cultural event', *Event Management*, 12 (3–4): 163–9.

Van Zyl, C. and Botha, C. (2004) 'Motivational factors of local residents to attend the Aardklop national arts festival', *Event Management*, 8 (4): 213–22.

Viljoen, J. and Dann, S. (2000) *Strategic Management*, 3rd edn. Melbourne: Longman.

Vogt C., Roehl, W.S. and Fesenmaier, D.R. (1994) 'Understanding planners use of meeting facility information', *Hospitality Research Journal*, 17 (3): 119–30.

Volrath, A. (2005) 'Eternity games', in D. Adair, B. Coe and N. Gouth (eds) *Beyond the Torch – Olympics and Australian Culture*. Melbourne: Australian Society for Sports History.

VolunteerNet (2011) Available at: http://www.volunteernet.org.nz/aboutus.php (accessed 29 August 2011).

Wainwright, M. and McDonald, H. (2010) 'Derry celebrates culture capital success', *Guardian*, 16 July 2010. Available at: http://www.guardian.co.uk/uk/2010/jul/15/derry-capital-of-culture-2013 (accessed 1 August 2012).

Waitt, G. (2003) 'Social impacts of the Sydney Olympics', *Annals of Tourism Research*, 30 (1): 194–215.

Waitt, G. (2005) 'The Sydney 2002 gay games and querying Australian national space', *Environment and Planning D: Society and Space*, 23: 435–452.

Waitt, G. (2006) 'Boundaries of desire: becoming sexual through the spaces of Sydney's 2002 Gay Games', *Annals of the Association of American Geographers*, 96 (4): 773–87.

Waitt, G. (2008) 'Urban festivals: geographies of hype, helplessness and hope', *Geography Compass*, 2 (2): 513–37.

Wale, D. and Ridal, A. (2010) 'Marketing events', in P. Robinson, D. Wale and G. Dickson (eds), *Events Management*. Wallingford: CABI. pp. 137–63.

Wall, G. and Mitchell, C. (1989) 'Cultural festivals as economic stimuli and catalysts of functional change', in G.J. Syme, B.J. Shaw, D.M. Fenton and W.S. Mueller (eds), *The Planning and Evaluation of Hallmark Events*. Aldershot: Avebury. pp. 132–41.

Walo, M., Bull, A. and H. Breen (1996) 'Achieving economic benefits at local events: a case study of a local sports event', *Festival Management and Event Tourism*, 4 (1): 95–106.

Walters, G. (2011) 'Bidding for international sport events: how government supports and undermines national governing bodies of sport', *Sport in Society: Cultures, Commerce, Media, Politics*, 14 (2): 208–22.

Wang, N. (1999) 'Rethinking authenticity in tourism experience', *Annals of Tourism Research*, 26: 349–70.

key concepts in event management

Wang, N. (2000) *Tourism and Modernity: A Sociological Analysis*. Oxford: Pergamon.

Warman, J. (2010) 'How music festivals are singing the changes', *Guardian*, 27 August 2010. Available at: http://www.guardian.co.uk/business/2010/aug/27/music-festivals-record-industry (accessed 5 August 2012).

Waterman, S. (1998) 'Carnival for elites? The cultural politics of arts festivals', *Progress in Human Geography*, 22: 54–74.

Webber, D., Buccellato, T. and White, S. (2010) 'The global recession and its impact on tourists' spending in the UK', *Economic and Labour Market Review*, 4 (8): 65–6.

Weed, M. (2003) 'Why the two won't tango! Explaining the lack of integrated policies for sport and tourism in the UK', *Journal of Sport Management*, 17: 258–83.

Weed, M. (2006) 'Sports tourism research: a systematic review of knowledge and a meta-evaluation of method', *Journal of Sport Tourism*, 11 (1): 5–30.

Weed, M. (2009) 'Progress in sports tourism research? A meta-review and exploration of futures', *Tourism Management*, 30 (5): 615–28.

Weed, M. (2011) 'The human impact of major sports events', *Journal of Sport Tourism*, 16 (1): 1–4.

Weed, M. and Dowse, S. (2009) 'A missed opportunity waiting to happen? The social legacy potential of the London 2010 Paralympic Games', *Journal of Policy Research in Tourism, Leisure and Events*, 1 (2): 170–4.

Weed, M.E. and Bull, C.J. (2004) *Sports Tourism: Participants, Policy and Providers*. Oxford: Elsevier.

Westerbeek, H.M., Turner, P. and Ingerson, L. (2002) 'Key success factors in bidding for hallmark sporting events', *International Marketing Review*, 19 (3): 303–22.

Wheatley, M.J. and Kellner-Rogers, M. (1998) 'The paradox and promise of community', in F. Hesselbein, M. Goldsmith, R. Beckhard and R.F. Schubert (eds), *The Community of the Future.*. San Francisco, CA: Jossey-Bass Publishers. pp. 9–18.

Whitford, M. (2004) 'Regional development through domestic and tourist event policies: Gold Coast and Brisbane, 1974–2003', *Journal of Hospitality, Tourism and Leisure Science*, 1: 1–24.

Whitford, M. (2009) 'A framework for the development of event public policy: facilitating regional development', *Tourism Management*, 30 (5): 674–82.

Whitson, D. and Horne, J. (2006) 'Underestimated costs and overestimated benefits? Comparing the outcomes of sports mega-events in Canada and Japan', *Sociological Review*, 54 (2): 73–89.

Wilks, L. (2009) 'Attending a music festival: the role of social and cultural capital', unpublished PhD thesis, Open University, Milton Keyes.

Wilks, L. (2011) 'Bridging and bonding: social capital at music festivals', *Journal of Policy Research in Tourism, Leisure and Events*, 3 (3): 281–97.

Williams, M. and Bowdin, G.A.J. (2007) 'Festival evaluation: an exploration of seven UK arts festivals', *Managing Leisure*, 12 (2): 187–203.

Williams, M. and Bowdin, G.A.J. (2008) 'Festival evaluation: an evaluation of seven UK arts festivals', in M. Robertson and E. Frew (eds), *Events and Festivals*. Abingdon: Routledge. pp. 86–121.

Wiscombe, C. (2010) 'Funding, sponsorship and financial management', in P. Robinson, D. Wale and G. Dickson (eds), *Events Management*. Wallingford: CABI. pp. 46–71.

Wood, E. (2005) 'Measuring the economic and social impacts of local authority events', *International Journal of Public Sector Management*, 18 (1): 37–53.

Wood, E. (2006) 'Measuring the social impacts of local authority events: a pilot study for a civic pride scale', *International Journal of Nonprofit Voluntary Sector Marketing*, 11: 165–79.

Wood, E.H., Robinson L.S. and Thomas, R. (2006) 'Evaluating the social impacts of community and local government events: a practical overview of research methods and measurement tools', in S. Fleming and F. Jordan (eds), *Events and Festivals: Education, Impacts and Experiences*. Eastbourne: Leisure Studies Association. pp. 81–92.

Wood, S. (2012) 'The power of celebration'. Available at: http://www.ifea.com/joomla1_5/index.php?option=com_contentandview=articleandid=180andItemid=306 (accessed 30 July 2012).

Woolcock, M. (1998) 'Social capital and economic development: toward a theoretical synthesis and policy framework', *Theory and Society*, 27: 151–208.

World Commission on Environment and Development (1987) *Our Common Future*. Oxford: Oxford university Press.

Worsfold, D. (2003) 'Food safety at shows and fairs', *Nutrition & Food Science*, 33 (4): 159–64.

Wortham, J. (2009) 'Social media overload allows web apps to shine', NYTimes.com, 15 March. Available at: http://bits.blog.nytimes.com/2009/03/15/social-media-overload-allows-web-apps-to-shine (accessed 16 February 2011).

WTO (2007) *A Practical Guide to Tourism Destination Management*. Madrid: OMT.

Yaghmour, S. and Scott, N. (2009) 'Inter-organizational collaboration characteristics and outcomes: a case study of the Jeddah festival', *Journal of Policy Research in Tourism, Leisure and Events* 1 (2): 115–30.

Yardimci, S. (2007) 'Festivalising difference: privatisation of culture and symbolic exclusion in Istanbul', EUI Working Papers, Mediterranean Programme Series, RSCAS 2007/35.

Yeoman, I., Robertson, M. and Ali-Knight, J. (eds) (2004) *Festivals and Events Management: An International Arts and Culture Perspective*. Elsevier: Oxford.

Yuan, J. and Jang, S. (2008) 'The effects of quality and satisfaction on awareness and behavioral intentions: exploring the role of a wine festival', *Journal of Travel Research*, 46 (3): 279–88.

Zeithaml, V.A., Berry, L.L. and Parasuraman, A. (1996) 'The behavioural consequences of service quality', *Journal of Marketing*, 60 (2): 31–46.

Zervos, H. (2012) 'The Olympic Delivery Agency and energy harvesting', *Energy Harvesting Journal*, 2 August. Available at: http://energyharvestingjournal.com/article /heated-trousers-sustainable-walkways-new-ball-game-at-london-olympics-00004630.asp (accessed 2 August 2012).

Ziakas, V. (2010) 'Understanding an event portfolio: the uncovering of interrelationships, synergies, and leveraging opportunities', *Journal of Policy Research in Tourism, Leisure and Events*, 2 (2): 144–64.

Ziakas, V. and Costa, C.A. (2011) 'The use of an event portfolio in regional community and tourism development: creating synergy between sport and cultural events', *Journal of Sport & Tourism*, 16 (2): 149–75.

Zukin, S. (1995) *The Cultures of Cities*. Cambridge MA and Oxford: Blackwell.

PROPERTY OF
SENECA COLLEGE
LIBRARIES
KING CAMPUS